Happy Ever After

Paul Dolan is Professor of Behavioural Science at the LSE. He is an internationally renowned expert in human behaviour and happiness. Amongst various other roles, he wrote the questions that are being used to monitor national happiness in the UK and has advised many governments, charities and corporations on how to influence behaviour to improve wellbeing. His debut book, *Happiness by Design*, was a *Sunday Times* bestseller and was dubbed 'the book that will make you quit your job'.

PAUL DOLAN

Happy Ever After

*Escaping the Myth of the
Perfect Life*

ALLEN LANE
an imprint of
PENGUIN BOOKS

ALLEN LANE

UK | USA | Canada | Ireland | Australia
India | New Zealand | South Africa

Allen Lane is part of the Penguin Random House group of companies
whose addresses can be found at global.penguinrandomhouse.com

First published 2019
001

Copyright © Paul Dolan, 2019

The moral right of the author has been asserted

Set in 10.63/14.18 pt Sabon LT Std
Typeset by Jouve (UK), Milton Keynes
Printed and bound in Great Britain by Clays Ltd, Elcograf S.p.A.

A CIP catalogue record for this book is available from the British Library

ISBN: 978-0-241-37495-5

Contents

Introduction   vii

PART ONE
Reaching

1 Wealthy   3
2 Successful   20
3 Educated   37
  Wrapping Up Reaching   55

PART TWO
Related

4 Married   61
5 Monogamous   81
6 Children   96
  Wrapping Up Related   114

PART THREE
Responsible

7 Altruistic   121
8 Healthy   138
9 Volitional   157
  Wrapping Up Responsible   174

  Conclusion   177

  Notes   187
  Acknowledgements   219

Introduction

There are countless stories about how we ought to live our lives. We are expected to be ambitious, to find everlasting love and to take good care of our health. The particularly dominant social narratives can serve to make our lives easier, by providing guidelines for behaviour, and they might sometimes make us happier too. But they are, at their heart, stories – and ones that may not have originated with present-day people in mind. As such, many of these stories end up creating a kind of social dissonance whereby, perversely, they cause more harm than good. They become what I will refer to as *narrative traps*, which together form the myth of the perfect life.

THE WORKING-CLASS HERO

Since this is a book about stories, let's start with an experience of mine. It's about a working-class kid who becomes a university professor and who is expected to change his behaviour in accordance with a (harmful) narrative about how academics ought to behave. A couple of years ago, I took part in an interesting panel discussion on 'emotion versus reason' at the 'HowTheLightGetsIn' festival in Hay-on-Wye. Walking across the field to get some food, I was approached by a man in his fifties. Our interaction started well, with him saying how much he liked my first book, *Happiness by Design*.[1] Then he asked, pointedly, 'But why do you have to play the working-class hero?' I requested clarification. He said, 'You do it in your book and, look at you, you're doing it now.' I had no idea what he meant by that, although I was singing 'Chim Chim Cher-ee' and dressed as a chimney sweep.

Ordinarily, I would embrace being a hero of any kind but, in this context, I was made to feel like an arsehole. The man proceeded to lecture me on how 'when you reach a certain level you *have* to modify your behaviour'. He told me that I should not swear: apparently I used the word 'fuck' twice in an hour-long panel discussion. This crime was made all the more heinous since the panel contained two 'middle-aged' women. You know: women, those fragile creatures who might have a nervous breakdown upon hearing an expletive used in a discussion as a means of emphasis.

So why shouldn't I swear? Perhaps because it is a sign of a poor vocabulary and/or low intelligence, and yet no such correlations have ever been found.[2] There *is* evidence, however, to suggest that students pay more attention to a teacher who swears, and are then encouraged to express their own opinions more freely.[3] Swearing is only ever harmful when it is used in an aggressive or abusive way, and not when used as a means of conveying excitement and emphasis, which is only ever how I use it in the workplace. In these circumstances the evidence shows that it does more good than harm, so the idea that swearing is bad is a fucking stupid one.[4]

This man was insistent that, in my role as a professor at the London School of Economics and Political Science, I ought to be setting a better example to those who looked up to me. And by better he meant consistent with the prevailing impression of a university professor. (Take a quick look at the website of any department you like at the LSE or any other leading university and the pictures of the faculty/staff will neatly illustrate what I am talking about.) He was appealing to a social narrative that placed the burden on me to act in a particular way based upon my middle-class profession. The LSE treats me very well, but the general expectation to act in accordance with the narrow confines of academic stereotypes still causes me some misery from time to time. I especially struggle with how seriously academics take themselves.

More importantly, stereotypes of exactly this kind deter working-class kids from going to university, by making them feel that they would have to suppress who they really are in order to fit in. Great strides have been made in the UK and the US to overcome a bias against accepting students from working-class backgrounds. The LSE has increased its proportional intake of working-class students by more than any other elite university in England. This is commendable.

But those cajoling working-class kids into higher education also need to consider that many of those kids really don't want to attend elite universities and mix with other kids who are different to them. Many working-class kids, especially boys, are reluctant to go to university because it involves hanging out with loads of middle-class folk, who think and act very differently, and being taught by middle-class teachers who cannot relate to their 'alternative' world views. And even if they do survive this new environment, they then risk feeling alienated from a working-class background where they had always felt at ease.

In my experience, the well-intentioned middle-class folk trying to get working-class children into higher education assume those kids have middle-class aspirations. But many don't. I never have. OK, so I have a middle-class occupation, and my kids are undoubtedly middle class. But many of my friends have never been near a university and I retain some of my working-class values and behaviours. I weight train with bodybuilders. Seeing a blazer or a pair of loafers at a bodybuilding competition is as rare as rocking-horse shit. I am proud of these differences, yet I appreciate that my life would be easier if I fitted in with expectations placed on academics (or, alternatively, on bodybuilders).

Social narratives make prescriptions about what people should want, do, think and feel. They influence us whether we like it or not. We fall into a narrative trap when we get so carried away with a social story that we expect everyone around us to conform to it. If I am to be called a working-class hero, I want it to be in a way that shows working-class kids that they can pursue an unexpected career and still be themselves, and not in a punitive way that stifles authenticity. When we learn how to spot the narratives that get in the way of our happiness, we improve our chances of taking control of the stories that have for so long controlled us. Once we accept that we can be trapped, we can begin thinking about whether and how to change what we do.[5] We might even, fingers crossed, end up with a few more bodybuilding professors.

WHAT'S THE STORY?

The kinds of stories I am interested in are those dealing with the way in which we *ought* to live our lives. This prescriptive definition of a narrative distinguishes it from most of what has been written about to date, which has focused on personal stories that help individuals to understand the vagaries of their own experiences and to form their own identities. Instead, my concern is with social narratives emanating from external sources, prescribed by others and adopted by you, and not necessarily informed by direct personal experience or positive feedback.

From a psychologist's perspective, social narratives are akin to established 'social norms'. There is no standard definition of a social norm but it usually contains some combination of these three elements: it comprises behavioural regularities; there is a sense of 'oughtness' to it; and there are sanctions associated with deviating from it.[6] As such, social norms have become fairly limiting behavioural rules that people are expected to follow, such as: 'If you are a professor at the LSE, then you don't swear', and so on. If we do not conform to what is expected of us, then we can incur some form of social punishment, be it as minor as an unsolicited verbal altercation.

An economist's starting point for understanding any kind of behaviour is in the study of preferences: well-defined desires for certain goods, services, experiences and states of the world. A distinction is sometimes made between revealed preferences (what people do) and meta-preferences (what they would like to do). You might never read literary fiction but would like to be the kind of person who does. A distinction is also made between individual and social preferences: those that are motivated only by personal well-being as compared to those that additionally account for the impact of our behaviour on others. My definition of a social narrative can therefore be seen as a 'meta-social preference': it reflects a desire for how we should all behave.

I have identified three broad categories of social narratives that I will refer to as 'meta-narratives'. These are labelled as Reaching, Related and Responsible, and all 'sub-narratives' discussed can be found within one of these three meta-narratives. With Reaching in Part One, I discuss the goals that we are meant to aspire to, to reach for unremittingly. We are expected to want to be: wealthy; successful; and well-educated. With Related (Part Two), I consider social narratives surrounding our most intimate relationships: namely, that we should: get married; be monogamous; and have kids. With Responsible in Part Three, I consider three narratives that place unique expectations on us to: be altruistic; be healthy; and act with volition.

All these narratives have withstood several generations of change. They have been shaped to varying degrees by power structures, cultures, laws, families, the media, historical practice and even evolutionary advantage. To some large extent they also map on to recent taxonomies of innate human motivations coming from social psychology, all of which basically assume that we are driven by 'primary' (i.e. unlearned) rewards.[7] Core motivations include: *hoarding* to collect resources (wealthy); *self-enhancing* to view oneself as worthy (successful); *understanding* for shared meaning and prediction (educated); *belonging* and *loving* for being closely connected to others (married and monogamous); *nurturing* to care for offspring (kids); *trusting* to view others as basically benign (altruistic); *comforting* to place one's body in optimal physical conditions (healthy); and *controlling* for perceived contingency between behaviour and outcomes (volitional). This gives the narratives a sense of universality, applicable across different cultures.

As well as satisfying some of our innate desires, social narratives have developed rules of thought and action that help to make a complicated world easier to navigate and make sense of. By looking to the narrative for clues about how to live, we are provided with a coherent path to follow. Not only do we want to fit in, but we can also get angry with those who do not. In fact, there is now a range of brain imaging studies to show that we feel pleasure when we can punish those who do not conform to what we expect of them.[8] We are even willing to pay (literally, in cold hard cash) to punish people who we think have violated social convention.

THE POWER AND THE STORY

It is likely that my festival friend had a strong inclination to support the existing social hierarchy: those who score highly on the trait 'social dominance orientation' (SDO) really dislike it when others do not adhere to a particular norm.[9] SDO is a measure created by social psychologists to determine the extent to which somebody endorses social hierarchies. An example statement is: 'Some groups of people are simply inferior to other groups.' Those who have a high SDO score are more likely to agree and therefore dislike people who are disadvantaged. And they are also more likely to occupy positions where there is an opportunity to put their discriminatory preferences into practice, such as by being in the police force. Stories, like 'professors must act in accordance with their professional stereotype', help to secure these hierarchies.

Social class is often used to define your place in the hierarchy. Social classes are defined according to economic and social status. They are most often proxied by occupation, but sometimes also by income and education, which are all highly correlated (and all make up elements of the Reaching narrative). In the UK, working-class jobs are lower skilled, lower status and lower paid than middle-class ones. In the US, the terms 'blue collar' and 'white collar' are used to represent the distinction between manual labour and office jobs. Basically, the 'better' the job, the higher the class.

I appreciate that this is a very simple definition of class, and that there are some differences in how class is perceived across countries.[10] The relevance here is that an analysis of class forces us to confront just who in society has power, and who is perceived to have it. Social narratives are used to preserve existing social hierarchies, and so it would be remiss not to consider the most powerful manifestation of hierarchies – categorizing people by social class – in a book about social stories. Some stories are more likely to become dominant because they emanate from, are reinforced by and disproportionately benefit those with power.

Perceptions of power matter too. In the UK, 60 per cent of people report being working class even though only about half as many people are in routine and manual occupations.[11] There has been a steady decline in households broadly defined as being working class since the 1980s, although the number of people identifying themselves as such has remained relatively steady. In the US there has been an increase in the number of those who see themselves as working class. According to a Gallup Poll conducted in 2015, nearly half of Americans considered themselves to be working class. This compares with only one third in 2003. The UK and US data suggest that, while the conditions appear to have got better for those at the bottom of the ladder, it may not feel like it.

In what follows, therefore, I will use the term 'working class' as shorthand for those with, or widely perceived to have, relatively less power, and 'middle class' for those with, or widely perceived to have, relatively more power. Where differences in values exist between groups of different power, it follows that social narratives will be more closely aligned with those with power than those without. Not only will stories about how to live align more with middle-class values than with working-class ones, but anyone moving up the social hierarchy will be expected to adopt the values of those with power and will be judged negatively if they don't.

In debates around societal equality and discrimination, it is notable that class has been neglected in comparison to gender, race, disability and sexuality. These other characteristics are all protected in the UK under the Equality Act 2010, which means that it is illegal to discriminate against someone based on these. Social class is not afforded the same protection, which means that there is nothing to prevent a company denying a perfectly good candidate a job simply because he or she comes from 'the wrong side of the tracks'. Similar protections for gender, race, etc., exist in the US; and, similarly, there is a lack of protection for social-class discrimination.

Further, and in contrast to other discriminated groups, there are very few advocates for the working class among the working class. We can't rely on successful working-class people because they have to disguise themselves as middle class in order to survive. So there simply aren't working-class role models to aspire to in many occupations. What's more, many successful working-class people will distance themselves, geographically and psychologically, from the people they grew up around once they reach a certain level of success. Successful women and black people might not always actively promote gender and race issues, but they are unable to distance themselves from other women and black people because these characteristics are more readily observable than class.

From the perspective of somebody who doesn't conform to professional stereotypes and who sits uncomfortably between classes, I recognize the difficulties and harsh judgement that come from rebelling against type. It can cause an initial period of suffering and doubt even if individual and societal misery is reduced in the long term. But understanding the narratives and the ways in which these can help and harm us is the first step towards making choices that are a better fit with who we are. If nothing else, being alert to when narratives can harm as well as help us will promote greater tolerance of those who do not conform to what is expected of them. And this is surely of long-term benefit to us all.

While a lot of attention will be focused on how the narratives might impact upon your own happiness, I will also urge you to consider how they affect the lives of others. Each of us wears different decision-making hats. In our role as partner, friend, parent, boss or policy-maker we rarely make decisions that affect our happiness alone. Whatever our position of power and place in the social hierarchy, it is good to help other people, and to resist judging them for the decisions they make. You might then care a little less about the judgements they make about your life, and possibly will even be judged less in return.

WHAT'S THE HARM?

It is my contention that the impact of any social narrative should be assessed according to how it makes people feel. It might sound good to be a high achiever but it might not feel good; and if it doesn't feel good, it really shouldn't sound good. We each need to pay attention to the realities of our experiences, because being in a great job in theory is no compensation for being miserable at work in practice. In a bid to be happy and not harm others, we need to align ourselves more closely with our experiences (which are fluid) and not with labels (father, professor, bodybuilder, etc.), which tend to be more rigid.

Many decision-making environments, such as when we are allocating scarce public resources, require that there is a normative standard by which to judge the goodness of actions, circumstances and lives. So I am suggesting that there be one over-arching social narrative to replace the many others discussed in this book: the real experiences of real people as they go about their real lives. This ought to take precedence over a load of stories that have very little recourse to, or relationship with, people's happiness. By focusing directly on experiences, we remove the stigma associated with being unwilling and/or unable to live according to the 'one size fits all' approach prescribed by a particular narrative.

Without the pressure to conform, you and your partner might be happier in a consensually non-monogamous relationship, or you might choose to be single, or celibate. Or you might decide that marriage, monogamy and kids are just the things for you. I don't give a damn what you do as long as you are happy and do not make others around you unnecessarily miserable in the process. A focus on experiences rather than narratives encourages many types of lives and lifestyles to co-exist, including (but not limited to) those consistent with the prevailing social narratives. While many of the arguments I make will be universally applicable, my focus throughout will be on the experiences of those living in the UK and the US.

I will focus on reports of how people feel where I can, but such data are scarce and so sometimes I will be obliged to rely on more widely available reports of life satisfaction. I am critical of these assessments, however, because the degree to which I am satisfied with my life will be influenced by what society expects of me; for example, do I have a job, is it a good job, and so on.[12] This means that if we find support for a social narrative in life-satisfaction data, we cannot be that confident about how it relates to the experience of happiness. But if life-satisfaction data do not support a narrative (for example when married women are no more satisfied with life than single women), then we can be more confident of the conflict between the narrative and the potential for happiness since the narrative has been fulfilled and yet satisfaction is no higher.

Much of the time the data simply won't allow me to be able to say with any degree of certainty what the world would look like in the absence of the social narrative. And if we find that happiness and marriage, say, are correlated, we rarely know which causes which, or whether both are caused by a factor that we do not have data on, such as personality. But my ambition here is to provoke conversation around what the data might be telling us rather than to provide a definitive answer. Besides, if decisions in life were only ever allowed to be made on the basis of watertight causal evidence, then not a lot would get done.

Happy Ever After focuses on when stories harm us. My position is that you should seek to reduce misery and suffering by as much as possible in the decisions you make that affect other people. This position is often referred to as the utilitarian one. It is reflected in the maxim 'the greatest happiness of the greatest number'.[13] For the purposes of this book, I will flip this maxim to become 'the least suffering of the least number', or what is otherwise referred to as 'negative utilitarianism'.[14] It allows me to give greater weight to benefits that go to those who suffer the most because the suffering alleviated by, say, £100 will be greatest for those who are the least well off. We can also minimize suffering by reducing inequalities if people are adversely affected by inequalities they consider to be unfair. (Most of us don't think that it is unfair that a company CEO earns a few multiples more than a hospital porter, but we do think a few hundred times as much is unjust.)

There is nothing inherently good or bad in a social narrative in itself; it can only ever be judged according to the costs and benefits of adhering to it in a given context. I therefore adopt a consequentialist position in contrast to a deontological one.[15] A consequentialist's view on theft would be that it is only ever wrong when it causes more misery than it promotes happiness, whereas a deontologist would be duty bound to argue that theft is always wrong because moral value lies in certain rules of conduct. A deontological perspective typically does not allow for the importance of context. And yet I would contend that it is morally right to steal to feed your hungry child.

In the purest form of consequentialism, each person's equal suffering is weighted equally.[16] This view of impartiality means that I should treat my own suffering, the suffering of my family and friends, and the suffering of strangers equally. But this form of consequentialism conflicts with common sense and possibly also with evolutionary advantage: it feels morally right to me that my family's suffering should count for more than yours does, just as your family's suffering should count for more to you. We are therefore required to develop some rules around which decisions and perspectives are legitimately partial and which ones require impartiality.

As a parent, I am allowed – even expected – to favour my own children over yours. I might buy my daughter the best pair of bouldering shoes or my son an expensive squash racket so that they are more likely to succeed in their chosen sports. Your children might be relatively disadvantaged by my decisions but I do not feel compelled to buy your kids new kit as well. But what if I were the coach of the bouldering or squash team and a donation meant we could buy new kit? It seems unfair for me to give it to my kids at the expense of yours. The fact that the money is mine in one case and not in the other makes a difference, of course, but so too does my role: partial parent on the one hand and impartial coach on the other.

While context always matters, as a first order rule, the additional weight I give to my children should be the same as the additional weight you give to yours. I therefore accept a view of consequentialism that allows for partiality but that also requires symmetry (where the additional weight we give to our children is the same). Partiality undoubtedly makes my life a little harder when considering the overall impact of different stories on people's well-being, but I will deal with the challenges it raises in a transparent way when the need arises.

ONWARDS

In identifying narrative traps, I am focusing on stories that continue to cohere with common sense from a deontological perspective but that quickly contrast with common sense in a consequentialist way. In so doing, I will at times ask you to suspend belief about what you think you know to be true. When it comes to weighing up evidence, we like to think of ourselves as deliberative and detached. We think carefully about the arguments and form an opinion or a belief in a dispassionate way. In reality, though, our beliefs often come first and then we search for evidence to support them. When the evidence supports a belief, we are proud of being right in the first place. But what about when the evidence goes against our belief? Well, then we are even cleverer at finding ways of explaining the evidence so that we can carry on believing what we did in the first place. We may then end up even more resolute in our original belief than we were before it was examined.

This is called confirmation bias.[17] Fingerprint experts are much more likely to make a match with a suspect whom they are told has confessed, as compared to when they are not told this, even though the evidence is the same in both instances. Writing this book has opened my mind to the nuances of narratives, and some of the evidence has 'unconfirmed' some things I thought to be true. I assumed that attending university would be unequivocally good for happiness and benefit wider society, for example, but the evidence does not strongly endorse either claim. I didn't think that divorce could actually be beneficial for children, but it appears to be preferable for many children than their parents staying together.

If by reading *Happy Ever After* you become even more entrenched in your views about a narrative, consider for one moment why this might be. It could be because you genuinely experience happiness in accordance with one or more narratives and have witnessed the same in those around you. Or it could be that you're apprehensive of the alternative because it's more challenging, more unknown or, perhaps, even more exciting. It was established a long time ago that homophobic men show more sexual arousal to gay sex than non-homophobic men.[18] Now, I'm not suggesting all homophobic men are in the closet, but I am proposing that behaviour and experiences are complex, even for those who identify strongly with a certain orientation. What I genuinely want is to promote dialogue around these narratives rather than simply to present a new set of rules to adhere to and identify with.

To aid this, I think it will be interesting for you to have an idea of just how much you believe in the narrative in question before we begin to probe further. So at the start of each chapter, I am going to ask you to choose between two lives. The choice is designed to be a simple trade-off between following the narrative and being happy. I recognize that the narrative could also make you happier, but these hypothetical examples allow you to see for yourself just how much the narrative matters even if it makes you miserable. And because a portion of the book focuses on the decisions we make on behalf of other people, I would also like you to think about the life you would choose for a friend of yours in each case, too. There are no right or wrong answers. There does not have to be any consistency within or across chapters but you might want to make a note of your answers and even revisit them at various points. At the end of each part, I will present some general population data on these questions so you can see how you compare to other people.

PART ONE
Reaching

The three chapters in this section – wealthy, successful and educated – examine social narratives that we can't seem to get enough of. Now, it should be obvious to anyone that the absence of any of these three can cause anxiety and misery. I will not suggest otherwise. The narratives suggest, however, that whatever our absolute levels of the positive attributes, we are expected to be reaching for more. The assumption is that ever more happiness is achieved with ever more money, more markers of success and greater intellectual validation. The trap comes from the fact that the happiness hit from adherence to these narratives gets ever smaller the further up the ladder you go and, eventually, can become reversed. To be happier we need to move from a culture of 'more please' to one of 'just enough'.

A just-enough approach has some similarities with the concept of 'satisficing', a rule for decision-making that involves searching the available options only until one of them meets an acceptable threshold. This is in contrast to 'maximizing', which is a standard assumption in economics. Maximizing involves searching until the very best option is identified by a process of elimination. The distinction was first put forward by Herbert Simon in the 1950s and has been popularized in recent times by Barry Schwarz. To illustrate, a maximizer booking a holiday will spend hours – days even – sifting through the best deals online within budget. They will weigh up all the options, taking account of all critical factors such as price, location, room size, breakfast offering, recent reviews and so on, and will then proudly announce 'I have found the best possible deal.' A satisficer will hit 'Reserve' as soon as they come across the right sort of hotel within budget.

The concept of just enough I have in mind here focuses directly on the happiness feedback provided by each decision. As such, it is less about accepting an option that is sub-optimal and more about finding an option that is optimal to you given its overall impact on your happiness and the happiness of those you care about. It is satisficing in the domains of wealth, success and education but it is maximizing of happiness.

I

Wealthy

Before we get going with this narrative, here are two questions for you to answer. Make a note of your answers and we'll come back to the questions at the end of Part One.

Please read the following statements and indicate whether you would choose Life A or Life B *for yourself*:

Life A: You are wealthy. You often feel miserable.
Life B: You are not wealthy. You hardly ever feel miserable.

Please read the following statements and indicate whether you would choose Life A or Life B *for a friend*:

Life A: Your friend is wealthy. Your friend often feels miserable.
Life B: Your friend is not wealthy. Your friend hardly ever feels miserable.

It has been credited with making the world go round on the one hand, and being the root of all evil on the other. The truth is that money can be whatever we want it to be, depending on how we use and abuse it. Money allows us to organize and collaborate on the trade of goods and services on a global scale. If it disappeared tomorrow, the majority of societies around the world would crumble. Without money in our pockets and bank accounts, each of us would be in real danger of going without food and shelter. And yet money does not have inherent value in itself: it is only ever an instrument for satisfying our wants and desires, and for pursuing happiness.

Getting richer is a pervasive goal. Governments around the world monitor the economic status of their populations through national surveys and with indicators such as gross domestic product (GDP), which is the monetary value of all goods and services produced by a country over a given period (it is usually calculated every three months). GDP is widely recognized as a very poor proxy for progress, however; all forms of economic activity add to growth, even the petrol you use in a traffic jam that only serves to pollute the planet and piss you off. Yet 'economic growth has become a fetish ... an altar on which we are prepared to sacrifice all.'[1] Such is the power of the narrative to get rich.

According to a 2008 Pew Research Center poll, over half of Americans say that 'being wealthy' is important to them.[2] An American Heartland Monitor poll from 2014 shows that half of Americans agree that being wealthy is a *necessary* component to living the good life.[3] The Brits celebrate their riches too. For example, the *Sunday Times* Rich List has publicized the wealthiest people and families living in the UK each year for the last thirty years. Think of all the people you know who are motivated by earning more money, even those who earn quite a lot already. We don't quite trust those who say that money doesn't matter that much to them.

There are, of course, social welfare considerations, too. The taxes on wealth and earnings can be used to address poverty, as well as to fund areas that the market might neglect, including healthcare and education. On the other hand, a focus on growth directs our efforts ever more towards the production and consumption of 'stuff' with questionable returns for anyone's happiness. As noted by Joseph Stiglitz in his book *The Price of Inequality*, individuals such as Albert Einstein make enormous contributions to social welfare and yet are not adequately rewarded by the economic system, and so the narrative of being wealthy may push other possible Einsteins into money-making professions instead.[4] The people at the top of the economic ladder, and who will feature consistently in the *Sunday Times* Rich List, are mostly those who have been lucky enough to exploit market forces, often with the added good fortune of inherited wealth, and often in ways that are not beneficial for society.

Strictly speaking, 'wealth' refers to accumulated assets in the form of savings, investments and property. It is tricky to measure. In this book I will draw mainly on income-based evidence. Over time, income and wealth have been consistently correlated: people who earn higher wages tend to accumulate more assets. At any one point in time, however, they can differ quite markedly; many retired people have low incomes but high levels of wealth, and some younger people have good salaries but no assets. As you consider the evidence please keep in mind that wealth is generally a better indicator of who is rich than income, because it better reflects true purchasing power.[5]

RICHER . . . AND HAPPIER?

What is the relationship between income and happiness? Well, if we use life satisfaction as our measure of happiness, then the association with income dwindles as income rises but – in most studies – never completely disappears.[6] The relationship between income and life satisfaction is never that impressive, though, especially when compared to aspects of life such as having positive social relationships, and good physical and mental health.[7]

Study after study, however, has shown that poverty makes people miserable.[8] To illustrate this, Kate Laffan, Alina Velias and I have been looking at the most miserable people in data gathered by the UK's Office for National Statistics (ONS) from a cross-sectional sample of nearly 200,000 people each year since 2011. The ONS asks four happiness questions that Richard Layard, Rob Metcalfe and I proposed, each rated on a 0–10 scale from 'not at all' to 'completely':

1. Overall, how satisfied are you with your life nowadays?
2. Overall, to what extent do you feel the things you do in your life are worthwhile?
3. Overall, how happy did you feel yesterday?
4. Overall, how anxious did you feel yesterday?

We might not all agree on the best question to measure happiness, but we probably would agree that a person who gives a score of four or less to each of the first three questions and a score of six or more to the last question is probably not doing too well. About 1 per cent of the ONS sample are miserable, according to this criterion. This equates to between 1,700 and 2,000 people in each of the five years for which we have data (and would scale up to about half a million Britons). Earning less than £400 per week (or about £20,000 a year) is one of the factors that increases the chances of being in the most miserable 1 per cent. Above £400 per week, the law of diminishing marginal returns kicks in. Once your basic needs are satisfied, your desire for ever-increasing amounts of money generates ever-decreasing returns of happiness.

Snapshot responses to questions like these don't really get at how people are feeling day to day. To help us explain the effect of income on experiences of happiness, Laura Kudrna analysed the American Time Use Survey (ATUS). I will refer to these data frequently throughout the book. This study has been running for over a decade and allows analysts to estimate the amount of time that people spend engaged in activities of daily life. In 2012 and 2013, the 20,000 or so people in the ATUS were asked to keep a diary of what they did over the course of a randomly chosen day, and then an interviewer called them the next day to ask some questions about the activities in their diary. Respondents rated the happiness, meaning, stress, tiredness, sadness and pain associated with each activity on a seven point (0–6) scale.

Take a look at the two graphs below, the first for 'happy' by income group and the second for 'meaning' by income group. They are actually quite similar. Happiness goes up with increases in income at the lower end of the distribution, but then it falls with higher incomes. People who earn between $50K and $75K experience more pleasure and more purpose than any other income group. Contrary to what most of us might predict, those earning over $100K are no happier than those with incomes of less than $25K. And it's worse for the rich folk when we look at purpose. Those with the highest incomes report the least purpose in their experiences. Perhaps 'having it all' makes what we do feel less meaningful.

So what about misery (stress, tiredness, sadness and pain combined), which we might care about more? From the graph below we can see that there are no significant differences in misery after $50K, but people are more miserable at incomes lower than this. This is an important reminder that not having enough money is a source of misery. Based on all of the results – from happiness, purpose and

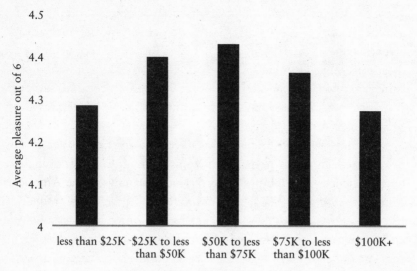

Figure 1: Happiness and income

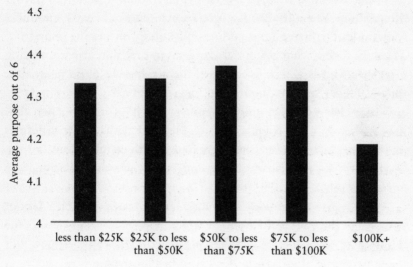

Figure 2: Sense of purpose and income

misery – it would seem that it is best to have 'just enough' income in the US, around $50–75K. At this point, people are protected from misery but they have not yet earned so much that they lose sight of purpose.

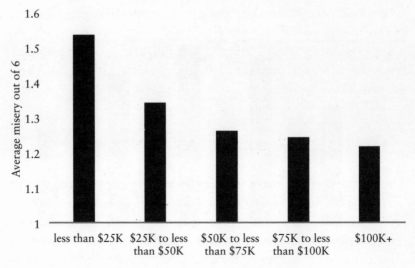

Figure 3: Unhappiness and income

These data consistently surprise people. While we cannot say any-thing about causality from correlational data, there is definitely something interesting, and perhaps not totally surprising, going on. The data suggest that being rich can lead to time and attention being directed towards activities that fuel the attainment of more wealth, such as longer working hours and longer commutes, and away from activities that generate more happiness, such as time outside and time with family and friends. This discrepancy between the big effect on happiness that we imagine increased wealth should bring and the small effect we experience goes a long way towards explaining the narrative trap of reaching for wealth.

Across various studies, it emerges that around $75,000 (about £50,000 in the UK) is the point at which further increases in income do not lead to further reductions in misery. This would be at about the 90th centile of income in the UK (and at about the 80th centile in the US). So actually, for the vast majority of the population, earning more money *should* alleviate misery. This is an important point that is often overlooked by relatively wealthy academics and comment-ators who say that money doesn't matter. It doesn't matter to those with some to spare, but it matters a bloody lot to those struggling to pay their monthly bills.[9]

But most people, including those on incomes above £50,000, truly believe misery would continue to fall with higher income above this point. And most people, irrespective of income, would continue to reach for more long after they have earned their fifty grand. This is the addiction problem.

LOOKING AROUND

The comparisons we make to other people can intensify the wealthy narrative trap. Imagine that you and I are colleagues and we earn the same salary. Imagine that you get a £200 a month pay rise. It feels good. Well, now imagine that you find out that I got double that. Your pay rise doesn't feel quite as good now, does it? In one sense, this is a bit odd because you can still use your extra money in ways that make you happier, and I have no great effect on your life or life-style. But in a seemingly more relevant sense, you don't really know how to feel about your pay rise unless you have something or some-one to compare it to.

A great deal of the research on social comparisons in economics assumes that the people we compare ourselves to are people who are similar to us in some way, such as age or gender. Psychologists, how-ever, have refined their theories more recently to show that we also make 'upward' and 'downward' comparisons with people who are better off or worse off than us according to some attribute, such as income (and that these people can also include our past selves).[10] And when it comes to income, most of our comparisons are upwards, to people who earn more than us.

In looking up, the higher the income of those near to us geograph-ically, the worse we think our lives are going. This has been shown in a number of countries, including the UK and the US.[11] There are exceptions, where no effect is found, though.[12] And other people's income is sometimes positively associated with life satisfaction, e.g. in some of the poorest parts of the world such as areas of rural China and small Latin American cities.[13] Resource-sharing within groups may account for some of these effects, but the biggest reason is likely to come simply from the expectation that you are next up to get rich.

When comparing ourselves to others, particularly in tight-knit or homogeneous communities, we see ourselves in them. This belief allows us to feel as if we have some control over our financial destinies. If we believe we have the ability to rise up the ladder, we'll feel better seeing what we believe we will someday become.

The importance of perception here is supported by other work which shows that how happy people feel is most affected by their perception of where they sit among various reference groups, rather than where they actually sit.[14] For example, one study has used a person's absolute income as compared with the average income of that person's neighbours to predict life satisfaction.[15] You've guessed it – we are happier when our neighbours earn less.

People's perceptions of their position in wealth and income distributions are often inaccurate. Those who have a little tend to overestimate their position, and people who have a lot tend to underestimate it. There is a general tendency to under-report wages in survey questionnaires, though. And this is further affected by how satisfied people are with their wages. Using a sample of workers from France, researchers compared how much employers said that the employees earned each month with how much the employees themselves said that they earned. Those who were less satisfied with their wages (the majority of people) tended to under-report the figure, but those who were more satisfied with their wages tended to over-report them.[16]

One of the difficulties in studies looking for the effects of other people's income on our own happiness is defining the 'reference group'; that is, the people we compare ourselves to. In Laura Kudrna's Ph.D. work using ATUS (and another sample of adults over fifty years of age in England) she tested over three hundred different ways of measuring the 'reference group', and her results suggest that studies finding no effect of relative status on happiness have most often used reference groups that are psychologically further away from us. The reference groups that mattered most consistently for happiness were others of a similar age in our area. When the groups to which people are assumed to compare themselves were defined only as those living in the same area, there was never an association with happiness, suggesting that people need to identify with their neighbours in some other way in order for social comparisons to matter for their happiness. Speaking personally, I am much more affected by what other professors at the LSE earn than I am by the average income of other people living in Hove.

Debt is a clear cause of stress and misery, and we can get ourselves into trouble by trying to keep up with those around us. In Canada, the government runs a very popular lottery. Research has shown that in the two years after a lottery win, the neighbours of those who win larger amounts are more likely to file for bankruptcy. Specifically, a 1 per cent increase in the size of the lottery win is associated with a 0.04 per cent increase in bankruptcies. Part of the explanation for this is that neighbours of lottery winners spend more of their income on visible goods such as cars and motorcycles in order to keep up.[17]

In Switzerland, researchers linked data on income satisfaction and life satisfaction from the Swiss Household Panel with regional information from the Federal Roads Office detailing the number of Porsche and Ferrari registrations per thousand of the population.[18] They found that the more Porsches and Ferraris there are in a neighbourhood, the less satisfied people in those neighbourhoods are with their salaries. There was also an effect on life satisfaction more generally, though it was smaller.

Envy can have a distorting effect, particularly when it comes to money. This has been demonstrated by a series of novel experiments conducted recently in the US.[19] In one experiment, participants were asked to take an envious or a neutral perspective when thinking of a person similar to them but different in one important regard, for example exceptionally wealthy. Participants were then asked to estimate the everyday ups and downs that person might experience in response to structured questions (e.g. if you were this person 'how frequent would little problems be for you, compared to you now?'). When an envious perspective was adopted, the everyday 'ups' dominated the 'downs' much more than when a neutral perspective was adopted; i.e. people thought of the wealthy as happier when they were in an envious frame of mind. A follow-up experiment showed that predictions about the everyday lives of those envied for their wealth were much better than those people actually experienced. So if you find yourself envying others with more money than you, think instead of their painful commutes, their screaming children and their enormous tax bills.

Getting richer does not necessarily bring more happiness, partly because we upwardly adjust the people we compare ourselves to. Looking up to those richer than us could serve to motivate us and give us hope, but most of the time it just annoys and discourages us and we are less happy with our lot, particularly if we start from a position of envy. But what if we thought of ourselves as part of the wider world? Let me assume that you are a Brit, you're single, and you take home no less than two grand a month after tax. For every thirty-three people on this planet, you are richer than thirty-two of them. Whatever your own circumstances, I bet if you faced the certainty of emerging into the world with your current assets or taking the chance of being in the financial position of any one of the other seven billion or so people on the planet you would bite my hand off to keep what you have. It might be quite good to remind yourself of that once in a while.

IF YOU'VE GOT IT, FLAUNT IT

People aspire to being rich for a whole host of reasons. One of the most prevalent is to spend money in a way that allows others to recognize your wealth. The need for recognition has been a key driver of the wealthy narrative trap for ever. We have always wanted to impress others, but this particular tendency began to really flourish in the mid-nineteenth century, around the time of the second Industrial Revolution. A whole new class of previously poor people started accumulating capital (the nouveau riche). With the arrival of wealth came the need to demonstrate their newfound status. When we spend our money demonstrably, we are engaging in 'conspicuous' or 'positional' consumption: consuming goods and services that demonstrate your status to other people.[20]

There are three key elements to status-seeking consumption. First, the goods must be limited in supply: if everyone could get the same pair of Valentino trainers, it would be much harder for you to show off your uniquely enviable position as their owner. Second, the consumption must be visible: if no one notices your trainers, because they have a discreet or forgettable design, others couldn't possibly know you were rich. Visibility can refer to physical visibility to other people and/or to social visibility, where our status is expressed in social cues. Going on holiday somewhere luxurious, for instance, is somewhat physically visible through a tan, but it is mostly socially visible. (I'm sure you have experienced a friend or colleague boring you to tears with stories of their adventure holiday, or endless photos of waterfalls and beaches.) The third element of status-seeking consumption is that there is a weak association between price and quality. If price goes up and quality remains unchanged and people still buy the article, they are buying it purely for the status it affords them. This is a fantastic marketing ploy that nearly all of us status-seeking humans seem to fall for; the relationship between price and quality is a lot weaker for lipsticks than it is for facial cleansers, for example.

There are many studies showing that status-seeking consumption improves life satisfaction.[21] In Russia, for example, the more people spend on clothing (a visible item) relative to the people they compare themselves to and interact with, the more satisfied they are.[22] A smaller number of studies, however, do show the opposite. In India, higher household levels of consumption on items such as jewellery, mobile phones, recreation and dowries are associated with lower life satisfaction.[23] One explanation for these results is a treadmill effect. People consume to keep up with others, but this encourages other people to consume more too. So, in a positional sense, everyone is spending more but standing still. (This is similar to the effect of having Porsches and Ferraris around your neighbourhood.)

Interestingly, the more inequality exists in a community, the more we show off our own status. One study by Lukasz Walasek and Gordon Brown first ranked US states according to the levels of income inequality within states and then looked at the most popular Google searches in those states.[24] They then presented sixty members of the public with the following statement:

Some things that people are interested in, or like to buy or find information about, are things that show how rich or successful they are compared to other people. These are sometimes called 'positional goods' or 'status goods'. Someone who buys such goods may be particularly concerned to demonstrate their social status.

The participants were then asked to judge whether the popular search terms fitted this definition. The results showed that, in more unequal states 70 per cent of the forty words used most frequently were related to status goods, such as 'Ralph Lauren', 'fur vests' and 'champagne punch'. In more equal states, none of the popular searches were related to status goods; instead the searches related to non-positional goods, e.g. 'chicken bake' and 'chick flick movies'.

We also see a difference in the extent to which different people on different rungs of the status ladder make their status visible.[25] As people climb the ladder, they may want their status to be recognized across the social strata, choosing status markers that are easily recognized by all (e.g. having a tan or a Hermès handbag). For social climbers, status visibility is essential. The purchasing behaviour of those already at the top tends to be different; they are more concerned with being noticed by others at the top, often in more subtle ways. A Birkin handbag, for example, is one of the world's most expensive handbags, and it has inconspicuous features recognizable only by a fashion-savvy elite.

HITTING THE ROOF

Let's turn to an item that most people will spend the most on – their house – and see how relative effects and showing off play a big part in this decision. This is not to say that owning your own home and/ or living in a bigger place will make you less happy (the evidence on this is thin and mixed) but, much like the other things that we reach for such as the designer bag, at some point keeping up with the Joneses becomes financially untenable.

Housing tenure and type is another nice example of a good that allows you to show off, both in terms of whether you own or rent and, more obviously, the kind of place and area you live in. Home ownership can be a desire with absolute value (you benefit from owning your own home irrespective of any comparisons you make to other people), but it also allows you to signal that you have 'arrived', or at least are in the process of 'making it'. It is a good that has relative (positional) benefits as well as absolute value.

It is now taken for granted in both the UK and US that a mortgage is better than a rental contract and it is something that the majority of people reach for. The British Social Attitudes Survey in 2010 found that, given the choice to rent their accommodation or buy, 86 per cent of participants expressed a desire to buy.[26] The figure was 87 per cent in 1999, so the housing market crash in 2008 hasn't made much of a dent in these desires. An American Heartland Monitor poll from 2014 shows that 56 per cent of Americans see home ownership as a very necessary component for living a good life,[27] although this figure is slightly lower among millennials (53 per cent).

It is not surprising, then, that the norms and status associated with home ownership influence people's decisions to take the plunge and to buy their own home. A recent study in the UK found that the greater the importance an individual's peer group placed on home ownership, the greater the effect on that individual's life satisfaction from getting a mortgage compared to renting.[28] The same study also showed that increases in home ownership among an individual's peer group led to decreases in life satisfaction for that individual. If your friends buy their own homes it dilutes the extent to which you stand out by buying yours.

One of the aspirational Hove mums that my wife, Les, knows asked her when we would be moving to a bigger house in a more 'desirable' area. She naively assumed that having a best-selling book and a minor TV career meant that I was raking it in. (Note to readers: this simply is not true. Note to publishers and TV companies: it ought to be true.) Our family of four lives in a five-bedroom house. Each of us has our own room and the kids have a playroom for fuck's sake. So why would we need a bigger house? Only to show off, which a lot of arseholes in Hove enjoy doing. (Did I mention the playroom . . .?)

If the benefits we derive from a good depend on what other people think about it, then its value is highly sensitive to shifts in narratives about what's important. Home ownership in the UK, for instance, was less than 50 per cent when I was born in 1968. Everyone I grew up with lived in social housing. There was no discernible desire to own a property among anyone I knew. This all changed in the 1980s with Margaret Thatcher's popular pledge of a 'property-owning democracy' made possible through the Right-to-Buy scheme. The scheme gave tenants of councils and some housing associations the right to buy their homes at heavily discounted prices. As a result, home-ownership rates in the UK rose steadily to around 70 per cent at the turn of the century. Smaller but broadly comparable increases were realized in the US.

Since then, home-ownership rates have been falling slowly but surely in both the UK and US, and are currently around 63 per cent in both countries.[29] It is possible that, over time, attitudes will fall in line with behaviours, as history attests. The strong social narrative in favour of home ownership might weaken, but it hasn't yet. However, given that average house prices in the UK are getting close to ten times the average income, reducing the social pressure surrounding home ownership would alleviate that particular strain for a great many people.

As well as who owns the house, does size matter? A bigger house can benefit us by giving us more room for more activities (such as playrooms), and it can also benefit us by the simple confirmation that we can afford a bigger house. From a large UK sample, a recent study found that, on average, a man's life satisfaction increased from upsizing (moving to a place with more rooms per person) but a woman's did not.[30] The authors of this study argue that those extra (empty?) bedrooms are a status symbol for men. In support of this conclusion, Bob Frank, the world's leading expert on status-driven consumption, has shown that the majority of people he surveyed said they would rather live in 3,000-square-foot houses while others live in 2,000-square-foot ones, than live in a 4,000-square-foot house while others live in 6,000-square-foot homes.[31] So, size matters; but only if yours is bigger.

Houses have got bigger over the years in the suburban US, but people haven't become any more satisfied with their housing over time. The positional nature of housing means that the happiness I derive from moving to that bigger home directly impacts how you feel about staying put in your comparatively smaller one. One study by Swedish academics estimated that about half of all the benefits we derive from additional expenditure on housing can be attributed to increased relative consumption.[32] Whether we gain in absolute or relative terms does not matter much to us, but our relative benefits make other people miserable by comparison and can lead to an arms race in which people fork out more and more, upsizing to bigger and bigger homes, not because they need or even use the extra space but in an attempt to outdo each other.

CONCLUSIONS

It makes a lot of sense to strive for more if you have very little. But being rich per se does not make us (or those around us) happy. The journey to riches for most people will be long, unpleasant and fruitless, so it makes a lot more sense to take the shorter path to 'just enough'. This requires noticing when decisions to pursue more money are driven by social comparisons and status, as opposed to those borne of the wish to have better experiences. For many of us the desire for income and wealth continues unabated even when we have plenty.

If anything, it feels like the social narrative of wealth is only getting stronger. Each generation is encouraged to strive for more than the one before. When I was a kid, no one thought of having more than one television in the house. The average British home now has about as many TVs as it has people. I remember being so excited when we got a colour television sometime around 1981. I know it was after 10 May 1980, as I watched West Ham beat Arsenal in the FA Cup Final on my twelfth birthday at our next-door neighbour's house because they had a colour set and we still didn't. (My twelfth birthday was the best day of my life – along with my kids being born . . .) We still only have one TV in our house (but it is a bloody massive high-definition one).

My main proposal drawn from this chapter is that if you are not struggling to make ends meet, rein in the social narrative that encourages you to endlessly pursue more money. Invest your time and effort into doing all you can to ensure that those who are struggling are provided with the living conditions, wages and financial support that will help them to cover the costs of their living expenses. (As we shall see in Chapter 7, helping other people is great for our own happiness.) The narrative trap of reaching for ever more wealth can be attractive and addictive. Failure to manage this addiction can lead to negative social comparisons, resulting in even greater consumption of material goods, which further raises living costs for us all.

A just-enough approach to wealth is not made any easier by the demands placed on us by family commitments, especially as your family grows, and social expectations. Social media, in particular, facilitates showing off beyond our wildest dreams. Even without the constant bombardment to reach for more wealth, 'just enough' can still sound like a weak counter-narrative to 'keep striving for more'. But even if it appears boring to accept that you (may) have enough wealth already, it can also be tremendously liberating. Once you have enough money to afford the basic things you want in life, you can stop constantly worrying.

Attending to being wealthy also means that we harshly judge others for being happy with what they have – we might call them unambitious or lazy – thus preserving the status quo and making it more likely that more people will be miserable with what they have. So we need to stop judging others as lazy, uninspiring or un-ambitious when they report being happy as they are. The narrative of reaching for wealth stigmatizes those who do not want more money. Let's instead celebrate those who choose to devote their time and effort to causes of social worth rather than question them for not accumulating more personal wealth. Social media could be a great catalyst for this too.

The desire for wealth has truly far-reaching consequences. It usu-ally means the over-consumption of goods, resulting in global greenhouse-gas emissions and unnecessary land, material and water use. Repeated spending on items that are easily replaced means more production and excess waste, both of which have serious environ-mental consequences. It has been suggested that we would need another economic crash, similar to the one in 2008, to have any sig-nificant limiting effect on greenhouse-gas emissions. So if you are going to spend your money on anything, try to spend it on something that will last.

If you are a parent, reinforcing the narrative at home that some money can be enough will help children learn from an early age that the relentless pursuit of money is not inevitable. When we asked our two children what they wanted last Christmas, they both replied that they didn't really want anything – except that a surprise might be quite nice. I was a proud dad in that moment (as well as sounding a little smug now).

If you are a policy-maker, perhaps you could start by publishing lists of the top taxpayers, rather than the top earners. When I searched for 'the world's richest person' on Google, the answer came up immediately (Jeff Bezos was giving Bill Gates a run for his money when I last looked). But when I looked up 'the world's highest tax-payer', the search returned lots of information on which countries had the highest tax rates. If we know that we are hard-wired to compete and to compare, then let's use this to write social narratives that we can all benefit from. This leads us nicely into the next Reaching narrative: that we should be successful.

2

Successful

Before we get going with this narrative, here are two questions for you to answer. Make a note of your answers, and we'll come back to the questions at the end of Part One.

Please read the following statements and indicate whether you would choose Life A or Life B *for yourself*:

Life A: Your job is very high status and people respect you for it. You often feel miserable.
Life B: You have a mundane job that is not held in high regard. You hardly ever feel miserable.

Please read the following statements and indicate whether you would choose Life A or Life B *for a friend*:

Life A: Your friend's job is very high status and people respect them for it. Your friend often feels miserable.
Life B: You friend has a mundane job that is not held in high regard. Your friend hardly ever feels miserable.

Following his suicide attempt, Stephen Fry claimed that his emotional breakdown was 'because he pursued success to the exclusion of everything else, imagining that would lead to happiness'.[1] Let us now turn to our second Reaching narrative, which is the constant pursuit of success and status. Success can come in many guises, but most people will focus on having a promising career or having a 'good' job. It is the most obvious way in which our success is judged, and so this is where my discussion will be directed. Around two-thirds of young people aged eighteen to thirty-four in the US currently agree that being successful in a high-paying career or profession is 'one of the most important things' or 'very important' in their lives, with the proportion agreeing with the statement now higher among young women than among young men.[2]

EMPLOYMENT

The first box to tick in the success narrative is to be employed, so let's start by looking at the effects of having a job – any job – compared to being out of work. The effects of unemployment on life satisfaction are about as big as the coefficients on a variable get.[3] Being out of work hits life satisfaction hard and, unlike many other life events such as divorce, there appears to be very little improvement afterwards. Life satisfaction never fully recovers from the effects of unemployment, even when those who had once been out of work are back in it again. It would appear that an individual's confidence and sense of job security are permanently scarred by unemployment, especially when there are multiple bouts of it.[4]

It has been shown that higher national unemployment is associated with lower happiness of the employed but with higher happiness of the unemployed, and (in some studies) especially for men.[5] This suggests that people who are employed are negatively affected by the threat of becoming unemployed, whereas people who are unemployed consider themselves to be doing all right when there are more people in a similar situation to them. This again illustrates the power of social norms, which in the case of work appear to affect men more than women, probably because of the historic emphasis on men being breadwinners.

There are mixed findings on the day-to-day experiences of the unemployed compared to those in work. Some studies show similar levels of experienced happiness between those in and out of work because the unemployed are not engaged in some of the less satisfying activities associated with work.[6] Research from Germany suggests that people who become unemployed also become more satisfied with their free time, hobbies and family life. But again these studies don't account for how meaningful people who are in or out of work report their experiences to be.[7] Notably, these studies do not take into consideration the additional contribution of purpose that many people experience at work. The activity of working is rated as highly meaningful by many people, as shown by my own research and several other studies.[8] So could it be that, even if the employed don't always feel any happier than the unemployed, they do feel that what they're directing their attention to is more worthwhile?

Our analysis of the ATUS data referred to in Chapter 1 found that the unemployed *do not* experience less meaningfulness, on average.[9] This may be driven by gender differences, as shown by Alan Krueger's analyses of the ATUS.[10] He found that women who are not in the labour force participate more in household activities than do men, and women experience these activities as meaningful. Men who are out of the labour force do fewer household activities, and experience less meaning than those in employment. Women who cite reasons other than home responsibilities for not being in the labour force report relatively lower meaning, too, but it is not unequivocally the case that the unemployed are miserable. In short, then, you don't need a job to be happy, but you do need one to think that you are. And if you are a man, you need a job to feel that what you do is meaningful, too – unless you also get involved more around the home.

That unemployment makes some people miserable in some ways is still consistent with a 'just enough' approach to the social narrative of success. A desire for a job can hardly be seen as getting carried away with the idea of success. Beyond having a job – any job – one of the most widely used measures of success is having a good job, and doing well in your career. So let's now look at types of job more closely.

OCCUPATION

One of the motivations for writing this book was the reaction I got to the following story I told in *Happiness by Design*:

> A few weeks ago, I went out for dinner with one of my best friends, whom I have known for a long time. She works for a prestigious media

company and basically spent the whole evening describing how miserable she was at work; she variously moaned about her boss, her colleagues, and her commute. At the end of dinner, and without a hint of irony, she said, 'Of course, I love working at MediaLand.'

This story highlights the very common inner conflict between the social narrative of success, which values status and recognition in a job, and personal experiences of happiness in the job, which will only be affected by occupational status when attention is drawn to it. My friend was experiencing pain and pointlessness at work, but the narrative she told about her job was totally unrelated. A job that makes us miserable is not a good job, but we can convince ourselves it is if it has high status. MediaLand is somewhere my friend had always wanted to work, her parents were proud of her, and her friends were a little bit jealous. So the narrative she created for herself comes from the broader social narrative of status. *Happiness by Design* wasn't intended to be 'The book that will make you quit your job', as the *New Statesman* attested. But it was for my friend (eventually) and for readers I have since spoken to.

The boss of a law firm I talked to about the book explicitly requested that I did not suggest to any of their employees that they should quit their jobs (a request I had to ignore, of course . . .). I have never been asked to talk to a group of florists but, if I should be, I am pretty certain that their boss would not request that I refrain from suggesting they seek alternative employment. OK, so lawyers probably have more alternative career options than florists, but it might still seem surprising, seeing that I tell the MediaLand story, that there is more concern about lawyers quitting their jobs than there would be about florists doing so.

The social narrative surrounding status suggests that being a lawyer is a 'better' job than being a florist. So surely a florist would be more likely to think about quitting their job than a lawyer would be? The former is lacking in economic status and the latter has plenty. But the MediaLand story also reminds us of another dimension on which one job might be 'better' than another: namely, how happy it makes them day to day. And it is here that florists seem to have better jobs than lawyers, with 87 per cent of florists agreeing that they are happy compared to 64 per cent of lawyers. These are the data I discussed in *Happiness by Design* and they come from a 2012 City and Guilds survey that interviewed 2,200 employees from a wide range of professions (there was a 2013 follow up for millennials that found pretty much the same thing).[11]

More recent data also suggest that the most conventionally 'successful' occupations are not ones where the happiest workers are to be found. In 2014 the Legatum Institute published a report combining data from the 2013 Annual Survey of Hours and Earnings and ONS data from 2011–13.[12] They looked to see which occupational groups were paid the most and which ones had the highest average life satisfaction. Predictably, chief executives and other senior officials were the highest paid, but they were no more satisfied than their secretaries, who were obviously paid much less. Some other professions whose members were happier than their bank accounts might suggest were the clergy, farmers and fitness instructors. There can be a lot of purpose in these roles (and quite a lot of pleasure too, if the fitness instructors I know are anything to go by).

There could well be issues with the 'selection effect' in that those who choose careers like floristry, on average, might be happier to begin with than those who choose to go into law. Prospective florists, again on average, might also be less affected by the narrative of success than prospective lawyers. We need good longitudinal studies (which follow the same people over time) to find out more. It would also be very interesting to find out if there are differences in the concerns for recognition among people who seek out jobs associated with recognition. We might expect that many of those choosing careers as lawyers care more about what others think of them than those who choose careers analogous to being 'just a florist'.

There are aspects of jobs like floristry, however, which make them more likely to generate happiness than working in a law firm. These include working with nature, regularly seeing the fruits of your labour, generally being around people who want to be with you, and feeling as though you have control over your workload. More than four out of five florists also say that they are able to hone their skills every day, according to the Legatum Institute report. So I reckon that some of the happiness difference between florists and lawyers is caused by the 'treatment effect' of occupation. The same can be said for members of the clergy, farmers and fitness instructors. Focusing on the likely daily experiences of the jobs we choose to take can help us avoid the unnecessary pain and pointlessness that often accompany adherence to the narrative of what a 'good' job looks like.

WORKING HOURS

The Reaching narrative not only applies to what jobs we have but also to how long we spend working. It suggests that we should work longer and longer hours so that we can be wealthier and more 'successful'. Increased economic growth during the twentieth century has been associated with more work. Those with more money and more prestigious jobs tend also to take on longer working hours and more responsibilities. As we get richer, we feel more intensely the need to keep up. The famed British economist John Maynard Keynes predicted that you would be reading this on one of the two days a week you are at work, or on one of the five days you are off sunning yourself, playing golf or watching TV. He predicted that increased economic growth would lead to increased leisure time. He was right about many things, but not this.

As incomes rise, it seems that we pay more attention to the income foregone from not working; and so we work more to capitalize on the increased value of our time. Time is money. Moreover, paying attention to time as money has been shown to diminish the pleasure experienced from leisure activities. Little wonder, then, that daily happiness in the US is actually lower for those on high incomes compared to those on middling ones. There is no time for enjoyment when you are using all of your time reaching to be rich.

Along with money comes status. Those in top positions often make statements that signal their long hours as a badge of honour. For example, Apple CEO Tim Cook recently told *Time* magazine that he starts emailing his colleagues at 4.30 a.m.; he is the first in the office and the last to leave. Since the 1970s, when there was not much difference in the number of hours worked by income, those on higher incomes have increasingly worked longer hours compared to those on lower incomes. Contrary to Keynes's predictions, then, long working hours have rapidly come to signal and legitimize class status among today's elite. The super-rich justify their superiority on the social ladder by fetishizing their appetite for non-stop work. They might earn high salaries but they really do deserve them, don't they?

When we look at the ATUS, happiness and purpose are both at their highest in the group working between twenty-one and thirty hours a week, and misery increases in tandem with the number of hours worked thereafter. The results are consistent across genders. When we look at the factors predicting who is in the most miserable 1 per cent of the ONS data, however (see pp. 5–9), Alina Velias assures me that working longer hours is on the list. On average, the most miserable work a couple of hours a week more than those outside the bottom 1 per cent group. Recall also that earning less than £400 a week is on the list too, so there will be a trade-off for many on low wages between earning enough money and not working themselves into the ground.

Overall, what constitutes 'just enough' hours will differ depending on the particulars of obligation and appetite. Many people do also choose to work long hours. Some people love their work so much that they want to spend as much time working as possible. I have felt like that at times in my career, and most of all when I have been working on my books, and I know many of my colleagues and collaborators have too. But this is a quite rare and extremely fortunate position to be in.

Many more people 'choose' to work long hours because the social narrative of long work hours is so persuasive. Most unpaid overtime (and perhaps some paid overtime too) is undertaken out of a desire to progress at work and not from any underlying pleasure or purpose from working those hours. The expectation of prolonged working hours permeates a number of different professions from banking, advertising and law to education and other public services, as well as poorly paid positions in the arts. There is huge pressure on staff to be the first one in and the last to leave, so everyone comes in earlier and leaves later.

Last year, I was involved in a TV series called *Make Or Break?* for Channel 5. A typical filming day lasted about sixteen hours, from leaving the hotel to returning, and this was for six days out of seven, over a period of four weeks. Now, I'm not asking you to feel sorry for me, because being a TV presenter is hardly the worst job in the world (although the four-hour daily round trip in a van across dirt tracks to sit around in the heat of the Mexican summer waiting to film was about as bad as it gets for an impatient git who melts in temperatures above 20°C). The long days were justified on the grounds that this is 'just how TV is', as if historical precedent and industry expectations were explanation enough for over-working people. Long hours in TV are seen as a badge of honour when instead they adversely affect happiness and, I suspect, productivity too.

As more of our time is spent working, the number of people affected by work-related 'burnout' has increased in recent years. A survey by eFinancialCareers investigating the hours worked by 9,000 financial workers in Hong Kong, London, New York and Frankfurt found that a typical week consisted of around 100 hours of work.[13] About 20 per cent of those surveyed claimed to be 'totally' burnt out. There has been quite a lot of news coverage recently of suicides among Japanese workers who put in long hours, literally working themselves to death. They even have a name for this phenomenon – *karōshi* (death by overwork). A recent survey reported by the BBC found that almost a quarter of Japanese organizations had employees who worked over eighty hours of overtime per month, a threshold above which the chances of dying prematurely increase significantly.

The 'tipping point' for burnout varies for individuals. A twelve-hour workday might be a breeze for somebody who only needs four hours' sleep a night, whereas it will be too much for someone who needs nine in order to feel rested. We should consider such individual differences and move away from the one-size-fits-all approach that is a consequence of the prevailing social narrative that just because you can work for twelve hours straight means your employees can or should, too. Averages can be useful for policy-makers because they can help inform us about the effects of a policy on large groups of people. But we must also be alert to individual differences and seek to accommodate these where possible. Striking a balance in between is probably the best starting point, leaving overtime or 'under-time' optional for a rise or reduction in pay.

Research suggests that establishing a satisfactory work–life balance is particularly challenging for women.[14] Despite their increasing prominence in the workplace, women with children still tend to see their duties as weighted in favour of home life compared to work life, and vice versa for men.[15] Even when a woman has a job, she is still expected to do more of the housework and childcare, and may feel a stronger obligation to do them. In some of my own work, I have shown that longer commuting time is associated with lower psychological health among married women, and hardly at all among men and single women.[16] This is almost certainly because married women still pick up most of the household duties when they get home, while the commute does not eat into men's time in quite the same way.

THE CLASS CEILING

We know that working-class people are discriminated against in the workplace right from their first day. In conducting interviews with thirteen elite accountancy, law and financial firms in the UK, the Social Mobility Foundation found that higher grades were demanded of state-school applicants than from their private-school contemporaries applying for the same job.[17] This is in spite of the fact that obtaining a given set of grades is easier in a private school, where the environment is much more conducive to exam success, than in state schools.

Even if someone from a working-class background 'makes it', they do not make as much; as colleagues from the LSE have shown, there currently exists about a 17 per cent difference in the salaries of those from middle-class and working-class backgrounds in highly prized professions such as law, medicine and finance. These data come from nearly 100,000 people who completed the 2014 Labour Force Survey, Britain's largest employment survey.[18] It draws on the class origins of people in these occupations, looking at how their income varies according to their background (whether or not their parents were in higher professional or managerial positions). This pay gap is about the same as exists between men and women. The 'glass ceiling' gets a lot of attention in the press, and rightly so, but the 'class ceiling' is hardly ever discussed. The LSE, like most modern institutions, has a diversity policy in relation to gender and race but, like most modern institutions, takes no account of class background in its faculty recruitment processes.

I found it very interesting that the 2017 coverage of who earns the highest salaries at the BBC in the UK focused almost entirely on the gender pay gap, and especially the fact that the highest-paid man (Chris Evans) trousers more than £2 million a year, compared to the highest-paid woman (Claudia Winkleman) who earns less than £500,000. There was a bit of coverage on the lack of representation of ethnic minorities in the list of those earning over £150,000. These are undoubtedly important inequalities worthy of discussion. But hardly anything at all was made of the fact that nearly half of the highest-paid presenters were privately educated. Apart from Sky News's Lewis Goodall, who drew my attention to this fact, there simply aren't enough journalists like him who care about class differences.

Although a blind eye has often been turned to class by organizations and the media, the barriers to entry to middle-class professions are pretty well documented. For the purposes of this book, I want to focus on the expectations that need to be fulfilled before somebody from a working-class background can be successful in a predominantly middle-class environment. This is a pernicious yet overlooked barrier to entry that prevents working-class people occupying middle-class professions, or from earning as much once in them.

To be successful in a 'good' job typically requires standing out from the crowd, which is something that middle-class people are much more comfortable with compared to working-class folk, who generally prefer fitting in.[19] Studies suggest that people higher up the class ladder are more independently oriented than those lower down the ladder, who are likely to be more group-minded.[20] For example, during a short interaction with a stranger in the lab, people of lower (self-reported) socio-economic status backgrounds displayed greater engagement cues (e.g. nodding and laughing) than those of higher socio-economic status backgrounds, who were more likely to display disengagement cues (e.g. doodling).[21] These skills allow for better understanding of others' opinions among working-class people.

Other studies have also shown a heightened awareness of social surroundings among working-class people. In one study, researchers stopped sixty-one people in New York City and fitted them with Google Glasses.[22] They then instructed these people to walk about one block. After their walk, they asked the participants which social class they thought they belonged to. The results showed that those participants identifying as higher class looked at other people less. A few other studies using similar methods with different people produced similar results. The higher up the social ladder you (think you) are, the less you care what's going on around you.

It is thought that working-class individuals are better attuned to their social environment because they have more to gain from other people than middle-class folk.[23] When resources are scarce, there is a real need to be able to depend on others and for them to understand that they can depend on you. Therefore, it benefits working-class individuals to be more vigilant and empathetic of the people around them; if you notice someone else in trouble, they will be more likely to notice you. Yet these important differences in class-based characteristics disadvantage working-class people in occupational settings where a high premium is placed on the more individualistic values of the middle class.

Like a number of unfair realities in the workplace, this one is also inefficient. While empathy (the ability to relate to others) has been shown to have downsides in the context of altruism (as we will see in Part Three), it can be an advantage in the workplace. Many scholars attest that having empathy is fundamental to good leadership.[24] Being attuned to the thoughts and actions of others can help leaders to predict possible outcomes before they happen. It also allows leaders to position staff in roles that match their skills and professional needs, making it more likely that they will be productive. In addition to this, an empathetic leader helps workers feel valued for the work that they do, which is important for happiness at work. So, a working-class trait that has considerable value can be neglected by companies in ways that can adversely affect the bottom line.

Working-class individuals have also been reported as having a greater sensitivity to environmental and social threats, due to being brought up in resource-scarce environments. For example, working-class kids display elevated heart rates and blood pressure in response to ambiguous and threatening social situations, such as the thought of someone laughing after they responded to being called on in class, or not being invited to a party.[25] This heightened vigilance is generally seen as a bad thing, but what the literature has failed to explore in its narrow focus on disadvantage are the potential upsides to increased vigilance, particularly within an organizational context. Perhaps if more working-class folk had been involved in the banking activities that led up to the global financial crisis, for example, the excessive risk-taking that resulted in the widespread economic downturn would have been mitigated.

For efficiency and equity reasons, then – and ultimately for happiness – we need to improve class diversity, and to celebrate class difference, just as, slowly but surely, we are doing with gender and racial differences. Diversity can cause tensions between groups but there are ways in which this can be carefully channelled for collective benefit. For example, working towards a common goal has been shown to bring people from diverse backgrounds together and reduce bias.[26] Exposure also helps in the right contexts: the more frequently we see people, the more we grow to like them. Employers should use these techniques to tackle the challenges of embracing diversity if they want to design a more efficient and inclusive workforce that makes all people, rather than just a select group, feel valued for their unique contributions – and happier as a result.

THE MYTH OF MOBILITY

From an efficiency perspective, there are some occupations where class diversity matters more than others. We would like people to be good at their jobs and, for many jobs, family background does not make much difference to work performance. If I am having a heart transplant, for instance, I want to be operated on by the best surgeon. Leaving aside the personal interaction aspects of the surgical process, I don't care whether she was born into a rich or poor family (though the former is obviously much more likely). Or if I am having my car cleaned, I want it be cleaned by someone thorough, and again I couldn't care less about his background (he is more likely to be working class, of course).

When it comes to politicians and policy-makers, however, being good at your job is a function of your family background. It is easier for us to act in the interests of those whose lives are similar to our own. No single individual can properly speak to experiences they haven't had, but a group of decision-makers collectively can. If over half of MPs have been to private school while 93 per cent of the general public have not, then I would argue that our representative democracy is not very representative at all. With the best will in the world, those who eat artisan bread (whatever the fuck that is) cannot understand the lives of those living on the bread line. This lack of representation is compounded by the fact that strong associations have been found between the decline in the proportion of working-class MPs and a decline in working-class turnout at election time.

So, unlike surgeons and car cleaners, who can come predominantly from middle-class and working-class backgrounds, respectively, our elected officials should be broadly representative of the populations they serve. The question, then, is which jobs require representativeness of the population served by that job in order to be done well. Note that I am referring to efficiency here and not equity: we need quotas in political representation to ensure that the job of representation gets done well, and not because it is a fair outcome for MPs to reflect the population they serve (though it could be thought of as fair as well as efficient).

Now, you might say that doctors should not predominantly come from middle-class backgrounds on the grounds of fairness. Even if the efficiency of a doctor were to be unaffected by her background, it is surely only equitable that we get more working-class kids into medicine? Most people would agree that we need more social mobility so that more working-class kids get the opportunity to become doctors (and, unless the patterns of demand across sectors changes, more middle-class kids get to be car cleaners). I have never been entirely sure about that. Let me explain why.

First, we will always need low-skilled jobs, such as car cleaners, as well as high-skilled ones, such as doctors. So we should pay much greater attention to improving the working conditions, pay and status of the low-skilled jobs so that people don't feel desperate to escape them – or dissuaded from joining them. Breaking free from the narrative of success will enable us to stop fixating on how to get a few people to move from low-end to high-end employment, so that we can each feel proud of what we do. The importance of this point may well be exacerbated soon as the brave new world of Artificial Intelligence (AI) and robots is set to radically transform the way we work and the kinds of jobs available to us. While we cannot predict the full consequences of this technological revolution, it is unlikely to diminish a skills hierarchy in the workplace, exacerbated by a status hierarchy, unless we rein in the narrative of success.

Secondly, the jobs that are supposedly aspirational usually pay more money but are often ones that make people miserable. Job satisfaction is positively correlated with income but the association is weak, and would be even weaker if we could diminish the power of the success narrative. We have already seen, even with the high status it is afforded, how being a lawyer may not be all it is cracked up to be. It seems bizarre to me that most people will see it as a good thing when the son of a relatively happy builder becomes a less happy banker. Social mobility should, in the very least, not be detrimental to happiness at work.

Thirdly, and related to the previous point, when we talk about social mobility, we are actually referring to market mobility in terms of socio-economic status, like getting a promotion or a new house. We do not mean mobility in terms of better social relationships such as greater volunteering or being more involved in family life. As a society, we should reorient ourselves towards the latter to diminish some of the power of a narrative that defines success in terms of income and occupation, so that, as individuals, we are each able to pursue success in ways that are best suited to our own experiences.

Fourthly, as I alluded to in the Introduction, the kind of social mobility that the middle class have in mind is that everyone wants to be middle class. But many working-class kids don't, and for good reason. As I will discuss in more detail in the next chapter on education, when working-class kids gain social status, they lose friends, networks and a sense of identity. I am, of course, aware that everyone can have it tough in their own way and that anyone can take a happiness hit whenever they switch between groups. For example, a public-school boy moving to a state school might well be bullied for his accent or his clothes. But moving down is universally seen to be a bad thing, whereas moving up is looked upon favourably and actively encouraged. And yet surely it is better to be a builder with friends you are connected to than a banker with colleagues with whom you feel no affinity.

Finally, and perhaps most importantly of all, the idea of social mobility promotes the notion that anyone can make it if they work hard enough. I became a professor at the LSE, so any working-class kid can; and if they don't, well, that's down to their own lack of talent and effort. This belief simply serves to prop up the existing system and its gross inequalities in opportunity and outcome. We will never have a level playing field and working-class kids will always be much less likely to 'succeed', no matter how hard they try. We are setting people up with unrealistic expectations, in terms both of what they can achieve and what will make them happy. And we are continuing to disproportionately praise and remunerate those who have simply been lucky enough to be born to the right parents with the right set of personal attributes. I will discuss this in greater detail in Chapter 9.

CONCLUSIONS

As we reach for success, we must be mindful of what it takes to achieve goals that will bring us status. Being in paid work is generally good for productivity, GDP and happiness. There are therefore good reasons to incentivize people to work – but not at any cost. In the UK in 2016, there were around a million people on 'zero hours' contracts. This means that they are not guaranteed work each week even though they need to be available to work, and they are not entitled to benefits such as sick pay. Most would prefer more stable conditions. In the US, workers generally do not even have employment contracts to protect them from being fired at their employers' will. There are also nearly 10 million people in the US classified as the 'working poor' because they have jobs but still fall below the official poverty level.[27] The 'just enough' approach means prioritizing those who do not have enough.

If you are a parent advising your children on what sort of job to pursue, consider encouraging them to think about the features of the job and the relationships they want to have with their colleagues. And while they are studying, suggest that they take subjects they enjoy rather than ones that may look good on their CV. It's often quite hard for a parent not to live some of your own life through your children. I say that all I want for my kids is for them to be happy, and I think that's true. But I also can't help myself from nudging them into sports that I think they should enjoy. I certainly hope that they grow up with a questioning view of their own about social narratives. And I can't help myself from thinking I would be a proud parent if they joined a protest group of some kind, because of the premium I place on questioning existing structures. I'm sure some of that will come across to them at some point. But so long as they are happy . . .

At the LSE and other universities, students are heavily marketed to by the big consultancy firms. These firms paint a glamorous picture of success. But many recruits work eighty-hour weeks throughout their twenties and, anecdotally at least, end up in 'golden handcuffs' in jobs they hate. Many jobs that are high in status are also long in hours. Schools and universities could do more to frame career choices in terms of personal growth rather than by which jobs will pay the most. They could encourage students to find out the answers to questions that are more likely to impact upon their day-to-day experiences on the job. How many hours does a typical employee work? Will I interact with other friendly human beings? Will I be expected to use one skill set or will there be an opportunity to use many different skills? How much autonomy is there in the work, and will I receive feedback? How long will my commute be? Is there a gym near the office? Does my office have natural light, windows that open and plants?

Employers have a role to play too. There is a concern that the 'happiness agenda' has been co-opted by corporations as a new form of social control. But it doesn't have to be this way if happiness feedback can be used to genuinely enhance employee well-being and productivity, and to guide employers in directions that facilitate these outcomes. For example, we know that people are happier and more productive when their work is valued, and employers could do more to communicate positive and timely feedback to their employees.[28] We also know that people who use a variety of skills on the job are happier in their jobs, and so we can create roles with opportunities to do this.[29] Happier people are more productive, and so the benefits of happier employees are generative.

Just as with the wealthy narrative, there will of course be individual differences in the degree to which people are motivated by 'extrinsic' rewards, such as status and success, compared to being motivated by 'intrinsic' goals, such as the desire to feel in control, competent and to grow as a person. We might be able to get people to care less about external validation for their efforts. But, akin to recasting the wealthy narrative, a more realistic and more effective way forward would be to create social narratives that encourage comparison to those whose jobs benefit society most, rather than to those with jobs that pay the most.

3
Educated

You know the drill. Here are your two questions. Make a note of your answers, and we'll come back to the questions at the end of Part One.

Please read the following statements and indicate whether you would choose Life A or Life B *for yourself*:

Life A: You are well educated. You often feel miserable.
Life B: You have only a basic level of education. You hardly ever feel miserable.

Please read the following statements and indicate whether you would choose Life A or Life B *for a friend*:

Life A: Your friend is well educated. Your friend often feels miserable.
Life B: Your friend has only a basic level of education. Your friend hardly ever feels miserable.

The third Reaching social narrative is that we should value and pursue being well educated. Because the best available data on education relate to years of schooling and qualifications, I will define it in terms of formal learning. I appreciate that this is a narrow definition, but it is difficult to collect data based on 'the school of life'.

We are now more educated than ever. There were about five hundred universities worldwide in 1945; there are over ten thousand now.[1] About one in seven people went to university in the UK when I was an undergraduate in the late-1980s; now it is almost one in two. In the US we see a similar picture, with just over one in three adults completing a four-year college degree now, according to the US Census Bureau.[2] This is seen by the overwhelming majority of people as a good thing. In keeping with the theme of 'just enough', however, I will argue that basic education is good for happiness, but its effects are questionable beyond this.

BETTER EDUCATED . . . AND HAPPIER?

In terms of economic returns, a university graduate can expect, on average, to earn about £200,000 more over their working lifetime than someone similar to them who has not been to university.[3] This gap has widened over the past few decades.[4] There is huge variation around this average, which is determined more by subject than by institution.[5] A good grade helps too. All in all, the costs of tuition fees, etc., which come in at around £50,000, would appear to be a price worth paying, especially since those costs can be repaid over time, and especially when a graduate's rate of repayment depends on their income. (A student loan is much more like an income tax than an unsecured debt on, say, a credit card.)

We should not think of education only as an investment in future benefits. It also provides consumption benefits (and costs) too. In other words, the experience of the education process can make people feel good (and bad) in itself. My own decision to go to university was based entirely on the fact that it sounded like fun, especially when compared to the prospect of taking a job that would probably mean getting up early every morning. I narrowed my choice of university down to those with a campus, which sounded quite cool to me at the time, and ones that were at least 150 miles away from London so that my parents couldn't just turn up unannounced. I ended up at Swansea University and had a great time. But if I had imagined university to be a worse experience than working, then I would not have gone.

Not everyone has a great time. In fact, the experience at elite universities, like Oxford, can be pretty challenging. In a recent survey conducted by Oxford University Students' Union, two-thirds of students admitted to missing lectures due to a lack of sleep. And before you put this down to partying, 44 per cent of students reported that they felt stressed all or most of the time. It's not much better at Cambridge. In 2014, 40 per cent of all students reading English had been diagnosed with depression. It could turn out to all be worth it in the end when you land that dream job because you studied at Oxbridge. But it would have to be bloody amazing to risk your mental health for, and I don't think we should be encouraging students to take that kind of risk.

It would be disingenuous to put all the blame for all this misery at the door of elite universities. The students who choose go to these institutions are probably pretty intense to begin with. Many of the students I have encountered at the LSE are under enormous pressure to perform well. Some of it is self-inflicted, and much of it comes from parents who have invested a lot in their offspring and expect them to get the highest grades. The students and their parents get carried away with the Reaching narrative of educational attainment way past the point at which it is valuable. And ironically, perhaps, in ways that are counterproductive for attainment anyway, since high levels of stress consistently impede performance.

Is university worth it as an investment in future happiness? Well, as with all happiness evidence, most of what we know about the effects of education comes from assessments of how well people think their lives are going overall. Remember that this is a far-from-ideal measure of happiness because it taps into the stories about how we should live our lives rather than into our direct experiences of living them. There is a lot of variation between studies but, overall, the direct effects of education on life satisfaction are small but significant. The overall effects of education are somewhat larger, however, due to the positive effect that education has on other determinants of life satisfaction, such as income.[6]

When Kate Laffan, Alina Velias and I looked at the most miserable people in the ONS data, we found that having a degree or leaving education after A-levels does not have much effect on the likelihood of being in the bottom 1 per cent of miserableness. What does seem to make a difference is basic education for girls. We found that one in three women in the bottom 1 per cent have no school qualifications, compared to fewer than one in twenty-five in the rest of the sample. The effects of education are a lot weaker for men.

A recent study using data from the British Household Panel Survey split the sample according to how satisfied people were with their lives.[7] The results showed that education had a positive effect on the life satisfaction of the least satisfied bunch, but a negative effect for the most satisfied folk. So if you are dissatisfied with your lot, education could be your ticket out of misery, but if you are pretty satisfied with life already education could make you feel worse.

What we ultimately care about in this book is whether or not education improves our experiences of pleasure and purpose and reduces misery, and we can again look to the ATUS for guidance. The graph below shows us experiences of happiness by level of education. In general, happiness decreases as education increases. Those in the lowest two educational groups – a high school diploma or some further education but not yet a Bachelor's degree – are about as happy as each other, and happier than other groups. Holders of Bachelor's degrees are happier than those with Professional or Doctoral degrees. The holders of Professional or Doctoral degrees are the least happy. They are about 0.35 units on the 0–6 unit scale less happy than those in the lowest two educational groups.

What about experiences of meaning? Can education enrich our experiences by making them feel more fulfilling, even if it does not bring about more good feelings and fewer bad feelings? This was certainly the case for the Greek philosopher Aristotle, who associated intellectual activity with his conception of *eudaimonia*, the virtuous, good and worthwhile life. He would have been somewhat

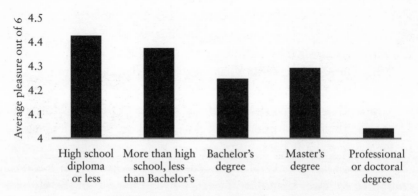

Figure 4: Happiness and education

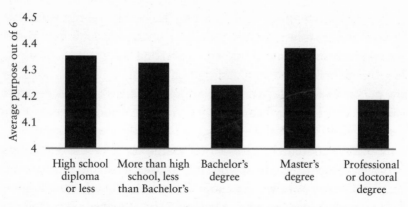

Figure 5: Sense of purpose and education

perplexed by the next figure. Purpose generally decreases with more education, although people with Master's degrees fare quite a bit better here. It is unclear to me why. Any ideas anyone?

As we saw in the 'wealthy' chapter, higher income is associated with less negative feelings even if it does not improve how happy people feel. So even if education does not benefit positive emotions, it is worth considering whether or not it reduces negative ones. The relationship between education and misery is shown in Figure 6. Higher education does not protect very much against feelings of misery. Those with a high school diploma or less are the most miserable, but not by much.

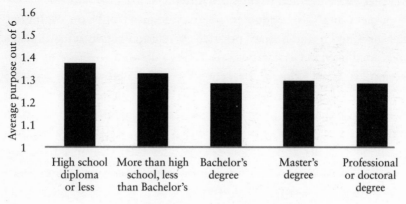

Figure 6: Unhappiness and education

As we also saw in Chapter 1, we are generally negatively affected by increases in other people's incomes. There are far fewer studies investigating the effects of relative education on happiness. I think that this is indicative of an assumption that social comparisons are less pervasive within education than for income. But what evidence there is does not really bear this out. In recent work using data from the UK, Germany and Australia, for example, there is a negative association between life satisfaction and average education using a reference group defined by region, year and age group. In other words, if a person improves their education but others around them improve their education by more, the individual is less satisfied with their life even though they are more educated in absolute terms. Everything is relative, it seems; at least when it comes to life satisfaction.

A NOTE ON INTELLIGENCE

As already noted, formal education is only a small part of what it means to be educated. There are some data on intelligence and happiness that are worth alluding to here. Overall, the concept and measurement of intelligence are highly controversial. Tests such as IQ tests tend to favour white, middle-class men and ignore emotional or social intelligence, which is more often correlated with women and the working class. For these reasons I won't dwell too much on cognitive capacity, but nonetheless it is worth considering whether those deemed to be more intelligent are also happier.

A meta-analysis conducted in 2017 focused only on evaluative measures and found a small positive correlation between intelligence (measured using a General Mental Ability questionnaire) and life satisfaction.[8] In 2012 – the most recent review of the literature at the time of writing – Ruut Veenhoven and Choi Yowon gathered up much of the research that had been undertaken on the relationship between intelligence and happiness at that point.[9] There were 23 studies covering nearly 10 nations and 16,000 people, and their overall conclusion was that there was no relationship between intelligence and happiness, which is consistent with prior reviews.

Of the twenty-three studies, seventeen included a measure that assessed people's experiences such as daily mood, sometimes alongside evaluations of things such as overall happiness, and life satisfaction questionnaires. Out of all seventeen studies assessed, only one study showed that more intelligent people also had better experiences. This took place around 1980, and it showed happier people were also more creative. In the study, almost 2,000 German adults were asked 'open questions about ideas that they associate with a certain city, profession or political concept'. People watching them rated how cheerful they looked. The results showed that more cheerful-looking people were able to list more ideas. So, here, it appears that creative intelligence is associated with better mood – or, at least, with looking like you are in a better mood.

In support of 'just enough', a lower childhood IQ is associated with increased risk of developing schizophrenia, adult depression and adult anxiety,[10] but too much intelligence can also be harmful. One study finds that those who demonstrate the top 10 per cent of 'manic features' (associated with bipolar disorder) have IQ scores around ten points higher when measured at age eight compared with those showing the bottom 10 per cent of manic features.[11] Manic features were measured at age twenty-two to thirty-three using the hypomania checklist HCL-32 questionnaire. This suggests that an exceptionally clever kid may be at greater risk of going on to develop mental health problems as an adult.

One study of around a million Swedish residents did manage to have a good go at understanding this better.[12] It found that male students with excellent school performance were four times more likely to develop bipolar disorder later in life; intriguingly, there was no such difference among women. Because school performance preceded the bipolar diagnosis, these findings suggest that intelligence plays a causal role in mental health problems. Having said that, the children could have had undiagnosed bipolar disorder at school and it is therefore still possible that their mental health problems drove their school performance. But either way, it's not so radical to conclude that there might be an experiential downside to over-thinking and self-scrutiny.

TAKE ME TO THE CLASS ABOVE

One of the reasons why we might not see such a strong association between happiness and education is that working-class people, who might be thought of as having the most to gain from education, lose their social networks and identities as they become better educated. People from similar classes share values, but these values differ across classes. Someone who attempts to integrate into a given class but who fails to conform to its respective value system can face great difficulties. As a result of having to fit into a different world, people who are socially mobile are often at risk of losing some of their sense of identity on the way up the social ladder.[13] Moreover, 'moving up' implies that there is something wrong with where they came from, and this can promote feelings of shame.[14]

The philanthropist Eugene Lang noted that working-class kids were more likely to go on to further education when their school-mates also received the same scholarship, while the economist George Akerlof has shown that social networks, and the identities associated with being a part of these networks, are considerations that students did not wish to give up.[15] This would explain why the students would be willing to progress to higher education if their friends came along too – they get to keep their mates and associated behaviours and values.

Qualitative studies have shown that the transition from school to university is tougher for students of low socio-economic status. For example, biographical reports from, and interviews with, lower-income students highlight the difficulty of forming a coherent identity while at university, as well as highlighting the sense of isolation and lack of confidence experienced by these students.[16] Students from lower socio-economic groups also report having a lower sense of belonging at university.[17] The feeling that we belong to the social groups in which we find ourselves is critical to academic performance and happiness.[18] This is one reason why many of the scholarship kids from poor backgrounds are not as happy as their equally high-achieving peers from wealthier backgrounds and are at a disadvantage when it comes to academic performance.

According to social dominance theory, the transition of working-class values into a middle-class world may actually threaten the middle-class majority.[19] If it were easy for someone from a working-class background to enter a middle-class environment, then the perceived stability of middle-class privileges would be under threat. Non-conformity on the part of the working-class individual therefore serves as a reminder of the threat that the middle class face from upward mobility. So, in an attempt to maintain their middle-class values, institutions have an incentive to perpetuate a sense of alienation among working-class kids.

By conforming to the rules, the working-class individual is assimilated into the middle-class group, and middle-class identity remains unchanged and unchallenged. Taking on middle-class values and acting in conformist ways legitimizes the myth that to be smart you must talk and look like a particular type of person. Failing to adopt this position makes it more likely that the individual will be rejected or ostracized from the group. It's no wonder, then, that working-class kids who want to retain their sense of identity can be made miserable by going to university. All of these seemingly small yet psychologically challenging conflicts add up, and collectively they form an understandable deterrent to going to university.

One of my current academic colleagues and friends talks as if he had a very posh upbringing. It shocked me to learn that he once had a strong Northern accent. He was ridiculed when he first attended university – by his tutors as much as by his peers – and so changed the way he spoke to fit in. Despite his objective success, he still resents feeling like he had to change who he was in order to survive in academia. It is entirely possible that the person most like my friend who did not go to university is every bit as happy as him – happier even – despite almost certainly earning less.

The loss of working-class networks, values and identities for those moving up the social ladder is supported by a longitudinal study from the UK using the British Household Panel Data. Upward inter-generational mobility has been found to be associated with feelings of isolation and vulnerability, mental health problems and lower life satisfaction.[20] Journalists, academics and working-class people from other career paths often mention a continued feeling of being an outsider.[21]

It is pertinent to note, therefore, that nearly all of the research assessing the impact of social mobility focuses on improved economic success, and not on the happiness costs incurred from moving between social classes.

EDUCATION IN CLASS

Let us now turn a critical eye to the experiences of the process of education by social class. If we were to adopt an evidence-based approach to education, we would be most likely to institute more collaborative approaches to learning, which have consistently been shown to enhance attainment.[22] Instead, teaching in education at all stages in the UK and US encourages independent working and competition over co-operation. As was indicated in the last chapter, working-class values are more group-based and less individualistic. Thus, arguably less effective middle-class values are promoted at the expense of more effective working-class values.

Take the application advice given by Yale University on their website, for example: 'pursue what you love and tell us about that. Be yourself.' Emphasis is placed on a student's ability to 'stand out'. All of these qualities are closely aligned with middle-class experiences of competence and there is a failure to recognize the disadvantage that this creates for working-class individuals, where social interactions are more about teamwork and co-operation and less about standing out. Yale could alternatively ask students to 'Tell us about a time you co-operated with others to achieve something you are proud of' or 'Tell us about a time you noticed a social problem and did something to ameliorate it.'

Nicole Stephens and colleagues in the US have carried out a series of valuable studies looking at the impact of cultural norms at university, and what can be done to address them. In one study they first established that universities do indeed value independence more highly than interdependence, through a survey of senior administrators in US universities who were asked questions about the degree to which certain statements were consistent with the values of the university.[23] Some statements were more focused on independence ('working independently') and others more on interdependence. In a follow-up study, Stephens found that working-class students were more likely to be motivated by interdependent goals than middle-class students, and that these motives were predictive of lower levels of academic attainment.

Now for the interesting part. New students at one private university were presented with statements about the mission of the university framed in either independent (individualist) or interdependent (collaborative) terms. They were then asked to solve anagram puzzles. The middle-class students in either group, and the working-class students in the interdependent group, all did just about as well as one another. But the working-class students in the group given the statement couched in independent terms solved significantly fewer anagrams.

Now for the really interesting bit. Stephens and her colleagues found similar results when conducting panel discussions and looking at academic performance as the outcome. In this study, participants were randomly assigned to one of two discussion panels, which differed according to whether the discussions highlighted how their backgrounds mattered for their college experience. In the standard, control condition, the framing of the discussion was not linked to the participants' backgrounds. For example, they considered: 'What do you do to be successful in your classes?' In contrast, in the 'difference' condition, the discussion drew out class differences, e.g. 'Can you provide an example of an obstacle that you faced when you came here and how you resolved it?' First-generation students in the difference condition had higher grades than did first-generation students in the standard condition at the end of the academic year, while there was no difference between conditions for those whose parents had been to university. We need more replication studies to test the robustness of these findings, but it's incredible that such a small intervention can have such a big effect.

So, there is a strong suggestion that working-class students would gain – and middle-class students would not lose out – if universities placed more emphasis on interdependence and collaboration in their mission statements and teaching methods. Our educational institutions should be allowing working-class kids to express their values – and to talk in their own accents. And this should apply to students of all ages, not just adults in higher education.

We also need to be alert to class differences in expectations, which can be reinforced by 'stereotype threat'.[24] This is when people think and behave in ways that conform to a negative expectation, such as low intellectual ability. Studies have shown that working-class students perform worse on intellectual tasks than middle-class students, e.g. on the verbal skills sections of tests.[25] This difference was only present, however, in cases where the tasks were described to the students as measures of their intellectual ability and not when the task was instead presented as non-diagnostic of intellectual ability. Negative expectations serve to promulgate class differences. Recent studies in the UK have shown a 27 per cent difference in grade attainment between middle-class and working-class children (as proxied by eligibility to receive free school meals) in English schools.[26]

Thankfully, though, in some of our own work (led by Ian Hadden) simple interventions in the form of 'self-affirmation tasks' show promise in helping to close these gaps. Self-affirmation is a process that involves prompting students to think about something of significant personal value as a way of reducing stereotype threat. We took two groups of students, aged between eleven and fourteen, from a culturally diverse comprehensive secondary school with an above-average population of children receiving free school meals. The first (affirmation) group were asked to write a short piece about two or three values that matter to them (e.g. family) and why. The second (control) group were asked to do the same but for two or three values that were unimportant to them but which might matter to someone else.

We then assessed performance on three mathematics tests taken by students across that year in addition to measuring levels of stress, stereotype threat, self-integrity and academic fit at the end of the year. We found that the self-affirmation writing task improved maths performance for free-school-meal students only, closing the existing achievement gap between these two groups by 50 per cent over the course of the year. This group also reported a significant reduction in stress levels at the end of the year. So it might be possible to effectively improve performance and reduce stress among working-class students simply by allowing the students to safely express values that matter to them.

A DEGREE OF SOCIAL BENEFIT?

Beyond individual benefits (and costs), a better-educated workforce is seen to earn more, contribute more in taxes, be more productive, create new jobs and drive economic growth. We believe that more education is better for society. A recent study from the LSE compiled data detailing the location of 15,000 universities in 1,500 regions across 78 countries between 1950 and 2010.[27] The authors found a strong positive relationship between the number of universities in an area and future increases in GDP per capita. The analysis suggests that if you double the number of universities in a given area you end up with 4 per cent increases in future GDP per capita in that area and a 0.5 per cent increase in national GDP. These regional effects are partly explained by population growth, as students come to town to study, eat and get drunk. But there are also positive spillover effects of universities too, whereby the increased supply of skilled graduates raises productivity in the firms they work in. The paper also shows that universities boost innovation, as measured by an increase in the number of patents registered.

There are other possible benefits that universities can bring. One of the most impactful is a reduction in crimes, such as burglary, theft and criminal damage, associated with increases in education more generally.[28] The fact that universities can attract international students exposes people to difference, which encourages creativity and reduces prejudice and discriminatory behaviour.[29] Higher education is also associated with more pro-democratic attitudes, including greater support for freedom of speech.[30]

We do not know what the counterfactual would have been, of course: it is entirely possible that the same resources could have been used in other ways to generate the same or greater economic growth for example subsidized vocational training for teachers and nurses, and so on. Alison Wolf has made a convincing argument that university provides students with the opportunity to signal that they are clever.[31] Accordingly, graduates will earn more money because they have shown that they can pass assessments and exams and not necessarily because they are more productive at work. As possible support for this argument, nearly one third of graduates say that they don't need a degree to do their jobs.[32]

Even if university is good for economic growth, the more important question is whether or not that growth is good for people. We are so committed to the narratives of growth and education that we ignore their downsides. These include environmental damage as well as increases in white-collar crimes such as corporate corruption and tax evasion.[33] Greenhouse-gas emissions are a necessary by-product of the quest for ever increasing growth, fuelled (no pun intended), to some extent, by the negative outcomes of higher education. So, if a university education does lead to higher growth, we must not automatically assume that this is beneficial growth, especially in developed countries like the UK and US. At the very least, the environmental damage it creates must be properly accounted for. As David Pilling has powerfully argued, 'Only in economics is endless expansion seen as a virtue. In biology, it is called cancer.'[34]

It is also worth considering that new technologies developed by educated people can be harmful as well as helpful, depending on how we use them. With our generally optimistic outlook, it is understandable that humans have the tendency to assume that all innovations, on balance, will be good for us. And perhaps even more so when the clever sods are the ones doing the innovating. Well, in spite of being an inveterate optimist, I'm not so sure. I reckon it is entirely possible that the human race will come to rue its development of Artificial Intelligence, as robots threaten to put the majority of us (including many of the clever sods) out to pasture.

PAYING FOR IT

I would like a system in which the costs of university are borne by those who benefit from it. On average, a university graduate earns hundreds of thousands of pounds more than those who never attend university. And it seems that students are pretty well informed about the returns accruing to education, particularly in the US. For the past fifty years, the fraction of high-school graduates attending college has risen and fallen in line with expected returns from a college education; that is, more people go when they can make more money from doing so. (The returns on education have remained relatively high in the US because completion rates have fallen, especially among men: so students know they should start college if they are to earn more money but many of them don't know how to finish.)

On this basis, students should be asked to pay for pretty much the full costs of their university education and taxpayers should not contribute very much at all. Fundamentally, I object to the idea that those who do not or cannot go to university should subsidize those who do through higher taxation. Higher education participation rates in the rich parts of London are two-thirds, compared to only one in six in the poorer parts of Bristol, Leeds and Nottingham. I can see no credible basis upon which builders in Bristol should subsidize the university education of the children of financiers in Finchley.

I appreciate that the 'psychology of debt' among students from working-class families can act as a barrier to applying, but the evidence on this is weak. If that were the case, applications from poorer students to universities should have fallen in the UK since tuition fees were first introduced in 1998, and fallen off a cliff in England and Wales since 2012 when tuition fees effectively trebled to £9,000 per year. They have not. In fact, the entry ratio of the most disadvantaged to the most advantaged groups has consistently increased over the last decade. The increase in tuition fees has increased access to higher education among poorer people because universities are no longer as constrained in their intake as they were before fees were introduced. It has increased at a faster rate than in Scotland, which scrapped tuition fees for home residents.[35]

Having said this, those universities that have been the most successful at widening participation are also those that are widely seen as being of the lowest status. Drop-out rates at these universities are very high, and working-class students are much more likely to drop out. About 3 per cent of students at the LSE drop out in their first year compared to 18 per cent down the road at London Metropolitan University. The difference in the perceived status of universities and the concentration of working-class students at those 'lower status' universities has led people such as Diane Reay to argue that class inequalities in higher education have shifted from being about exclusion from the system to exclusion within it.[36]

So let's do away with subsidies for higher education except for subjects of clear social value and where we might want to encourage more working-class students to participate. Public resources should still be used to subsidize those who pursue socially useful careers, such as teaching. Scholarships and fee waivers can also be made available to encourage students, especially those from working-class backgrounds, to go into these professions; and also into professions, like the arts, that are currently dominated by students from wealthy families.

The social narrative of reaching for ever more education is so powerful that many politicians and commentators (nearly all of whom have been to university) take it as given that public subsidies for higher education represent a fair and efficient use of public resources. Yet such subsidies unfairly disadvantage those who do not gain from university by, firstly, having to pay for those who do and, secondly, missing out on the resources used to fund higher education which could have generated a social benefit elsewhere.

I should make clear that we absolutely must pursue, and publicly fund, innovative and impactful research. About a quarter of the expenditure on research and development in the UK flows through the higher education sector, compared to about one-sixth in Germany and the US. These differences may go some way towards explaining why the UK performs very well at generating intellectual property, which our universities are great at, but much less well at turning ideas into impact, which our universities are generally quite poorly attuned to. Arguably, some of the research that will have real world impact can be more effectively pursued away from universities in research centres.

CONCLUSIONS

There is a fairly weak association between the level of education we attain and how we feel. In this, as with so many other issues, we must be careful about causality. It is possible that the most educated people are unhappier to start with. It is even possible that their unhappiness caused them to pursue some form of validation through education, without which they might be even worse off. The same could also be true of wealth and success, but, just as with these other Reaching narratives, we can at least ask whether the 'just enough' approach to education might have positive outcomes.

In general, a 'just enough' approach to education would see the public sector invest more in early years education. It genuinely saddens me that the UK currently spends twice as much on higher education as it does on education for children aged under five. Children from working-class backgrounds start showing significantly lower levels of cognitive development than their middle-class peers before they start school.[37] Early intervention programmes go a long way towards counteracting some of the educational inequalities that exist between social classes,[38] even though some of the huge effects of early years interventions that were first established by James Heckman have been reduced (by Heckman himself) as the follow-up of students extended over longer periods.[39] And while the UK does now spend more per student in schools than in universities (staggeringly, it was the other way round as recently as the 2000s), spending per pupil has stagnated in real terms for the last decade.

We need to dispel the myth, promulgated by those who have university degrees and can't imagine a life without one, that higher education is the only route out of poverty and into a good life. Rather than devoting so much to those going to university, we need to properly consider those who do not go. For both efficiency and equity reasons, we need to redirect discussion and resources towards further education (or continued education as it is called in the US) in the form of vocational training and apprenticeships for those who wish to start specific careers, such as accountancy and engineering. Anecdotally, there are many teenagers out there who would much rather undertake vocational training but who feel their parents exerting considerable pressure on them to go to university. Cuts in spending on further education have been accompanied by a stigma attached to pursuing post-sixteen education that does not lead to university.

Above all else, the real route out of poverty is to pay a living wage to the millions of care workers, teaching assistants, cleaners and labourers. And to afford these jobs the status their impact on society deserves. These are the kinds of jobs that future economic growth will depend upon most, but they are underpaid and undervalued by society because of our obsession with graduate jobs.[40] Or rather, with jobs that now require graduates.

Overall, more graduates do generate social benefits but these are not as overwhelming as the narrative would have us believe. It is entirely plausible that similar benefits could be generated at a much lower cost to the public purse and private bank accounts by redesigning primary, secondary and tertiary education in ways that promote innovation for social returns, civic participation, and so on.

There is a lot to be improved in our education system, such as making it more accepting of different cultures and learning styles. It is well established that white working-class boys, in particular, feel especially alienated by education systems that try to force those kids to adopt middle-class values and behaviours.[41] This is unfair and inefficient, and it simply doesn't have to be this way. We must create different experiences for those who go into higher education and alternative (i.e. better) narratives for those who do not. But at the same time, we need to know when education stops serving its purpose, particularly when it comes to our happiness. It's not big and it's not clever . . . to be miserable.

Wrapping Up Reaching

We have become ever more obsessed with wealth, success and education. Let me stress once more that poverty can cause great misery, and the increase in 'deaths of despair' (from drugs, alcohol and suicide) among low-income and poorly educated middle-aged white people in the US in the twenty-first century has been ascribed to these people feeling left behind economically.[1] But at the same time, and in ways that illustrate a sharp distinction between those whose incomes have grown and those whose have not, many of us have gone way past the point at which these benefits contribute towards the reduction of suffering. We probably have something akin to an innate desire to pursue these three narratives, but the power of Reaching has resulted in us becoming addicted to more money, success and knowledge. The social narratives have magnified our desires.

A lot has been written about how a lack of goals and motivation can be harmful to the lifetime outcomes of people, but much less has been written about how being too goal-oriented can be harmful too. Constantly setting goals can cause anxiety and more serious mental health problems. The point here is not to stop setting goals altogether but instead to reframe our goals in ways that bring about the most happiness. Wealth, success and education are all worth striving for, but only up until the point at which the feedback from our experiences tells us that we have enough.

You can use these insights in the decisions you make on behalf of other people. As a parent, for example, you can advise your children to maximize their happiness (subject to having enough wealth, success and education). Far too many parents place far too much emphasis on their kids excelling academically or in sport or in playing a musical instrument or whatever. Excellence does not have to come at the expense of enjoyment. Indeed, we are most likely to enjoy what we are good at and to be good at what we enjoy. But when parents focus almost entirely on their child's attainment, it is impossible to see how this does not crowd out the joy of the experience. I can already see some of the kids who play squash with Stanley losing their passion for the game because a pushy parent cares much more about the result than the pleasure from playing (most often a dad who also plays squash and who wants to live out his own, usually failed, ambitions through his kids).

Now you could say that it's easy for me not to care about how successful my kids are because, by dint of their privilege, they will do just fine whatever happens. It is hard for me to completely rule that out as a possibility, but I am convinced that Les and I encourage rather than push Poppy and Stanley. I am not aware of ever being burdened by the expectations of my parents, and they were happy for me to pursue any career path – or not to be driven by a career at all. I'm sure I am happier with my life as a result. If it worked for my relatively poor family when I was a kid, it can work for my relatively rich family now.

As a politician, if you are really interested in tackling inequality to ensure that as many people as possible have 'just enough', then you need to ensure that the rich stop using, as Stiglitz puts it, 'their political influence to cut taxes and curtail government spending'. Additionally, you need to properly engage with everyone to help us all overcome our societal addiction to the meta-narrative of Reaching. This requires interventions analogous to those found to be effective in the treatment of individual addicts. Here are three steps. The first is acceptance. You must accept that many of your fellow citizens are collectively addicted to asking for more please when they are either already past the point of just enough or would like to keep asking for more please if they were ever to get to that point. (This remains the best explanation for why poor people vote for tax cuts for the rich: they want to cut taxes for when they are rich.)

The second step is to not get discouraged when some people don't listen. Many of those most addicted to the narrative will also be the least likely to believe you when you try to nudge them away from over-reaching. It is easy to blame addicts but their actions are driven largely by the power of the narrative trap. So carefully consider how some of your own policies might be egging people on rather than reining them in. The third and final step is to act now. It's tempting to say let's first deal with unfair inequalities in wealth, success and education, and after that we can try to convince people about their addiction. But helping some people and reining in others are inextricably linked. The preferences and behaviours of all citizens determine what we are all expected to be reaching for. By directly questioning the narrative trap, we can shape the nature and extent of the desires of everyone.

The more people are convinced by the 'just enough' approach, the more likely they will be to limit their material consumption, and favour redistributing resources away from those with more than enough towards those with little. A diminished desire to consume will also mean that we will be better placed to tackle some of the critical and seemingly intractable collective-action problems of our time, such as climate change. There have been five occasions in the past when the planet has undergone change whereby the diversity of life has dramatically fallen. There is every possibility that we are creeping towards a sixth extinction, which could even see *Homo sapiens* become extinct.[2] The chances of this are reduced if we can avoid falling into the trap that ever more wealth, success and education – and growth and consumption – will lead to ever more happiness.

If nothing else, I hope to temper the judgements we make about those who choose not to carry on Reaching. There is next to nothing in the happiness data to suggest that addiction to this meta-narrative is good for us or those around us. In addition to the goals we set for ourselves and others, we also make decisions about how we relate to other people. These choices are of interest in their own right and so in the next part of the book, I consider the 'Related' meta-narrative and its constituent sub-narratives.

But before that, let's see how your answers to the questions at the beginning of each chapter in this part of the book compare to what other people think. In an online survey Amanda Henwood, Laura Kudrna and I asked two hundred people from each of the UK and the US the same questions that you were asked. The results are shown below.

The first thing to say is that each narrative is supported to some extent, even if it means being miserable (since people often trade off their happiness for the narratives). In both countries, being educated matters more than being wealthy, which in turn matters more than being successful. All three Reaching narratives matter more to Americans than to Brits. The biggest difference we see across the countries is concerning wealth, where twice as many people in the US compared to the UK are seemingly willing to be miserable in order to be wealthy. Amazingly (to me at least), exactly half of Americans would choose to be miserable in order to be educated. And for each question in each country, people are less willing to sacrifice their friend's happiness for the sake of a Reaching narrative.

This might be because, cynically, while we want our friends to be happy, we don't want to risk them reaching further than us. Or perhaps, and I reckon that this is more likely, it is easier for us to visualize the impact of being miserable when we step back from our own egos and detach ourselves from how we come across as a result of failing to adhere to the dominant social stories. We don't imagine our friend facing quite the same obstacles we would in order to live an authentic life.

% people choosing Life A (narrative) over Life B (happiness) when chosing for **themselves** and for **a friend**

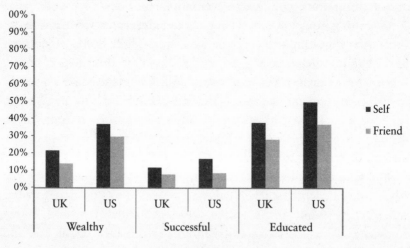

Figure 7

PART TWO
Related

The three chapters in this section are all social narratives about our personal lives and how we ought to relate to the people who are closest to us. We are expected to get married, be faithful to our spouse and have children with them. As an alternative, I am not suggesting that you never marry, that you live polyamorously and don't have kids. Rather, you should not be judged harshly if you opt for one or more of these routes, and you should not judge how others choose to live their lives either. Remember that breaking free of narrative traps can mean choosing to marry, be monogamous or to have kids – but only because one or more of these decisions suits you, not because the social stories dictate that you should.

The critical question is, of course, whether or not a world where these narratives are abolished or seriously curtailed leads to less misery overall than one in which they retain a vice-like grip over us. No such data can provide a reliable answer, but what there is might shift your current perspective. So, as throughout this book, I suggest allowing the feedback of your experiences, and of those you consider to have similar preferences to you, to decide what is right for you and for the people you care about and are responsible for.

4
Married

Here are your two scenarios. Please make a note of your answers, and we'll come back to them at the end of Part Two. Please read the following statements and indicate whether you would choose Life A or Life B *for yourself*:

Life A: You are married. You often feel miserable.
Life B: You have never married and never will. You hardly ever feel miserable.

Please read the following statements and indicate whether you would choose Life A or Life B *for a friend*:

Life A: Your friend is married. Your friend often feels miserable.
Life B: Your friend has never married and never will. Your friend hardly ever feels miserable.

Think back on your bedtime stories as a child and I bet these words are lodged somewhere in your brain: ' . . . and they fell in love, got married, and lived happily ever after.' These imagined happy endings stick with us as adults. An overwhelming majority of us report considering marriage as part of our ideal lifestyle and we often project this preference on to others too. An unmarried forty-year-old is 'unlucky' or has yet to meet 'the one': as if being married is something for all of us, and that there is some one – *one* person – out there for every one of us. Yeah, right . . .

Marriage is still viewed by many as constituting one of life's basic achievements. In our own analysis of survey responses from over 7,000 members of the German population, which have been collected every two months since 2013, over 90 per cent of people said that they considered a long-lasting marriage to be very important in their lives. It made no difference whether these people were very happy, very miserable or anywhere in between.

FINDING THE ONE

If I was writing this book even a decade ago, I would be discussing finding a mate at work, in the supermarket, in a bar, or maybe through a friend. But not today. Through dating apps, we can look at hundreds of prospective dates without leaving the house. The evolutionary biologist and sex researcher Justin Garcia has suggested that there have been two major transitions in heterosexual mating in the past four million years. The first he identifies as having happened during the agricultural revolution, when humans began to settle in one place and marriage emerged as a social contract. The second, he suggests, is now. With the rise of the internet there has been a radical shift in dating and mating practices.

On the face of it, the availability of so many possible partners sounds thrilling, but the reality is often more disappointing. Social networking sites can exacerbate our fear of missing out, for one thing. With so much choice, we can feel burdened to make the most of it, and feel like we are not taking every opportunity if we don't. Dating has become like shopping. We are now presented with people much like new shoes on our screens; we shop for the most attractive and add them to our dating basket. But with so much choice, filling up our baskets is not enough. New faces pop up all the time, with better hair, firmer abs and sexier hobbies. The old items in our basket lose their lustre. The people on our screens are commodified: easily disposed of when a better, or simply newer, item comes in store. And we never stop shopping.

While many economists still worship at the altar of choice, psychologists have alerted us to the psychological costs incurred when we are presented with too many choices. This has been neatly captured by Barry Schwartz's concept 'the paradox of choice', whereby more choice makes us feel worse off as we agonize over our options both before and long after we've made a decision.[1] So one of the consequences of having lots of choice over who to date (just like any other decision) is that any decision can feel like a mistake in comparison to all the other available options. And when it comes to love, the stakes are impossibly high. So you might intend to settle down at some point, but that point may never come.

Moreover, it would seem that much of this might not be good for our happiness. In a study unrelated to romance, students at Harvard University were given twelve photos as part of a photography course and asked to pick the best two, one of which they could keep.[2] The first group was told that their choice was reversible, while the second group was told that they could not change their mind. Two-thirds of students chose to be in the first group but the results indicated the second group reported feeling happier with the choice they made.

So where does this abundance of choice leave those looking for love? For the shy and awkward types, the busy city slicker or a single parent with not much time to hang out in bars and nightclubs, making contact online can lead to a meeting in real life that would never have taken place otherwise. Dating apps allow people to fine tune their preferences in ways that were previously unachievable. Users can filter prospective dates by age, profession and desire to have babies, for example. And the good news is that studies suggest that relationships that started online are sometimes more successful (at least in terms of a reduced likelihood of getting divorced) than those that started out by meeting in person.[3]

In this way the age of modern romance is great for those who would have found it hard to find a mate back in the day when people like me had to walk up to a woman in a bar and face the very public shame of rejection. The problem is that many of us are now keeping our options open even once we have settled down. Interviews with over 17,000 users of the dating app Tinder revealed that two in five of its users are people already in relationships. Like most dating apps, Tinder is cleverly set up in a reward-type format whereby you receive a dopamine hit each time you achieve a 'match'. The average Tinder user logs into the app for a scrolling session eleven times a day. The dopamine hit of a new match keeps you coming back for more even when you are in a relationship.[4]

WHAT'S LOVE GOT TO DO WITH IT?

Once we find our partner (thanks or no thanks to digital technology), that person is expected to provide, well, pretty much everything: from sexual fulfilment to the sharing of household tasks. This expectation can be quite harmful for us. For example, those who believe in soulmates (a belief that people are either meant for each other or they aren't) tend to be less committed to their partner when faced with difficulties (as if a disagreement confirms their incompatibility).[5] Moreover, those who believe in romantic destiny (as measured by a Romantic Beliefs Scale that asks people the extent to which they agree with statements like 'there is only one person whom we can truly love') are often more anxious in relationships and less likely to forgive romantic partners for their wrongdoings.[6]

In the discussion here, I distinguish between: 1) passionate love, which is experienced in the early stages of a relationship and more closely resembles lust, even addiction; and 2) companionate love, which can form as a deep commitment to someone once the passionate love has subsided. In so doing, I will draw mostly on love as a biological phenomenon, which serves to explain the transition from feeling passion to seeing someone as a companion. Love as social narrative then overlies this 'natural' progression. Given the way that love is portrayed in literature, film and the media, the prevailing narrative clearly places a high premium on its passionate aspect, most often in manipulatively uplifting ways – see Disney.

In one study of love as biology, participants who were in the early stages of a relationship in the US were put into an fMRI scanner and shown a photo of their loved one.[7] The activation in the brain was similar to that found when someone anticipates making money – and when experiencing a hit of cocaine. There have actually been a few 'scanning love' studies. One shows that people are better able to withstand pain when they are picturing someone they feel passionate love for compared to viewing a picture of an equally attractive acquaintance.[8] Part of the explanation for this is that the association of the partner with reward reduces the experience of pain.

Passionate love involves such phenomena as lust, attraction and attachment that are all meant to bring two heterosexual individuals together to procreative ends. My focus therefore will be principally on male–female relationships. Passionate love is associated with many changes in cognition, emotion and behaviour.[9] For the most part, these changes are consistent with the disruption of existing activities, routines and social networks to orient the individual's attention and goal-directed behaviour towards a specific new partner. If passionate love is reciprocated, then there's something to be said for the disruption it causes. Experiences of passionate love have been linked to personal growth and to motivation. Those butterflies in your stomach get you out of bed, encourage you to go to new places and to try new things.

But those experiencing passionate love also often report experiencing extreme lows too, and these can be unpredictable and therefore use our attention in ways that make people miserable. Love can lead to lots of intrusive thoughts about the loved one, which can get in the way of good experiences. Some of the psychophysical responses include anxiety, shyness and sleeplessness.[10] There is often an imbalance in the relationship (one will be more 'into it' than the other) as well as emotional dependency on the loved one, each of which can manifest itself in possessiveness, resentment and jealousy.

All of this does rather undermine the socially constructed idea of romantic love as being exclusively blissful. Cocaine has many psychological and physiological benefits but we don't look on it quite as fondly as we do love, yet their effects on the brain, and on many subsequent behaviours, are remarkably similar. Love is a drug: and like many addictive drugs it has certain benefits and some quite serious side effects.

Thankfully, passionate love only lasts between one and two years, provided you are in regular contact with your partner. Italian researchers have identified distinct differences in hormone levels (e.g. higher cortisol levels, associated with stress) in the blood of volunteers who claimed to have fallen in love in the previous six months relative to those who were single or had been in a relationship for over three years.[11] If a relationship lasts beyond a couple of years, then companionate love takes root. This is essentially where a strong bond exists between two people but where passion is no longer the driving force. Other brain imaging studies have shown that as the length of time in love increased activation in specific emotion-related regions decreased, confirming the inevitable decline of passionate love.[12]

Biologically, only companionate love is sustainable in the long-run, and so the distinction between passionate and companionate love resonates across sexual orientation, genders, cultures and relationship types. Indeed, when passionate love lasts for a long time it becomes destructive, whereby the physiological reactions accompanying the initial stage of love disturb the usual flow of an individual's life.[13] For example, increases in arousal associated with passionate love reduce cognitive control, making it harder for people to focus on important tasks.

By the time they get married, most couples would have transitioned from passionate love into companionate love. But the 'happily ever after' narrative continues to set unrealistic expectations about life together, leaving people ill-prepared for the fact that mundanity will get in the way of the fairy tale. The problem with the social narrative of marriage is that it is an expression of both passionate *and* companionate love at the same time. The social narrative is that you should marry in the name of passionate love, which should, by and large, then last for ever.

When we think about the narrative of love, most of us will smile and feel good, yet many of us will experience love in a negative and damaging way. This disconnect can lead to people behaving really badly in the name of love. For example, 'I only get jealous because I love you.' No, you get jealous because of the kind of person you are in certain environments and not because of how someone else makes you feel. It is true that some people try to evoke feelings of jealousy in their partner, but their partner is ultimately responsible for how they react to this.

Social media has done little to help with jealousy and control. Once in a relationship, research shows that women are more likely to use Facebook to display their affection than men, and they also consider public online declarations of affection to be more appropriate than men do.[14] While Facebook relationship declarations can be viewed as a sign of love and commitment, they are also used in strategic, controlling ways to warn off other potential mates. This idea follows from the finding that those who report using social media to promote their relationships also report having lower self-esteem than those who do not.[15] The same group also claim to use Facebook more for the purposes of self-expression than validation, although this finding should be treated with caution given that most of us are pretty oblivious to the real reasons underlying our behaviour.

Love gives us an excuse for staying in a relationship that causes us harm – it's much easier to explain away staying put with 'But I love her' than to get out. Love has often been cited as a defence by perpetrators of domestic abuse hoping to gain sympathy from judges. And sometimes it works. Jane Monkton-Smith, a criminologist and domestic-homicide specialist, has analysed seventy-two cases in which convictions of manslaughter were mitigated by claims such as 'how much the perpetrator said they loved the victim'.[16] Perhaps the most infamous case in recent memory was the murder of OJ Simpson's wife, Nicole Brown (as well as Ron Goldman: wrong place, wrong time). Her murder was foreshadowed by domestic abuse and claims from OJ that he loved Nicole but that she drove him crazy. He said of the crime: 'Even if I did do this, it would have to have been because I loved her very much, right?' There is nothing to admire about the word love here.

So the way in which we conceptualize and deploy love has a significant effect on what we do and how we feel. People will often say it is better to have loved and lost than never to have loved at all, implying that love with heartbreak is superior in some way to never having experienced love in the first place (although this line from Tennyson's poem in fact refers to the love the poet felt for a close friend who died). We pity those that have never been in love.

'TIL DEATH US DO PART

Once we have found someone and fallen in love with them, we should marry them. We are so keen to show off about our wedding that it's quickly become a staple social media event. The ability to share your wedding with virtual friends must have played some part in contributing to the increasing costs in the last decade. Not only do the wedding guests get to witness, envy and comment on your wedding, but your 'big day' can now be seen via sites such as Facebook and Instagram by many multiples of those who actually turn up to the day. Perceptions of your economic and romantic status can both be enhanced by an expensive, elaborate and widely disseminated celebration of your love for one another.

But you are likely to be wasting your money, and not just because marriage does not do much for happiness. It has emerged that the more you spend on getting hitched, the greater your chances of getting ditched. If we take spending $10,000 on a wedding as the reference point, you are twice as likely to get divorced if you spend more than $20,000 and half as likely to if you spend less than $1,000.[17] So the next time you marvel at the many hundreds of orchids hanging from the ceiling of the venue, ask yourself why the couple has chosen to publicly display their love in this way.

Apart from the joy and expense of the big day, does marriage actually make us happy? Data from the German Socio-Economic Panel, which has followed the same people over about twenty years now, show that the year before and the year after the wedding are especially enjoyable in terms of life satisfaction.[18] But the benefits don't last very long: just about as many people in this study report ending up less satisfied from being married as report being more satisfied. Different studies show different long-term effects, but the consensus is that there is generally a small but robust positive effect of marriage on life satisfaction. It is worth noting, however, that some of the differences in reports of life satisfaction between married and single people are also due to reverse causality; in other words, it has been shown that more-satisfied people are more likely to get married in the first place.[19]

Most studies looking at the effects of marriage use life satisfaction measures or global evaluations of happiness as their happiness measure rather than experience-based reports. This is important because marriage is a social narrative to aspire to, and so there is a general positive evaluation surrounding the very fact that you are married, regardless of the state of your relationship. Even the relatively short-lived measurable benefits of marriage could be entirely due to the fulfilment of a social narrative. Equally, the single people in these studies might be comparatively unhappy because of the stigma surrounding being single. We therefore need to look more closely at more experience-based measures of happiness, including purpose, and at other outcomes, such as health, that might not be so directly influenced by the narrative trap.

The correlation between marriage and experiences of happiness is quite weak. In the American Time Use Survey (ATUS), there is some information on the relationships people are in. We know whether they have never been married (33% of the sample), or are married (50%), widowed (5%), divorced (10%) or separated (2%). Among some of those who are married, we also know whether their spouse was present or absent during the interview.

The average reported 'pleasure' for each group is shown in the graph below. People who are married do not experience significantly more pleasure relative to people who have never been married unless their spouse was also present in the interview. It appears that people are more likely to say they feel happy if their spouse can hear what they are saying. Or it could simply be that their spouses put them in a better mood, which influences how they recall their experiences yesterday. (My money is on the former.)

When the spouse is present at the interview, people who are married are also happier than people who are divorced. When the spouse is not present, however, there is no difference in pleasure between the married and the divorced. In fact, as long as married people's spouses are absent for their ATUS interview, there are no significant differences between people who are married and any other group. Have we really deluded ourselves to think married people are genuinely happier? It certainly seems to be a story that we tell our spouses.

The average purpose by relationship group is shown in Figure 9. Here, we see that the never married experience the least purpose relative to any other relationship group. This is a significant difference, but none of the other groups differ significantly to each other in terms of experienced purpose. Since most of the married sample would have been hitched for more than a couple of years, this suggests that companionate love can in fact feel meaningful, fulfilling and worthwhile, even if it does not do much for pleasure.

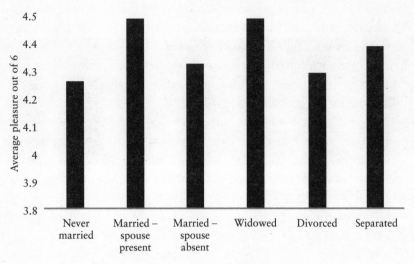

Figure 8: Happiness and marriage

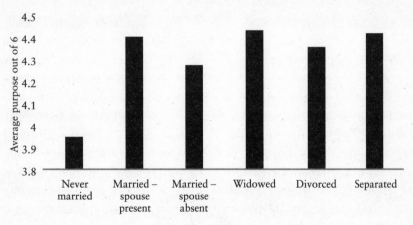

Figure 9: Sense of purpose and marriage

The results for misery are shown below. People who have never been married experience less misery than the divorced and separated. Better not to have loved and lost then, it seems. Married people with their spouses present for the interview report being less

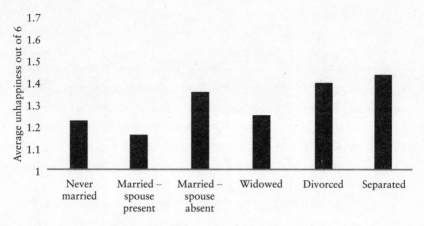

Figure 10: Unhappiness and marriage

miserable than married people without their spouses present, which again suggests that people report better experiences when they otherwise risk offending their spouse.

These data do mask some important differences between relationship groups. We don't know about people who are in long-term cohabiting relationships and who are not married, for example, or whether some of the people who have never been married are actively dating or recently going through break-ups. We need more data like these, and more data on the experiences people have in their daily lives, to better inform us about how well people in different sorts of relationships are doing.

There are other potential benefits to marriage besides happiness. On average, married people (and to some degree cohabiting couples) are wealthier and healthier than single people:[20] the argument is that couples support each other and encourage each other to seek promotions and pay rises, and medical help where necessary.[21] Moreover, having a partner is theorized to act as a buffer against negative events in life because your partner's social support can help you to get through tough times.

The health effects of marriage are greater for men than for women. Men 'calm down' a lot when they marry and stop taking so many risks with their health. Insofar as this is good for them, they therefore benefit from marriage. In contrast, there really do not appear to be any health-related reasons to marry if you are a woman. The risks of many physical and mental health conditions are higher among middle-aged married women than they are among their single counterparts. Moreover, if the marriage isn't going well, research has found that this negatively impacts women more than it does men, suggesting that if we think about marriage as a gamble men can expect to have more to gain and less to lose from saying 'I do'.[22] As Scarlett O'Hara remarked in *Gone with the Wind*: 'Marriage, fun? Fiddle-dee-dee. Fun for men, you mean!'

Why do women marry then? Well there are some financial benefits from doing so if a husband can earn more than his wife, as well as tax breaks. If a woman does marry, I suggest she has her own bed. Studies comparing the sleep quality of couples sleeping apart versus together using objective sleep measures such as polysomnography or actigraphy have shown that people typically sleep better on their own, and the effect is especially strong for women.[23] This is one of many examples of where he needs her more than she needs him. Sleep is a very important determinant of daily moods – more than salary or how much sex you're having – so more couples would surely be happier if they gave up on the silly (and actually relatively recent) idea that sleeping apart is a bad thing.[24] You're asleep for God's sake: do you really need someone next to you? Certainly not every bloody night, that's for sure.

'TIL THE DIVORCE COURTS

OK, so you have met someone, fallen in love, married, been happy for a while . . . and now you want to get out. Over two in every five marriages in the UK end in divorce, according to recent records from the Office for National Statistics.[25] Before this, there is usually a period of separation, during which time people report the lowest levels of life satisfaction and the greatest experiences of misery in the ATUS data reported above. The uncertainties of whether or not to get back together again, and what life will be like afterwards if you do or don't, make for a pretty horrible time. After that, however, your attention is focused on dealing with a future that can be better planned and managed. It is no surprise, then, that happiness bounces back a fair bit once the divorce papers are signed, and continues on up until you move on completely as a single person or with someone else (who is nearly always seen as being better than the previous partner).

We don't predict much of this, imagining that we will remain very distressed for a very long time if we break up.[26] Many people are also scared of being single. Studies have shown that people who tend to agree with statements such as 'I feel it is close to being too late for me to find the love of my life' are more likely to experience greater dependence in unsatisfying relationships.[27] While we don't have evidence on how happy these people would be if they weren't already in unsatisfactory relationships, I'd suspect their happiness would rise as they begin to adapt to their newly found single status, or new partner, if the marriage narrative wasn't always looming.

We really cannot overestimate the impact of narrative surrounding the magic of marriage, and the marital bed. It starts with young girls hearing about handsome princes saving (largely passive) princesses. Presently, four out of five divorces in the US are filed by women, according to the National Center for Health Statistics:[28] the narrative may nudge them into marriage but, once there, they eventually realize the raw deal they are getting and want to get out. In contrast, the same gendered pattern does not hold for cohabitation, where both men and women are equally likely to end a relationship.[29] This suggests that there's something special about the (historically subordinating) institution of marriage that women want to escape from more than men.

Interestingly, it appears that women are less likely to experience the worst of the negative impacts of divorce, e.g. men are ten times more likely to commit suicide following the dissolution of marriage than women.[30] The greater ability of women to cope following divorce is thought to be because they generally have better support networks than men, and are also more willing to ask for help. It probably also has something to do with the fact that in most cases the divorce was their decision in the first place. We know from the psychological literature on resilience that feeling as if we have more control over a negative event can help us to cope better.[31]

Divorce hurts the children of couples who separate though, right? Well, yes, to a degree. Researchers from the University of Virginia have shown that children of divorced parents do experience negative emotions, including anxiety, shock and anger, in the short-run; however, for the vast majority of kids these feelings have dissipated within a couple of years of their parents' divorce.[32] The sociologist Paul Amato has also looked into the long-term impact of divorce on children by comparing children of divorced parents to those with married parents at different ages, following these individuals into adolescence.[33] The children were compared on measures including academic achievement, emotional and behavioural problems, delinquency and self-concept. Only small differences were found between the groups. Those born into high-conflict relationships report greater happiness as adults if their parents split up compared to those whose parents stayed together. So, on balance, it's probably better to be the child of divorced parents than to be the child of parents who stayed together and who argue a lot.

The characteristics of the children themselves and the coping strategies they adopt influence the extent to which they suffer from their parents' divorce.[34] More easy-going children fare better, as do those who seek social support rather than look for ways to distract themselves. But how the parents behave towards each other, take care of themselves, and talk about the divorce is arguably even more important. Co-operative parenting, low inter-parental conflict and good parental mental health are key drivers of how children fare, whether their parents are together or not, and so the litmus test is really whether there is likely to be more of those good things in or out of the relationship.[35] Talking about divorce as a liberating, rather than limiting, life event will also go a long way towards determining how children will cope.

The social story of staying together for the sake of the children potentially harms the children more than accepting when a relationship has gone wrong and walking away from it in a way that preserves the kids' happiness. We should perhaps start using the word 'congratulations' for divorce, as well as for marriage.

POOR SINGLETONS

Perhaps we should also use the term 'dodged a bullet' for those that remain single. Despite damaging fairy tales, the 'married is best' narrative remains pervasive. One study in Israel asked people to look at comparable biographical accounts of both married and single people (created by researchers) and then to rate the extent to which they displayed a number of thirty-three traits.[36] Yes, you guessed it: the majority of people assumed the married folk scored higher on traits relating to happiness (e.g. in love with life and content) than the 'depressive', 'lonely' and 'shy' singletons. No matter how single people were described and what great things they had experienced and achieved, people were insistent that their happiness must have been overstated.

What's particularly interesting about this study is that the researchers also chose to vary whether or not the single people had chosen their relationship status. Those who had chosen to be single received even lower positive trait ratings than those who would have preferred to be married, despite the former living the life they had favoured. It's as though the choice to be single is too great an affront on our collective ethics to have stemmed from a position of sincerity. It's almost a provocation.

What I found most troubling was that marriage was celebrated both by those in relationships and single people. In other words, singles uphold the notion of committed relationships even though they suffer 'singlism' and negative stereotyping as a direct result of endorsing the marriage myth. This is perhaps because only 4 per cent of singles realize that they are being stigmatized.[37] Another perversion of this particular social narrative.

Single people also experience discrimination in professional contexts. Married people generally get first dibs on holiday times and are the last to be asked to relocate offices. Employers often assume that single people are more time rich than married people, and expect them to put in more hours and effort relative to their married counterparts. So single people work harder and are not rewarded for it, the assumption being that they have no other meaningful commitments and are therefore less likely to be put out.

Outside work, discrimination continues. Singles are excluded from a host of 'couple specific' deals on insurance, hotels, gym memberships, banks accounts and mortgage payments. Laws and other regulations, such as the UK's marriage tax allowance, which allows married couples to transfer nearly £1200 of their personal tax allowance to their spouse, discriminate against singles further. (This particular allowance sees couples benefiting from paying up to almost £240 less tax a year relative to single people.)

Our insistence on advocating committed relationships through marriage may be caused in part by a desire to defend overarching power structures, such as government, political frameworks and religion. Power structures represent codes and practices that bring a sense of reliability and familiarity to our lives. Threats to those power structures, which, as noted in the Introduction, are referred to by psychologists as 'system threat', can cause us to feel uneasy and act to defend the systems that we generally consider to work in our favour.[38]

Consider this experiment from Canada.[39] One half of the participants were asked to read a critique about how Canadian society was suffering economically, politically and socially compared to other countries. This was designed to activate a system threat. The other half did nothing at this stage. All the participants were then presented with a study suggesting that single people experience just as many benefits as those in committed relationships. The researchers then recorded the extent to which participants criticized the study. They found that men primed with a system threat defended committed relationships much more relative to men in the control group.

This suggests that highlighting a flaw in one part of the system makes men feel inclined to defend another part of the system: 'Well, our country is being run by a mad man, and our international relations are fucked, but hey, at least marriage is still on the cards – let's support that.' The same results did not hold for women, though. In general, men have more to gain than women from existing power structures and systems (such is the nature of gender inequality), and so it is not surprising that they defend these systems, including marriage, more vehemently when they are perceived to be under threat.

In contrast, women tend to value their relational identities more strongly than men, and marriage provides a positive identity.[40] A study conducted in America got people to either feel secure or insecure about their relationship potential by getting them to fill out a fake personality questionnaire. Subjects were given a score pertaining to their relationship capability as part of their questionnaire results. Half of the group were told that their 'lifetime romantic relationship will be very likely to be successful and have [a] positive experience' (non-relationship identity threat condition) and half were told that it will be 'very likely to be unsuccessful and have a negative experience' (relationship identity threat condition). Those made to feel insecure about their relationship potential responded by endorsing committed relationship ideals more enthusiastically than those made to feel secure about their relational potential. There's a certain irony in the fact that the narrative of committed relationships should be upheld more by those who are often experiencing the opposite.

It will not be time wasted if we reappraise how we see single people relative to married ones. Single people are more likely to foster social connections that bring them fulfilment, whereas married people often find themselves with less consciously chosen social networks, such as a spouse's family members.[41] Single people are also more likely to participate in social events and to volunteer.[42] By contrast, married and cohabiting individuals tend to become more socially isolated, even without the excuse of children. The longitudinal nature of these data suggests this relationship is causal, with those entering marriage more likely to lose existing connections than those who do not marry. Similar results are also highlighted in Bella DePaulo's recent review of 815 studies investigating singledom, which revealed that singles are more socially connected than their married counterparts who appear to have become more insular.[43] This is not to say that wider social networks are always good for us, just that there might be some important upsides to being single that the marriage narrative ignores.

CONCLUSIONS

When it comes to the social narratives surrounding love and marriage, we are wilfully over-optimistic. Any given relationship is much more likely to end than it is to result in living happily ever after.[44] We have to come to terms with those odds. We expect passionate love to be nothing but pleasurable (when in fact it can be quite damaging, just like any other compulsion) and to last for ever (when, for the vast majority of us, the high dies after about a year), and our spouse to satisfy all of our needs (which no one human being ever can). Against this background, as Esther Perel, the well-known psychotherapist who has written a lot about marriage, has asked, 'Is it any wonder that so many relationships crumble under the weight of it all?'[45]

When a relationship ends, particularly a long-term one, so many people are heard to say 'what a shame' or 'such a waste'. But if for the most part during that relationship both partners were happy, how can it be a shame or a waste of time? A break-up is most likely to be in the best long-term interests of both parties. How many of you are knowingly with someone now who is worse than a previous partner? We are highly adaptive creatures who are very good at moving on. So if in doubt, best get out. Don't let the narrative fool you into staying past the point it would be better for you to get out. You are likely to get over it more quickly than you think you will, and will probably find someone you're happier with and better suited to.

As with many of the other narratives, non-conformity to this narrative results in stigmatization – and being single is something to dread. In *Make Or Break?*, the Channel 5 TV show I hosted, we brought eight couples to an idyllic holiday setting to test their relationships. Fifteen of the sixteen participants were in their twenties (the exception was Steve, at the ripe old age of thirty-two). A lot of airtime was devoted to Holly (aged twenty-two) and Karl (aged twenty-six), and to whether their four-year relationship was going to, well, make or break. They are both fun and attractive people and, if they were to split up, they could have a great time as singletons until one day, maybe, they meet someone else. So the pressure they placed on their happiness being so wrapped up in staying together – and the degree to which the viewers were invested in this – grossly overplays the consequences of a break-up.

The evidence I have covered in this chapter attests to the fact that singledom and singletons should not be vilified; if anything, they should be celebrated. Singles have more time to devote to meaningful activities that can benefit society, and they leave more of their money to charity in their wills. The one-size-fits-all approach currently on offer ignores the ways in which we are different and the many different ways in which we are capable of finding fulfilment in and out of relationships. The less prescriptive we are about what forms love and commitment should take, the better off we will all be.

There are many decision-makers that can start to tackle the narrative traps of love and marriage. Parents could warn their children about the dangerous fairy-tale narrative that love always means living happily ever after. This would then result in less psychological, financial and health-related support being required for the acceptance of, or perhaps more likely still, eventual fallout from, a less than perfect marriage. Schools could do more to provide teenagers with the basic facts on love: that you can expect the passion to diminish would be a good place to start. This will help youngsters to see through the fog of social narratives so that they can make more informed choices. Employers have a duty to ensure that any flexible working policy is available to everyone, no matter what their personal circumstances.

The legal system also needs to rethink how it deals with marriage and divorce, and the welfare of children affected by both. There are good libertarian and egalitarian grounds for the state to stop incentivizing marriage (e.g. by removing the tax breaks for married people that are not available to single people). It can instead allow for a range of different contracts between two or more individuals, so that people can specify the rights and responsibilities in the relationship that best suit their unique set of circumstances. Where the state does intervene in family matters, it should focus directly on strengthening the relationships that each parent has with their children. In this way, governments can focus on what really matters – strong parenthood to the benefit of children – without having to interfere in the relationship between the parents.[46]

Divorce law should shift its focus away from attribution of blame and towards ensuring effective support for children. When an intimate relationship breaks down it is often the case that one or other partner, or perhaps both, are seen as responsible for the potential break-up. And that one or other, or perhaps both, are seen as responsible for doing something about it. But it could just be that the individuals are not suited together and should quickly move on. The consequence is a break-up, but the cause does not have to be a question of fault.

Rather bizarrely from a happiness perspective, if you want a quick divorce in the US or the UK, your only options are to accuse your spouse of infidelity or unreasonable behaviour. Attributing blame expedites the process, even if there are no hard feelings. This, of course, only serves to reinforce the narrative that divorce – or, rather, the end of a marriage – is a process that ought to be painful, shameful and, by extension, avoided. If you decide that you do not want to play a role in the blame game and opt for a 'no fault' agreement, you and your partner must commit to living apart for a minimum of two years. At the end of this period, you must both sign to say that you want the divorce. A failure to do so by either partner results in a protracted divorce process governed by the non-compliant other. A one-year 'no fault' divorce default would seem to be a better policy.

We should seek to mitigate the happiness hit to all involved when a love story comes to an end. Research in the US has found that parental conflict is lower, communication and co-operation is greater and paternal involvement is higher when agreements over custody are made through mediation rather than more adversarial processes. Governments could therefore do a lot more to ensure the smooth running of custodial negotiation processes by informing parents of the evidence on effective communication and offering support in this regard. Let me now turn to the behaviour that we rely on to save us from the divorce courts: monogamy.

5

Monogamous

Before we get going with this narrative, here are your two questions. Please make a note of your answers, and we'll come back to the questions at the end of Part Two.

Please read the following statements and indicate whether you would choose Life A or Life B *for yourself*:

Life A: You are in a monogamous relationship. You often feel miserable.

Life B: You are in a non-monogamous relationship, which you and your partner both agree to. You hardly ever feel miserable.

Please read the following statements and indicate whether you would choose Life A or Life B *for a friend*:

Life A: Your friend is in a monogamous relationship. Your friend often feels miserable.

Life B: Your friend is in a non-monogamous relationship, which they and their partner both agree to. Your friend hardly ever feels miserable.

Once we are hitched, the idea of sex outside marriage must be ditched. While attitudes to sex before marriage have relaxed over time, views about monogamy have not changed much in the last few decades in the UK or the US.[1] According to the UK National Survey of Sexual Attitudes and Lifestyle data (2013), around 70 per cent of women and 63 per cent of men think that infidelity is 'always wrong'.[2] Intriguingly, this is up from 53 per cent and 45 per cent, respectively, in 1990. A study conducted by the Pew Research Center suggests that Americans are even more averse to infidelity, with 84 per cent of people agreeing with the statement 'married people having an affair is morally unacceptable', compared with 76 per cent in the UK.[3] France, Germany, Italy and Spain were among the most tolerant nations in this study. Eastern European countries also seem to be more tolerant of affairs, while Muslim countries appear to be the least tolerant of all.[4]

Monogamy is a valid life choice; it's just that it shouldn't be the only aspirational one. Much of the view about the wrongness of infidelity stems from a general belief that it is inherently immoral; that is, a deontological view without recourse to its consequences. The wrongness of infidelity is one social narrative that really has remained unchallenged for a long time. It is the only 'sin' that is repeated twice in the Ten Commandments: 'Thou shalt not commit adultery' and 'Thou shalt not covet thy neighbour's wife'. All religions in their own ways judge extramarital relationships harshly, and most implicitly or explicitly judge women most harshly of all.

NO SEX PLEASE, WE'RE MARRIED

When our spouse becomes as familiar to us as a sibling – when we've become family – we cease to be sexually attracted to each other. None of us lusts after our partner as much after six years as we did after six months. The dominant social narrative, however, is that our desire to have sex with our partner should continue unabated. In his fascinating book *Everybody Lies*, Seth Stephens-Davidowitz analyses data from Google searches, showing that searches in the US for 'sexless marriage' are three and a half times more common than searches for 'unhappy marriage' and eight times more common than the number of searches for 'loveless marriage'.[5]

Beyond evidence from Google searches, the limited existing data are open to all sorts of bias too. Even in response to questions as straightforward as how often people have sex, stories about how frequently we should be having sex get in the way of establishing the facts. Much like in real-life conversations, in surveys men have been shown to report much higher frequency of sexual activity than women.[6] Threaten to bring a lie-detector machine into the interview, however, and many of the differences between men and women disappear.[7] And it appears that an increase in women's reported sexual activity is doing most of the work to close this gap. This tendency for women to give (presumably) more accurate reports when the need to be truthful is made more salient than the need to align with social convention is a clear indication of the myth that women are far less driven by sexual desire than are men.

With this important caveat about the quality of the data in mind, we do know that the frequency with which couples report having sex shows no correlation with overall life satisfaction, but some correlation with how satisfied they claim to be with their partner.[8] It seems that this correlation is an inverted U-shape, with optimal marital satisfaction associated with sex once a week, and lower satisfaction with less and more frequent sex than this. It would presumably be good if the partners had compatible sex drives but I am unaware of any data that speaks to this point.

The frequency with which couples have sex does correlate convincingly with their instinctive reaction towards one another.[9] Those who reported having sex with their partner twice a week or more reacted more quickly to positive words and less slowly to negative ones after seeing an image of their spouse. The opposite was true for those who had sex once a week or less. The priming of positive associations also promotes relationship satisfaction. This was shown in a recent US study where couples were asked to view a brief succession of images of their partners paired with positive or neutral stimuli once every three days over the course of six months. Positive and neutral stimuli were a mix of words (e.g. 'wonderful' or 'straw') and pictures (e.g. a sunset or bucket). Those trained in positive associations reported increased marital satisfaction over time relative to those trained in neutral associations. Satisfied couples probably enjoy sex more, and more often.

The gendered story around sex is that men both want and enjoy sex more than women. Well, our analysis of a group of six hundred Germans using diary reports of happiness suggests a different reality so far as enjoyment is concerned. We find that men experience less pleasure during sex compared to women. These effects are meaningful by the standards of happiness research: 0.6 units' difference on a 0–6 scale (i.e. a 10 per cent change) when asked how happy they felt while engaged in intimate activities.

Women are more likely than men to lose interest in sex in long-term relationships, and to lose it sooner.[10] It is unclear why, though. Perhaps a woman's idea of passionate sex is more closely associated with novelty; or perhaps women associate sex with high-intensity emotion more than men do, so that when the feelings of passionate love go, the interest in sex with that man diminishes. Whatever the explanation, we should not fall into another trap of assuming that as women are married for longer or as they get older they inevitably lose interest in sex more quickly. It's just in a long-term relationship with the same man that a woman's interest in sex seems to wane.

It's hard to get causal evidence on the effects of sex on happiness because happier couples might be at it more often in the first place. To probe this, one study conducted in the US took one hundred hetero-sexual couples and randomly assigned them to one of two groups: the first group was told to double the amount of times they had sex over the next ninety days. The second group of couples received no instructions to change the frequency with which they had sex. The results showed that the first group became less happy and enjoyed sex less.[11] Being told to do something – even something pleasurable – takes the fun out of it.

WIRED TO CHEAT

Evolutionary biologists have posited that sexual variety – prompted by a short window of passionate love – evolved to prevent incest and inbreeding in ancestral environments.[12] This serves to mitigate the risks of infant mortality and birth defects. Social monogamy, rel-ating to a life-time pair bond, is observable in around 3 per cent of mammals but is frequently accompanied by extra-pair copulation, i.e. a bit of fun on the side.[13] Complete monogamy, partners choosing to have sex with only one person for life, only occurs as the default arrangement in one species: owl monkeys, who mate once a year when the females are most fertile.

Robust evidence on sexual infidelity is hard to find, for obvious reasons, but this has not stopped us from knowing that infidelity is widespread. Some recent research estimates rates of at least one sexual affair over the course of a marriage in the UK to be at least one in three for men and one in four for women. In the US, the numbers of men reporting infidelity has remained around 25 per cent for the last couple of decades; for women the figure is around 15 per cent.[14] I assume the actual numbers are higher in both countries.

There are countless stories about differences between the sexual attitudes and behaviours of men and women. What about the evidence? A BBC study, using a large dataset of over 200,000 online participants, examined cross-cultural patterns in sexual desire across fifty-three nations.[15] The survey found that women were typically far more variable in their sex drive than were men. This gender difference remained consistent across nations, suggesting that the variability in sex drive among women tends to be less influenced by cultural construction and more by biological factors. In the same study, women were also found to be more variable in their self-reported openness to sex (clumsily called 'socio-sexuality' in academic literature) than men across nations. Unlike sex drive, however, socio-environmental factors such as gender equality and economic development were found to explain these gender differences in socio-sexuality.

The greater variability in the reports of women compared to men might go some way towards explaining why (high sex drive) promiscuous women are often judged more harshly by (low sex drive) women as well as by (insecure and controlling) men. Social class seems to play a part here too. It has been shown that middle-class women will call working-class women sluts in order to assert their economic and social advantage.[16]

There is some exciting new evidence from researchers at Oxford University to suggest that, on the spectrum from monogamy to infidelity, the distribution within men and women might be bi-modal rather than normally distributed; that is, two groups might emerge within each gender.[17] The researchers looked at two separate datasets to show this. The first contained data from six hundred Brits and Americans who answered the Socio-sexual Orientation Inventory, which measures people's proclivity towards engaging in sexual relationships without an emotional commitment. The second dataset contained information on the index- and ring-finger measurements of 1,300 Brits. The ratio of these measurements is called the 2D:4D ratio. It gives an indication of how much testosterone people have been exposed to in the womb and is linked to sexual promiscuity: the lower the ratio (i.e. the longer your ring finger is relative to your index finger), the higher your testosterone levels and the more sexually promiscuous you are likely to be.

To determine whether or not men and women differ in their self-reported and biologically determined sexual tendencies, the researchers ran tests on these two datasets. The best fitting models were those that split each of the men and women into two groups. While there are some gender differences in the 2D:4D ratios pertaining to phenotypic mix, they are not as exaggerated as some people might think. Men are more likely to be promiscuous rather than monogamous by a ratio of 57 to 43, and women are more likely to be monogamous than promiscuous – but only slightly more so, at a ratio of 53 to 47. In simple terms, the evidence implies that some men are more predisposed towards being dads than cads, and some women are more predisposed to being mothers than lovers.

That there are more cads than dads may not surprise many of you, but the high proportion of lovers among women might. We have been fed a narrative that men are hardwired to 'spread their seed' while women are 'naturally' a lot less inclined to stray. The UK's latest major survey on sexual behaviour, the 2000 National Survey of Sexual Attitudes and Lifestyles, suggests a 6 per cent difference between men and women, which is not that much – especially when we account for the fact that women typically under-report their sexual activity.[18]

It is certainly not as different as the harshness with which women who cheat are judged compared to how we view men who do. Sure, we judge men badly, but women who cheat are severely chastised, especially when they have children. There can be no doubt that men have sought to downplay women's sexuality in many ways across societies over a very long time. So I suspect that breaking free from the narrative of monogamy will reduce the suffering of women most of all. They would certainly be able to express themselves more freely with less judgement, and smash once and for all outdated ideas around sex being something which men enjoy and women endure.

The challenge, of course, is that a man cannot know for sure that the child he is bringing up is his. The more likely his partner is to cheat, the more uncertain this becomes. A child requires a huge commitment of resources, and a father would like that commitment to be towards his genetic offspring. So it makes good sense for men to suppress the sexual behaviour of women. A man may benefit from monogamy too, by investing attentional resources into saving, bringing up children and increasing economic productivity for the sake of children he knows are his.[19] This is also thought to reduce intense competition for young females and in so doing reduces male aggression and the spread of sexually transmitted infections. But my point, as always, is that we can surely accommodate different ways of living without the world falling down around our ears.

We should also consider that sexuality can be quite fluid, especially among women. Heterosexual women get turned on by looking at a much broader range of sex acts than do their male counterparts.[20] While men become aroused looking at sex acts that are aligned with their sexuality (heterosexual men looking at women, homosexual men looking at men), self-identifying heterosexual women can get turned on by watching women masturbate, as well as by watching men.[21] Only one third of the sample, who all identified as lesbians at the start of the study, engaged in exclusively lesbian sexual activity throughout.

DESIRED TO CHEAT

What are the motivations to cheat, beyond biology? Those having affairs often feel guilty, but they also report feelings of being wanted, an increase in self-esteem, 'feeling alive', and having new experiences – as well as sexual satisfaction.[22] Misery in a marriage can act as a catalyst for an affair too, of course. Some studies have shown a clear negative correlation between marital satisfaction and infidelity.[23] The effects appear to be stronger for women than for men, and among those who have an affair, women are significantly less satisfied in their marriages than are men. Overall, marital satisfaction appears to account for about a quarter of the variance in infidelity.

As with all behaviours, the 'pull towards' the new behaviour (the desire for someone new and exciting) is more salient to some people whereas the 'push away' from the old behaviour is more salient to others (there is something missing in my marriage). There would appear to be a slight gender difference in the importance of these factors, with 'pull' factors mattering more to men and 'push' factors more to women.[24] Affairs may be driven by factors such as a greater propensity for sensation seeking among men[25] and lower levels of reported relationship satisfaction in marriage among women.[26] Interestingly, there is some suggestion that a man's likelihood of an affair is unrelated to the length of the relationship, but that a woman's increases the longer she is in the relationship.[27]

There are many other factors at play which affect people's propensity to have an extramarital relationship. Just like so many of our other behaviours in life, infidelity is also related to opportunity.[28] Those living in big cities, where the likelihood of getting caught is lower due to the possibility of increased anonymity, are more likely to report having an affair. And those who engage in infidelity with co-workers are not necessarily unhappy in their primary relationships; rather, they are acting on the opportunity available to them outside their domestic context.[29] This view of 'infidelity as opportunity' might help to explain the closing gender gap in rates of infidelity as greater numbers of women have entered the workplace over the last fifty years.

It has been shown that people with more money are more likely to cheat.[30] Income might be a marker of something else that contributes to infidelity. For example, individuals with higher incomes might be considered to have higher status, to travel more, or to interact professionally with more interesting people. Studies also show that powerful men and women are more likely to be unfaithful.[31] For example, in a study assessing a large number of professionals in varying positions of power (from junior workers to CEOs), those who perceived themselves as having more power reported higher engagement with, and willingness to engage with, infidelity. Increasing income might also make it easier to hide the additional cost of hotels and restaurants from a personal perspective as well as professionally – costs of entertainment or other expenses incurred as a result of being with a third person being seen as normal.

According to anonymous online survey data from the Netherlands, one in ten people in non-management roles report having engaged in infidelity.[32] For those in top management positions this figure rose to four in ten. The study controlled for gender, age and education differences as possible contributing factors. Interestingly, it was found that attraction to secrecy (breaking social convention) mediated the link between power and infidelity. It seems that power liberates people from the chains of social conformity, thus making infidelity more likely.

With the advent of technology, infidelity has also started to crowd the digital space. To gauge public attitudes towards digital infidelity (the use of digital media to initiate and/or maintain affairs), one study analysed 124 personal narratives from an online infidelity social support group in the US and asked hundreds of people about their attitudes towards digital infidelity.[33] Researchers found that sexual exchanges were considered to be the biggest predictor of whether interaction would be classified as cheating or not – even if these exchanges were virtual. Little wonder, then, that spying on your partner's online activity has become standard practice. And little wonder, too, that real as well as virtual infidelity is most likely on the increase.

THE IMPACT OF INFIDELITY

It is worth reminding ourselves that infidelity will mean different things to different people. A couple might agree that sexual intercourse with someone else is off the cards but that kissing somebody on a night out is OK. At the other end of the spectrum sits US Vice-President Mike Pence, who was reported to have declined dinner with another woman on the basis that his wife was not going to be present. On *Make Or Break?* the couples were separated and forced to spend the night with someone else's partner. Even after a month, and with TV cameras watching their every move, some of the men were still sleeping on the floor.

There are of course good consequentialist reasons to be concerned about infidelity, however defined. Those who find out about their partner's affair often feel rage, loss of trust, decreased personal and sexual confidence, damaged self-esteem and fear of abandonment, and suffer damage to other relationships such as those with children, parents and friends.[34] While a small percentage of couples may benefit after an affair (through closer marital relations, increased assertiveness, realizing the importance of good marital communication, and by placing higher value on family), an affair generally has adverse, long-lasting effects.[35]

Besides sexually transmitted infections, the most obvious fallout of an affair is a break-up. Infidelity makes an independent contribution to the prediction of divorce, regardless of which spouse was perceived as having caused the problem, and is cited as the primary reason for separation in about a fifth of divorce cases, according to Grant Thornton's annual survey of seventy-six family lawyers in the UK.[36] There is other evidence, however, suggesting that affairs themselves do not cause divorce, but rather that the overall level of relationship satisfaction, the motives attributed to infidelity, the level of conflict generated over the infidelity, and the attitudes held about long-term infidelities play significant roles in the decision about whether or not to split up. [37]

The real effects of infidelity cannot be separated from the social narrative of how awful it is. The partner who finds out about the affair is expected to be angry and should, according to a majority of their peers, leave their partner out of self-respect. Recall the public outrage at Hillary Clinton after she decided to stay with husband Bill after his widely publicized sexual indiscretions. Many were completely baffled as to why she hadn't filed for a divorce despite knowing about his intimate encounters with other women. Donald Trump capitalized on this widespread disapproval by positioning Hillary's tolerance of Bill's infidelity at the forefront of his political rhetoric against her, labelling her an 'enabler'.

As with many areas of human behaviour, intentions are a poor indicator of future action. In one study conducted in the US, 60 per cent of participants initially threatened to leave their primary relationship as a result of the disclosure of infidelity, but less than a quarter of those couples actually separated.[38] Half were actively working on their relationship through therapy, and the rest were unable to take effective action, changed their minds, or decided to 'give their spouse another chance'. This study highlights two things. First, we can never reliably say how we might behave in the future based on a hypothetical set of circumstances: what we say has little correlation to what we do. Second, we are capable of adapting to a changed set of circumstances. Our psychological immune system kicks in when we find out about infidelity and helps us to ameliorate its initial impact and to make sense of it. Many couples have come out of affairs claiming to be stronger for it. Many more would if only we kept our opinions on their particular relationship to ourselves.

What about the effects on the partner who has the affair? Well, they are judged very harshly and are expected to show regret and shame. They are seen to be in the wrong, irrespective of the context surrounding the infidelity. The perpetrator is usually loath to see themselves as someone who cheats. This produces cognitive dissonance, whereby your attitudes are inconsistent with your actions. The literature on cognitive dissonance shows that it is much easier to change what you think about your actions than it is to bring your behaviour in line with your beliefs. The evidence supports this, showing that those who engage in extramarital relationships are pretty good at explaining away the affair so that it sounds acceptable.[39] As a result, while many do feel considerable guilt, many feel no other negative emotions at all.

Once you have engaged in infidelity, there is also the question about whether or not to admit it. The upside of lying is that you can avoid hurt and conflict. The downside is that you can feel guilty, which affects how you relate to your partner. Indeed, studies have shown that people report feeling less intimate during conversations in which they are withholding the truth.[40] Lying is more taxing cognitively than telling the truth.[41] When we lie, we must first think of the truth and then remind ourselves of our fabrication or construct one in the moment. During this time, we are also often weighing up the costs and benefits of the lies we are telling and considering the likelihood that we might get found out. Generally speaking, the costs of lying are given much greater prominence than the benefits, and this can lead to people telling their partner the truth when it might have been in both their interests not to air it.

In the case of infidelity, it is for each person to decide whether or not to come clean depending on their own specific context. There can be no general guidance here. On the one hand, telling your partner will draw attention to the issue and make it a big deal. On the other hand, not telling them might make you feel guilty and act in ways that further damage the relationship, particularly if your sense of connection with your partner is bound up with the belief that you should be honest with them. I'm sure at this point many of you are screaming that people shouldn't cheat in the first place. But we are dealing here with what to do once an affair has occurred and, as we have seen, they occur pretty frequently.

OPEN UP

One way in which people can be more tolerant of infidelity is to choose to be in a relationship that is consensually non-monogamous (CNM). About 5 per cent of heterosexual individuals in the UK identify themselves as part of a CNM relationship, an arrangement in which all partners involved agree that having multiple sexual and/ or romantic partnerships is allowed.[42] Each couple will have their own rules about exactly what is and what is not permissible, but they have one thing in common: namely, that, within those rules, infidelity to some degree is acceptable.

Research suggests that individuals in CNM relationships report relatively high levels of trust, honesty, intimacy, friendship and satisfaction, as well as relatively low levels of jealousy, within their relationships as compared with individuals who have never engaged in CNM relationships.[43] One study asked 175 people in CNM relationships to freely describe the benefits of being in this kind of relationship, and then compared the answers to a similar study of people in monogamous relationships.[44] The three key benefits that emerged as being unique to CNM relationships were: diversified ways in which personal needs can be fulfilled; variety in non-sexual activities (if one partner doesn't share your love for skydiving or playing bridge, another might); and personal growth relating to a greater ability to explore separate, individual identities. These benefits have also been reflected in more recent empirical findings.[45] For monogamous relationships, uniquely listed benefits included better sexual health and a perceived sense of moral superiority.

There is obviously potential for strong selection effects and self-reporting bias here, but you should at least consider which lifestyle and associated benefits suits you best. Being in a CNM relationship carries a moral stigma, although people typically judge cheating in monogamous relationships more harshly than cheating in CNM relationships.[46] A CNM relationship might also be preferable for individuals who prefer not to be constrained by the polarized dichotomy of sexuality which posits that sexual attraction should be limited to one gender. By granting people more autonomy in their sexual choices, CNM relationships give people greater freedom to explore a more fluid form of sexual expression.

What about the children of those in CNM relationships? Unfortunately there isn't much evidence on this but there do appear to be some important benefits to children from living in such environments. In a longitudinal study, CNM parents reported that their children were able to have more one-to-one time with adults.[47] This meant children spent less time in day care, which would mean reduced expense and increased time with family members. It is also likely to be beneficial for language development; more parents means that parents will be less fatigued, which facilitates more engaged discussions with the children, and being interested and engaged in your child is shown to have a positive impact on language acquisition.[48] Other research has shown that children benefit from having multiple role models in their lives who can help with homework or inspire their hobbies.[49] The dissolution of CNM relationships could be potentially damaging, though, as the children may find themselves being emotionally pulled in multiple directions.

Given the power of the social narrative of monogamy, it is not surprising that children whose parents' seemingly monogamous relationship broke down as a result of infidelity tend to grow up with concerns about their own partner's ability to commit to them. The burden of monogamy is a harmful one given the prevalence of cheating; it exacerbates the impact of a separation that might have otherwise been far easier to cope with if monogamy wasn't positioned as the linchpin of the relationship. It is at least plausible that CNM might be a viable alternative to monogamy when it comes to transparency and satisfaction, both of which create a happier home life for children too.

Yet the social narrative of love and (monogamous) marriage is so powerful that those in CNM relationships are perceived not only to have less valid relationships but also to be fundamentally flawed people, even in ways that have nothing to do with their sexual or romantic profile. For example, researchers from Michigan University found that those in CNM relationships are considered to be less likely to floss than those who are monogamous.[50] In broader terms, a correlation is made between their 'looser' morals and a lower standard of hygiene.

CNM relationships are more commonplace among gay men but not among gay women. There is perhaps a greater recognition by men that other men may cheat and a better understanding of the distinction between sex and love. There might be some interesting parallels here between CNM relationships and homosexual ones. As with most progressive change, it might just take a while for the rest of us to get the hang of accepting difference. But once we get there it wouldn't surprise me if far greater numbers of people started to embrace CNM relationships more openly. In fact, there's already been a documented rise in Google searches relating to CNM relationships over the last decade in the US, so we shall see what happens.[51]

Part of this potential change might be due to online dating, which has made it easier than ever for open-minded people to seek out like-minded individuals for a relationship. The dating site OkCupid has recognized the growing prevalence of this trend by building a 'search as a couple' function into the site. According to the data that the site collects, 42 per cent of its customer base say that they would consider dating somebody in an open relationship.

CONCLUSIONS

It is hard to argue with the contention that we should each be free to choose the kind of relationship that suits us. Monogamy works for some of us some of the time, but not for all of us all of the time. We have to be more accepting of our basic human desires while at the same time being thoughtful in our solutions about how best to manage them. This is not a philanderer's charter, just a recognition of some basic facts about the human condition. Challenging the importance of the narrative of monogamy and its relevance in our own lives may go a long way towards curtailing some of the social costs incurred by those who do not fit with social convention, and allow them to make choices about their relationships that may make them and their partner(s) happier. There are many good options to choose from, with monogamy being just one.

Once we accept this, we can have more open and honest discussions about the kinds of relationships we would like to be in, rather than just falling into an assumption of monogamy by default. As with most behaviours, we should design institutions and policies that reflect human and social development, as opposed to clinging to morally charged historical guidelines. This might involve removing infidelity as an immediate ground for divorce, for example.

It certainly requires ways to support people who choose to be in non-monogamous relationships, such as finding ways to provide the same tax breaks to people with multiple partners that most married people are entitled to, and allowing multiple people to be involved in end-of-life care. For example, this might function as a separate CNM contract that entitles people to the same allowances as married couples but spread across those in the relationship. Some legal systems are already set up to recognize multi-person unions. The Netherlands has already proposed a multi-parent law, whereby up to four parents can claim legal rights to a child, although this law is yet to be passed. Multiple parenting is legal in California and in the Canadian provinces of British Columbia and Ontario. Looking at how the legal systems of different nations were set up to embrace the LGBT movement could yield important insights into similarities (and differences) that individuals in 'new' kinds of relationships might face in trying to achieve social parity.

Monogamy might suit most of us for long periods in our lives. But it is not deviant to deviate. We need to interrogate an ideal that seems to have no basis in biology, behaviour or happiness. We do, of course, need to consider the impact of our intimate relationships on children. Speaking of which . . .

6

Children

Before we get going with this narrative, here are two questions for you to answer. Please make a note of your answers, and we'll come back to the questions at the end of Part Two.

Please read the following statements and indicate whether you would choose Life A or Life B *for yourself*:

Life A: You are a parent. You often feel miserable.
Life B: You are not a parent and never will be. You hardly ever feel miserable.

Please read the following statements and indicate whether you would choose Life A or Life B *for a friend*:

Life A: Your friend is a parent. Your friend often feels miserable.
Life B: Your friend is not a parent and never will be. Your friend hardly ever feels miserable.

After you have fallen in love, married and proved your commitment by not straying, what next in the narrative of your life? Well, kids, of course. It's the final step to becoming a fully fledged adult. And quite rightly, you might say: without the biological imperative, our species would die out. We may also need young workers to support old retirees, although this is a more questionable economic challenge. It does not follow that evolution should be used as a social stick with which to beat those who do not want children, or as justification for pitying those who cannot have them. Just because species survival requires new generations, this does not place the burden on *every* member of society, especially now given the challenges of planetary overpopulation.

Our general endorsement of procreation means that those who do not want children, especially women, may feel compelled to have them because society demands it and, they're told, they might regret it for ever if they don't. The narrative trap surrounding kids comes from the fact that having children is not unequivocally good for happiness. Indeed, kids can cause considerable strain and anxiety for many parents – and many parents can cause great misery for their children. Moreover, those that don't have children can lead very pleasurable and purposeful lives, despite being undermined by a narrative that suggests they can't.

If you are in any doubt about how pervasive the having kids narrative is, just think about how many work colleagues send round pictures of their newborns. I am never going to meet the apple of their eye, so what compels them to share their child's birth weight or ridiculous name with me? Because they have to show off their narrative success. Yet if they reflected for a moment, they would see how selfish this is: not just by assuming that I care about their procreative capabilities, but also by failing to account for the impact their pictures might have on colleagues who can't have children, or who may have had other traumatic experiences around conception or childbirth. In the UK, one in five pregnancies are terminated and one in five result in miscarriage. I bet those sending out pictures of their gurning newborns do not give these statistics a moment's thought.

The children narrative is also making its mark on our digital footprints. Social media has contributed to the sharing of baby and family images that fetishize motherhood. There is even a new term for this phenomenon: 'sharenting'. The average parent will display almost 1,000 images of their child online before they reach the age of five, according to a recent survey of 2,000 parents commissioned in the UK.[1] Parents obviously favour images that present their children in a positive light, making other parents worry that their experiences of having children don't measure up.

While we embrace sharing our experiences of parenthood, very little is said of the burden placed on our planet by the exponential rise of populations, which is nothing to show off about. A picture of an adopted child would really be something worth celebrating but I don't recall ever having been sent one. Rather than being recognized for their decision to improve the life of an existing child, people who adopt are usually assumed to have compromised because they can't have children of their own, so they hide away their loving deeds while parents parade their self-propagation. Let's consider these issues in more detail.

AN IMPERATIVE?

The first thing that probably comes to mind when considering the reasons people embark on the journey of parenthood is biological instinct. Our bodies are designed for procreation, and the need to preserve the survival of our species is surely one of our main reasons for being here. The desire for children is human and there are strong biological and evolutionary arguments for why this is likely to be true for most people.

What isn't true, however, is that this biological drive is or should be innate in everyone. There is no 'biological imperative' for all individuals. Maternal instinct, for example, is not universal. In her review of historical evidence, Maria Vicedo Castello concludes that there is no evidence supporting our assumptions that all women have an innate desire for children.[2] If the desire to bear children were inherent in us all, Vicedo Castello explains, we would see birth rates remain consistent over time (controlling for medical advances, of course). Yet birth rates tend to fluctuate with cultural shifts in attitude.

The reality now is that if we all wanted children, the survival of our species would become problematic. The planet is already stressed and we depend on fertility rates falling for environmental stability. It seems odd to me that childbearing is presented to people as a lifetime obligation when, seen from the macro level, conformity to this will impede the lives of those same people. If the happiness of humankind was our primary concern, it would be more helpful to systematically limit the numbers of children being born. This could be achieved using illiberal methods, such as the one-child policy in China. Alternatively, we could all take the more humane, liberty-preserving route of questioning the children narrative.

Another problem with the biological imperative argument is that it assumes that we should want and have children that carry our DNA. This makes the prospect of adoption far less appealing relative to biological parenthood, even though this option is likely to result in far greater welfare gains for those involved and for society. Imagine being asked right now to choose between saving a sentient being from a lifetime of misery or giving life to someone who does not yet exist. The former should be a no-brainer, but the latter is what nearly all of us opt for.

The biological imperative argument also ignores the prospect that we can override our biological instincts through consideration of other factors, such as social impact. Yes, we may feel inclined to want children but that doesn't necessarily mean that we can't change our mind once presented with the facts in this chapter. It is interesting that we pick and choose when biological instinct should and should not dominate over other factors. For example, as we have seen in the previous chapter, many of us are reluctant to accept the role that biological instinct might have on our propensity to cheat in committed relationships, yet when it comes to kids biological instinct is very rarely downplayed. This is a clear example of how narratives cleverly shift our perspective on what is and is not acceptable.

Perching parenthood on a pedestal promotes this assumption that having children is following a more 'natural' course than being childfree. Negative stereotyping associated with not having kids sees individuals branded as self-interested, materialistic, emotionally underdeveloped and less caring. As an example of this, Pope Francis deemed societies with low birth rates 'depressed societies', insisting that 'not to have children is a selfish choice'. Those on the receiving end of negative associations like these typically report feelings of incompleteness and the belief that others regard them as desperate, pitiful and selfish.[3] Stigma is greatest for those who are voluntarily as opposed to involuntarily childfree.[4] The voluntarily childfree are more likely to be regarded as self-centred and socially awkward, whereas involuntarily childfree people are met with a degree of pity.[5]

Pitching voluntary childlessness (and even adoption) as against nature's imperative also prevents it from becoming a legitimately alternative pathway, placing unnecessary restrictions on the options available for people to improve their happiness. It implies that a woman is not complete without a biological child when in fact there are many other routes to fulfilment. In an Australian study exploring the lived experiences of childless women through in-depth interviews, participants consistently reported feeling as if their decision was unnatural and undervalued. Our restrictive definition of womanhood means that those who eschew motherhood tend to be constructed as deviant 'others' in cultural discourse.[6]

The children narrative further exacerbates the misery experienced by people who want but can't have children. Signalling this narrative as the most desirable path puts pressure on couples to achieve this milestone. We know that focusing on unattainable goals is particularly bad for our experiences and evaluations of happiness. Emphasizing having kids as the most socially desirable option also devalues the many other opportunities available to those who do not have children, such as helping others.

Much of what is typically understood as a biological imperative can also be viewed through the lens of social context. As has been a key theme of this book, our beliefs, behaviour and feelings are highly influenced by what those around us do, often in ways that we are unaware of. In the US, nine out of ten adults say that they have kids or are planning to, and this number has remained relatively unchanged over the last decade.[7] Importantly, though, behavioural patterns have shifted against these expectations. While historically about 10 per cent of the population were documented as childless, nowadays the figure is closer to 20 per cent.[8]

One major reason for this change is that women are trying for children later in life when fertility rates are lower. Some of my own research into extending IVF deadlines has shown that delaying having a child by one year can lead to 6 per cent fewer pregnancies.[9] The contraceptive pill, the women's movement and better job prospects now all mean that women are no longer expected to have children young. But they are still expected to have them.

It goes without saying that the social expectation to have children is especially incumbent upon women. If you conduct a quick Google search for girls' and boys' toys you will notice the extent to which parenthood plays a prominent part for girls but not for boys. Her toys are prams, dolls and doll's houses; his toys are weapons, superheroes and construction games. Childless heterosexual women tend to be portrayed by the media as lonely and unhappy, living half a life. Jennifer Aniston is a good example: whatever else she might do in life, she is nonetheless pitied for her childlessness. There are some small differences in how childlessness is viewed across nations, but in every country for which data are available, women are judged more harshly than men for not having children.

Another social layer that prevents people from exploring the 'no kids' option is pressure from close friends and family. If you are a young couple that have been together for a number of years, particularly if you have just tied the knot, you will no doubt be accustomed to the frequent whispers of parents, grandparents, siblings, uncles and aunts asking you when you will have children. This social pressure can drive people towards having children, even if it may not be in their own best interests. Indeed, many people list the pressure to provide grandchildren for their parents as a reason for opting in to parenthood.

Although there's no experience-based happiness data on this, it appears that having grandchildren increases life satisfaction, particularly for grandmothers.[10] We are all at liberty to make life choices on the basis of what will make our parents happy, and to sacrifice some of our own happiness in doing so. But I would rather parents keep their noses out of their kids' lives when it comes to the life-changing decisions that will directly impact their happiness for years to come. We can't avoid imposing our preferences to some degree, of course, but I am determined that Poppy and Stanley never get any suggestion from me about whether or not I would like grandchildren. It's interesting that little scholarly attention is devoted to parents' impact on their adult children's behaviour and happiness. I suspect, just as in childhood, it can be quite transformative.

REASONS TO BE CHILDFREE

Despite the prevailing social narrative of having children, an increasing number of people across the world have decided that child rearing is not for them. Greater economic and social freedom has created a climate in which this decision has been made easier for women. Qualitative research in which couples answered structured interview questions about their decision to remain childfree shows that most couples arrive at this conclusion over time and after careful deliberation.[11]

An important contributing factor to this decision-making process is the time commitment. Children represent a lifetime of work and they take up a lot of your time. People that decide not to be parents can devote time that would otherwise be spent caring for their children to other activities. Indeed, there appears to be a positive relationship between voluntary childlessness and investment in other life domains. For example, 42 per cent of charitable foundations are created by people without children.[12] It is thought that endeavours like this appeal to childless people since they provide an alternative means through which to 'leave a mark'. Results from the Survey of Health, Ageing and Retirement in Europe, which is a longitudinal study of over 20,000 over-fifty-year-olds in ten European countries, also show that older childless people are more likely than older parents to give both their time and money to charity.[13]

Being socially connected to others is a powerful means by which humans can fulfil the fundamental needs of belonging and closeness. Greater perceived social support has a positive impact on the quality and solidity of romantic relationships.[14] And so it is not surprising that increased opportunity to develop relationships with other adults is also high on the list of reasons why people decide to remain childfree.[15] You only have to do a quick search online to find special hubs and forums devoted to living a childfree life. Non-mothers can communicate in these spaces and share the benefits of their childfree experiences. They may mourn not having children but, overall, these are somewhat more enjoyable exchanges than those taking place on equivalent spaces for uneasy mothers such as Mumsnet, where parents compare the colour of their children's faeces and how little they've slept.

Having said this, it is true that motherhood also offers a specific window of opportunity for increased socialization. For example, new mothers may find it easy to form new friendships with other mothers due to their shared experience. Studies show that parenthood can help to increase social connections with friends, family and communities.[16] One study from the US also found that new parents experience better levels of social integration (measured as frequency of contact with friends and relatives) than non-parents, probably because of the attention that having a child brings.[17]

Many people also cite the financial burden as a reason for not having children. They are bloody expensive. The average cost of bringing up a kid in the UK from birth to age twenty-one is close to £250,000. So, Poppy and Stanley, that's half a million you will have cost us. We know from Part One that having loads of money isn't all it's cracked up to be, but being pressed for money can also make us miserable, and the presence of children makes money worries much more likely. Financial strain affects working-class families disproportionately for obvious reasons.

The other salient reason for not having kids, alluded to earlier, is their undeniable impact on the environment. This is barely referenced in public discourse, though the results are astounding. Oregon State University researchers compared the potential impact of completing six 'green' activities with the simple decision to have one less child.[18] The six environmental habits included driving a more fuel-efficient car, halving annual car mileage, fitting double glazing, using low-energy light bulbs, replacing an inefficient fridge, and making sure all paper, tin and glass was recycled. Adopting all six pro-environmental activities can reduce your carbon footprint by an impressive 486 tonnes. But researchers found that simply having one less child could reduce it by 9,441 tonnes – potentially twenty times more effective than adopting what many of us would conceive to be quite inconvenient environmental measures.

And, of course, it is the kids we so desperately want who will suffer the consequences of climate change. By the time children born today are teenagers, we are expected to see a surge in droughts, flooding and extreme weather conditions. UNICEF believes that current figures for child malnourishment will rise by 25 million as a result of climate change. And a further 100 million children are expected to suffer from extreme food scarcity by 2030.

KIDS AND YOUR HAPPINESS

So do children really make people happy then? Well, our children certainly ought to according to the narrative. And, despite all the good reasons given above for not even having them in the first place, we can get into trouble if we suggest otherwise. I have been on the receiving end of some pretty nasty online abuse for saying that they 'do bring pleasure from time to time but I was a pretty good pleasure machine before they came along. And they have given me something important to worry about, and not in a good way. But they do bring me a huge amount of purpose.' Here are a couple of the kinder comments: 'I feel sorry for the children . . . Yuck.'; 'Also his attitude to his own children is very selfish. Twat!!' (I appreciate both exclamation marks.)

Unsurprisingly, I still agree with my former comments. My kids do bring me purpose. But I am letting them know that they are not responsible for my happiness. I hope they find this liberating, and that they can be their own people. Les and I chose to have them, and we are the ones responsible for how they make us feel. Too many parents expect their kids to make them happy and that is a huge burden for their kids to bear. Poppy and Stanley are free to make our lives miserable, as they did as babies and as I'm sure they will be only too good at again when they become teenagers.

I strongly suspect that those who criticize me for stating the bleeding obvious are overcompensating for the ways in which their own kids make them sad in ways they never expected. In any event, it is at least worth noting that while people will often say that their kids make them happy, they will also say how much they have sacrificed for them (sometimes to the children themselves). As we shall see in Chapter 7, I'm not at all convinced that happiness and sacrifice go together that well.

A recent review assessing the associations between parenthood and life satisfaction concluded that, according to most cross-sectional and longitudinal data, people without kids are at least as satisfied with their lives as those with them.[19] So even when using measures such as life satisfaction that will contain some reporting bias in favour of the narrative (as with marriage), it appears that the notion that kids should make us happy is not powerful enough to override the fact that they actually don't much of the time.

Longitudinal data assessing people's transition into parenthood can help us to examine the extent to which certain highs might be mitigated by other lows. For example, one study using the German Socio-Economic Panel data found that the positive effect of being a parent on life satisfaction is offset by financial costs.[20] It is not surprising, then, that higher income levels can act as a buffer against the negative well-being effects of parenthood.

The age at which you have kids seems to play a part too. In large longitudinal studies of Brits and Germans, young parents between the ages of eighteen and twenty-two tend to experience declining life satisfaction that does not improve above pre-birth measures of life satisfaction.[21] The middle age group of parents (between twenty-three and thirty-four years old) experience a rise in life satisfaction during pregnancy and in the first year; however, life satisfaction reverts to pre-birth levels in the two years after birth. Mature parents (aged between thirty-five and forty-nine) report increases in life satisfaction before the birth of the child and in the year of birth, before returning to just above or at pre-birth levels of life satisfaction subsequently. Other large studies, using data from eighty-six countries, have found comparable results.[22] Before the age of thirty, the associations between parenthood and life satisfaction were negative; between thirty and forty there was no association; and after the age of forty children make people more satisfied on average. So the evaluative benefits of having children certainly appear more promising the older people get. Ticking off that milestone feels better once you step back from it, even if it was pretty miserable at the time.

The number of kids you have matters too: in short, don't have more than two unless you want to be really dissatisfied with your life. The law of diminishing marginal returns is everywhere. And then what about the effects of the gender of the children? Well, most data suggest no effect on life satisfaction, although there are some behavioural data from the US to suggest that parents of daughters are more likely to get divorced.[23] The researchers suggest that this may actually be driven, at least in part, by the fact that female embryos are better equipped to survive stressful pregnancies, rather than being solely attributable to daughters causing more strife. Some more research from Melbourne, however, shows that daughters are only associated with higher divorce rates in their teenage years, which casts doubt on this explanation.[24] There is probably something about the teenage years of daughters that places a significant strain on the relationship. I can't wait.

I digress, a little. Back to the misery of parenthood, which comes through in larger studies that use measures other than life satisfaction. A large, nationally representative study of 13,000 people in the US, using data from the National Survey of Families and Households, has shown that parents living with children at home experience more depression than non-parents. Parents were also coded according to whether or not they had biological or adopted children under the age of eighteen, and there were no differences between these groups.

Women seem to experience more misery than men from having kids. According to the mental health charity Mind, one in five mothers experience a serious mental health condition following childbirth.[25] This problem is exacerbated by the assumption that we aren't supposed to feel this way – our kids should make us happy, right? Men are also affected by an increased risk of mental health problems following birth, though to a slightly lesser extent.[26] Mothers are also more likely to experience greater stress and anxiety than their male partners.

According to a recent Norwegian study of 85,000 mothers, having children triggers a three-year decline in self-esteem.[27] In this study, first-, second-, third- and fourth-time mothers were asked to complete a questionnaire prior to, during and several times after giving birth. Researchers found that first-time mothers' self-esteem decreased in the lead-up to having a child, then increased until the child was six months old, before decreasing again up to the final questionnaire when their child was aged 36 months. The consistency of this trend across sub-groups of mothers (first-, second-, third- and fourth-time mothers) is suggestive of a standard trend in the population. I suspect that the increase in self-esteem recorded in the first few months after birth will be due, at least in part, to the increased purpose experienced by having to look after the baby. The subsequent blip probably reflects adaptation, as well as a likely drop in familial interest and social support.

For first-time mothers, relationship satisfaction has been found to be high during pregnancy, but then to undergo a sharp decline after the birth of the child, with a gradual decline in the following years. For second-, third- and fourth-time mothers, this decline in relationship satisfaction was more gradual. Some of the factors that contribute are likely to include reduced quality time to spend on the relationship and increased conflict relating to childcare. In any event, if you do have kids living at home, you can look forward to your marital satisfaction reaching one of its peaks after your offspring have finally moved out of the family home.[28] Context matters, of course; for some couples this 'empty nest' time can increase the likelihood of separation.[29]

By now I bet you are crying out for some data on experiences of happiness. In a diary study of 1,000 American women, Daniel Kahneman and colleagues found that taking care of children is the twelfth most enjoyable activity . . . out of sixteen. Housework is only marginally less pleasurable.[30] Eating and exercising (though not at the same time) are a whole lot more fun. Some of my own research assessing the levels of pleasure and purpose associated with different activities among German participants revealed that time spent with children was, on average, not very pleasurable – but it was quite purposeful.[31] You certainly have more fun with friends, and you can gain more purpose from volunteering.

Children grow up, of course. A child with physical, emotional, behavioural or lifestyle problems has an ongoing detrimental impact on the happiness of their parents.[32] Other research shows that adult children that have experienced at least one psychological, behavioural, financial, employment, relationship or addiction problem are the strongest predictor of a mother's depression.[33] Successful children (as measured by parents' responses to open-ended questions regarding their children's achievements), in contrast, do not do much to improve parental well-being.[34] Losses loom a lot larger than gains in so many aspects of life.

YOUR KIDS' HAPPINESS

Once you have children, how should you bring them up to give them the best shot at being happy? Well, the short answer is that we don't have reliable data to know for sure. Carrying out randomized controlled experiments with families is almost impossible. There is a strong narrative that a child ideally has both a mum and a dad, but especially a mum. What evidence there is shows significant advantages to maternal care in the early years of a child's life, but researchers often fail to compare this with only a father being present in these early years, therefore failing to distinguish a mother as the superior caregiver.[35] There is a wealth of evidence supporting the importance of the father's involvement on positive child development.[36] In addition, a recent review of existing studies on child outcomes conducted in Melbourne has shown that children of same-sex parents do just as well as other children on a number of well-being measures.[37] The idea that women should devote their lives to child-care makes sense if the alternative is neglect. But if, in a mother's absence, the child receives high-quality care from others, then positive outcomes become more likely.

The way in which you interact with your children is crucial to their development. And here social class plays a big part. In the early years, it's all about communication. One study in the US assessing the household communication of forty-two families with kids found that over the course of one week, kids from middle-class backgrounds were exposed to 215,000 words, compared to 62,000 words for kids from working-class backgrounds.[38] By age three, class-related factors accounted for 36 per cent of the variance in vocabulary. Moreover, the middle-class mothers tended to communicate for the purpose of prompting conversation with their children whereas mothers of low socio-economic status tended to communicate for the purpose of directing behaviour. This further widens the ability gap between children from middle- and working-class backgrounds.

Research also suggests that how a mother interacts with her child can alter the development of serotonin functions, which are associated with empathy.[39] People who report being neglected by their parents as children have been shown to exhibit decreases in central serotonergic neurotransmission as adults, which is thought to make them less empathetic towards others.[40] Animal studies employing stringent experimental methods have demonstrated similar findings; that is, separating newborn babies from their mothers influences serotonin receptor expressions.[41]

Parent–child interaction can also influence your subsequent romantic relationships. This is what Attachment Theory, formulated in the late 1960s by British psychoanalyst John Bowlby, posits. According to Bowlby, we belong to one of three attachment styles that we display as children: secure, ambivalent and avoidant.[42] These were categorized according to how two-year-old children react when their mother leaves the room and then returns. Securely attached infants typically experience distress when their mothers leave the room but seek them out on their return and are easily comforted. This attachment style is representative of most of the population. Ambivalently attached children experience distress following their parent's departure but approach them on their return with some initial resistance. Avoidant children display no signs of distress when left by their parent and show little interest in their return. (A fourth attachment style – 'disorganized' – has been added more recently. This is characterized by behaviour such as approaching the mother with back turned upon her return.)

These early developing attachment styles are associated with adult intimacy.[43] So those who develop secure attachment styles in early life tend to be more comfortable, secure and trusting in subsequent relationships. This again represents the vast majority of people. Those who develop ambivalent early attachment styles tend to worry about whether their partners love them and want to stay with them. Finally, those that develop avoidant early attachment styles tend to experience nervousness when forming new relationships and find that others tend to expect a higher level of closeness than they feel comfortable offering. Early socialization has a long-lasting and pervasive impact on our subsequent interactions with those we are closest to.

Being securely attached is associated with higher levels of life satisfaction and also with higher experiential happiness. A recent study in Spain found that anxiously attached individuals experienced greater stress and perceived social rejection as compared to securely attached individuals.[44] Individuals with an avoidant attachment style, by contrast, experience a decreased desire to interact with others when alone, as compared with securely attached individuals. But, as others have noted before me, we must be careful not to over-infer the extent of this impact; while attachment appears to have some effect, it is but one piece of a much larger jigsaw that determines our adult behaviour.

CHILDREN AS ADULTS

Once a child is born, a two-way system of communication is established between parent and child. Just as people shouldn't feel pressured into having children they don't really want, children shouldn't feel pressured into staying in contact with parents who cause them misery. Yet we have to really swim against a tidal wave of social narrative if we are to remove ourselves from family that really harms us. There are some pretty horrible parents out there, but their kids tolerate an enormous amount of suffering because 'he's still my dad'.

One explanation for why we find it so hard to reject familial relationships lies in attachment. In studies looking at emotional attachment in rats, it was found that the neural circuits associated with fear and avoidance become suppressed when rats are in the presence of mothers that neglected or physically injured them as a pup.[45] An evolutionary explanation for this is that infants remain attached during abusive periods because it is more beneficial for an infant to stay attached to a caregiver that abuses them than to not receive any care at all. A similar biological attachment circuit may exist in children, which will remain a powerful motivator of action in adulthood.

Biological antecedents are then reinforced when those who refuse to make peace with a failing parent find themselves being judged harshly by other people. It is fine for us to dump partners who treat us badly but not to stop talking to our parents, who might cause us or our own children more long-term damage. So far as social welfare is concerned, particularly where grandchildren are involved, many children do remain in contact with a bad parent irrespective of the consequences for themselves and their own family. We need to get out of the narrative trap, which in this context suggests that we should put up with family treating us in ways we would not tolerate from friends.

Parents might think twice before behaving badly if they thought they might actually lose their child as a result. To some large extent, and despite the personal stories we might tell otherwise, we treat other people as they allow us to treat them. So if a parent knows that their child will stop talking to them if they continue to behave badly, then, insofar as that parent benefits from contact with their child, they have an incentive to modify their behaviour. There is no real incentive to behave differently if contact is unconditional. The social stigma attached to breaking free simply reinforces the status quo.

Erroneously, a parent's love for their child is considered to be unconditional. In reality it is more often the child who endures a parent's bad behaviour towards them. It is true that a parent will often continue to 'love' a child even if that child behaves appallingly: witness the number of mothers who will go and visit their sons who are in prison for rape, murder and other serious crimes. But a parent will often withdraw their emotional support from a child who is perceived to be treating them badly or who rejects their love. So, I find it interesting to observe that, while a parent may forgive an adult child for causing other people great pain, they will be much less forgiving of even the slightest pain to them personally caused by that same child. This is a very partial, and quite perverse, form of utilitarianism indeed: the parent perceives any harm inflicted on them as a greater harm than any inflicted on others.

Recent analysis conducted by my team using the panel data of 7,000 Germans found that people in the saddest 5 per cent of the population report consistently low satisfaction with their family lives. In over a third of these cases, reported levels of satisfaction with family life decreased further as time went on, suggesting that if family issues are bad to begin with, they are not likely to improve. None of us should feel under any obligation to maintain harmful relationships, be that with partners or parents.

CONCLUSIONS

Happy and fulfilled lives are often supported by, but certainly do not require, children. There are good reasons not to have children, both at the micro and macro level. It is not helpful, therefore, to push the 'have your own kids' narrative on everyone. Finding a way to celebrate rather than undermine people's decisions to remain childfree by loosening our hold on the social narrative can have a positive societal impact. Our current approach involves repaying childless individuals with interrogation and social sanctioning.

Having children should be a personal choice since it has such dramatic consequences for how people spend their time and money, and yet we continue to incentivize having children. Current policies include financial support for families with children, long maternity leave and increasingly long paternity leave, as well as subsidized childcare for many. A day rarely passes without a news report on how ridiculously expensive childcare is, i.e. how expensive it is for middle-class families to pay to have their children looked after by someone else.

Support for these policies is further enhanced by the suggestion that a lack of children means fewer people to look after the elderly. To confront this worry and address their low fertility rates, countries such as Denmark and Japan are actively encouraging baby-making. They have set up key initiatives to ensure that there is a stable workforce to support those out of work. For example, travel companies in Denmark are encouraging people to pack their bags and go on holiday following some preliminary evidence that holidays increase people's likelihood of having kids by 46 per cent. Danish holiday firm Spies is offering three years' worth of free nappies to couples that conceive on a holiday booked through their website. These holiday bookings even come with a useful 'how to' guide to help couples maximize their chances of conception while abroad.

There is no reason why we need to jump straight to incentivizing pregnancy, however, without at least first considering other policy options to deal with the dependency ratio (the number of people above and below working age compared to those of working age). Putting more pension-saving policies in place to ensure adequate funds for later life and/or increasing the retirement age would be good places to start. We know that work can be an important source of purpose in people's lives and can prevent loneliness in older people, and so with the right kind of work for older generations we could improve overall happiness without doing further damage to an arguably already overpopulated planet.

Given the financial, social and environmental costs of parenting, policy-makers could do more to drive home the consequences of having children. This would ensure that people are a little better prepared for the downsides of parenting as well as for the fleeting moments of joy. This would allow people to make better happiness-enhancing choices, and it would also make for better parents. Governments, institutions and individuals should work together to acknowledge the many benefits and social good that come with pursuing a childfree life. The childless among us engage in more charitable giving, more environmental protection, and greater intergenerational equality through donations than their selfish friends with kids. So let's celebrate people without as well as with children. We are all grown-ups.

Wrapping Up Related

No man is an island. We are social creatures who benefit greatly from our connectedness with others. But many of the narratives surrounding how we should relate to each other are far too prescriptive. Get married, stay faithful and have kids. If these life choices work for you, then great. However, there is no one-size-fits-all approach to conducting relationships with our partners, parents, children and ourselves, and there never has been. Each of us should instead decide what works best for us, and not be judged harshly for doing so.

The contradictions between what the narrative tells us we should feel and what we often do feel creates a lot of unnecessary grief for those who are forced to go along with what is expected and for those who are unwilling or unable to do so. Telling single people the pinnacle of life is to find 'the one' and they just need to 'keep looking' is as condescending as it is inaccurate. Equally, when we refuse to acknowledge that it is possible and perfectly normal for people to be able to maintain successful intimate relationships with more than one person at the same time we are ignoring the evidence that many people do and that there's nothing inherently harmful about it. As for kids, well, Planet Earth could do with fewer people making a mess of it, and so, if anything, we should be creating narratives around how fulfilling life can be without having children, and for which there is good supporting evidence.

I can imagine that some of you would predict that reducing or removing any one of the Related narratives would lead to a breakdown in social cohesion. You might even view them as some integral part of the fabric of society. Analogous to 'body politic' views about institutions like the monarchy, you might even think that breaking away from any one Related narrative would have adverse knock-on effects for the other narratives and for civil society generally.

Similar arguments have been made throughout history about behaviours that today we accept as mainstream. The most obvious parallel is with the fears that decriminalizing homosexuality would lead to some sort of contagion effect whereby many more people would 'choose' to be gay. These fears were largely motivated by bigotry and prejudice. They were also completely unfounded. I think the same motivation lies behind many people's unwillingness to accept non-monogamous relationships. And I think these fears would also turn out to be without any merit. I reckon that it is no more likely that consensual non-monogamy will replace monogamy than it is that homosexuality will replace heterosexuality.

Keep in mind, too, that the counter-narrative that I am proposing is not the opposite of the prevailing one. To restate, it is to base what we do on the flow of pleasure and purpose over time. And this means that the happiest ways for you to relate to other people might make someone else miserable, and vice versa. If you prefer your relationship to be of the monogamous kind, backed up by a marriage certificate in a drawer somewhere, I am not asking you to choose differently for yourself.

I am, however, asking that you adopt a more open mind when it comes to your judgements of others. Greater tolerance of those who make less conventional choices in their romantic lives can only be a good thing for how we relate to each other. The only way to judge the lives of other people is according to the principles that they should use to judge you: are they happy and acting sincerely; and, compared to how they might otherwise conceivably behave, are they minimizing the misery of those affected by their decisions?

Against this background, it is worth bearing in mind that the narratives are applied differently to men and women. Marriage benefits men more than it does women, yet women are much more pitied for not having found their Prince Charming. Monogamy doesn't seem to suit almost as many women as it would work for, yet people are much more appalled when a wife cheats than when a man does, especially if she has children. A woman who chooses not to have kids is seen as much more cold and calculating than a man who makes the same choice, and she is the subject of much more pity than a man if she cannot have them.

But whatever groups we belong to or identify with, I'm pretty sure that we can be happier if we pay more attention to the feedback from our experiences rather than basing our decisions and judgements on outdated, socially constructed codes of morality. For some decisions, of course, we do not have any personal experience: a childless person has no experience of the impact of children. This is where other people come in handy: talk to people like you and find out what it was like for their own experiences of pleasure and purpose.[1] But equally, take what people proclaim to be key drivers of their happiness with a pinch of salt, and judge their experiences for yourself. This way you can avoid getting caught up once again in the narrative trap.

OK, time to find out how your answers about the set of Related narratives compare to the people in our study. The graph below presents the results. Again, all the narratives are seen to be more important than happiness by a significant minority of people. Overall, though, fewer people are willing to make themselves miserable in order to live according to the Related meta-narrative than they are the Reaching one. This time, more respondents in the UK are willing

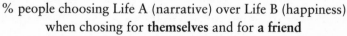

% people choosing Life A (narrative) over Life B (happiness) when chosing for **themselves** and for **a friend**

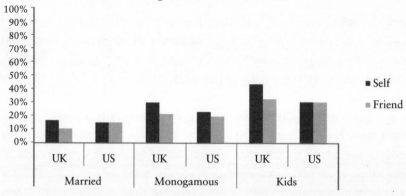

Figure 11

to be miserable to adhere to the narratives than in the US (recall that for Reaching it was the other way round). This is especially true for having children. So it seems Brits want families while Americans want money, suggesting the narrative trade-offs are informed by different value systems. And, as before, respondents are more likely to avoid the narrative trap on behalf of other people (except in the US on this occasion, where there is no difference).

PART THREE
Responsible

Aside from the social narratives surrounding work and family life, a well-adjusted 'grown-up' is also expected to behave responsibly. Responsible here means being altruistic (to be motivated to some extent by selflessness), healthy (to prioritize physical well-being and a long life) and volitional (to act with free will in ways that allow us to be held to account for our actions). I hope to show that pure altruism is a social construct with no discernible benefit compared to good deeds motivated by self-interest. I will also discuss the reasons why we might justifiably be motivated by concerns other than living as healthily as possible for as long as possible. Finally, I explore the possibility that none of us has anywhere near as much free will as we would like to think. This final part goes to the heart of how we judge human behaviour: we should do so on the basis of impact and not, as the Responsible meta-narrative insists, according to intent.

7

Altruistic

Before we get going with this narrative, here are your two questions. Please make a note of your answers, and we'll come back to them at the end of Part Three.

Read the following statements and indicate whether you would choose Life A or Life B *for yourself*:

Life A: You regularly donate anonymously to charity. You often feel miserable.

Life B: You regularly donate to charity and show off about it. You hardly ever feel miserable.

Please read the following statements and indicate whether you would choose Life A or Life B *for a friend*:

Life A: Your friend regularly donates anonymously to charity. Your friend often feels miserable.

Life B: Your friend regularly donates to charity and shows off about it. Your friend hardly ever feels miserable.

Every day, around the world, individuals act in ways that help other people. In the US in 2015, charitable giving by individuals far outweighed that of foundations and corporations put together: $268 billion compared to $75 billion. In the same year, Americans volunteered nearly eight billion hours of their time. That same year in the UK, £9.6 billion was donated by individuals, a mean donation of £37 a month, and one in seven people reported having volunteered.

Altruistic acts, big and small, should be celebrated and encouraged. So where's the narrative trap here? Well, it lies in the idea that people ought to be motivated, foremost, by altruism. These acts should contain no personal benefit *at all*. They should be *purely* altruistic. But by not recognizing and accepting the importance of self-regard, this narrative can get in the way of the very thing it is trying to promote: namely, less suffering through more kindness.

LOOK AT JILL ON TOP OF THE HILL

Let us consider my two friends, Jack and Jill. Jack earns around £30,000 a year and donates 2 per cent of his annual net salary to charities. He donates mostly to charities in developing countries, with the majority of his money being used for deworming and providing malaria nets in high-risk areas. Jill earns the same as Jack and also donates about 2 per cent of her net salary to charity. All of her money goes to breast cancer charities in the UK. Both Jack and Jill are much more generous than the average Brit: over the last thirty years or so, UK households donated an average of about 0.5 per cent of their disposable income to charity.

Jack and Jill are, however, completely different in how they publicize their giving. Jack basks in the glory of his philanthropy. His friends, acquaintances and pretty much anyone within earshot is well aware of his generosity. He uses every platform possible to publicize it, and the benefits that come from it. He talks about it in the pub after work, on nights out with friends, and on dates. One of his recipient organizations even did a feature on Jack in their widely circulated newsletter to celebrate his efforts. In contrast, Jill donates anonymously. Only her very closest friends know, and you sense that even that recognition causes her some discomfort. She genuinely would rather it go completely unnoticed.

There is a temptation to believe Jill is more altruistic than Jack. And perhaps that her discretion makes her a better person than him. I bet some of you instinctively think a lot like Maimonides, the twelfth-century rabbi who famously constructed the Eight Levels of Giving, in which giving anonymously is more commendable than being recognized for it. I think the rabbi got it wrong. A primary focus on the motivation of the giver is, at best, a distraction; instead, we ought to focus solely on the impact of the gift.

Any hierarchy of altruism based on motivations on the part of the giver leads straight into a narrative trap. In seeing pro-social acts that are cleansed of self-interest as somehow better than those that are selfishly motivated, we not only lose sight of how the act might benefit the recipient, but we also implicitly (and sometimes explicitly) discourage people who might personally benefit from helping others from doing just that. The upshot is less philanthropy overall.

The narrative of pure altruism is pervasive, however, so let us consider the reasons for Jack's and Jill's generosity. Let me quickly discount two explicitly evolutionary reasons for caring that cannot usefully explain charitable giving in this case. The first is kin selection, where we only help those we are genetically related to: neither Jack nor Jill are related to the recipients of their donations. The second is reciprocity, where group members all help each other out (I don't much like reviewing academic papers, but I do it because other academics take the time to review mine). Jill might possibly benefit from a breast cancer charity at some point but Jack certainly can't expect any reciprocity from the beneficiaries of his donations. This then leaves two reasons why Jack and Jill might behave in the ways they do: external recognition and internal reward.

SHARING IS CARING

Jack seeks external recognition for his charitable giving. He runs the risk of being seen as a show-off, but he will also be viewed as a more desirable romantic partner. In one study, over two hundred straight women in their twenties in England were shown photographs of handsome, and less handsome, men and given descriptions of their behaviour in scenarios where they had an opportunity to be kind or not, such as when passing by a homeless person.[1] The results showed that the attractive and kind men were rated the most desirable whilst the unattractive and unkind men the least so (no surprises there); but also that being rated as unattractive and kind was more desirable than being seen as attractive and unkind.

In reading about Jack and Jill, some of you will have immediately thought that their behaviour was consistent with their gender – men typically show off more than women. In a study which explored the online charitable contributions of men and women, men were found to donate almost four times as much when the request for donations included a picture of an attractive woman, and even more again when they could also see that other men had made large contributions prior to them. In contrast, women's donations were unaffected by the attractiveness of the person asking and by the donations that other women had made.[2] While this is just a single study, it is suggestive of the notion that men's generosity evolved largely as a mating technique, while women's appears to be independently motivated. We know that the more altruistic a man is, the more sexual partners they report having – and, if in a relationship, they have sex more often.[3]

Other research has found that not only do we expect women to behave more altruistically than men, but we punish them to a much greater extent when they don't. David Rand and his colleagues at Yale University have suggested that these higher expectations and greater punishment of women might be behind the results they find in their work on gender differences in automatic helping responses. Their meta-analysis (which involves data from twenty-two studies) finds that, while men were always less generous than women irrespective of how much time they had to make decisions, women were disproportionally generous when they had to make a quick call.[4] Women default into being 'good'. Give them a bit more time to make an informed choice, and their generosity decreases. But not all women's 'goodness' decreases to the same extent over time. The decrease is far greater for those women who identify as having relatively more masculine traits, such as dominance and independence, rather than feminine traits such as warmth and tenderness.

While I was writing an early draft of this chapter, David Beckham's email account was hacked and some fairly lively emails about him being denied a knighthood, despite his extensive charity work, were splashed across the news. Beckham was of the opinion that it was a 'fucking joke' that the 'unappreciative cunts' on the Honours Committee had passed him over. The witch-hunt that ensued was vicious and particular attention was paid to this 'revelation' that

Beckham's charity work wasn't born entirely out of self-sacrifice but was partly motivated by a desire for recognition. The vitriol aimed at him in the days after was immense. Swathes of people took to Twitter to weigh in on the #Beckileaks scandal, with 'phony', 'pathetic' and 'goldendick' being just some of the clever terms being thrown around. Journalist Piers Morgan, in particular, had plenty to say. He took to Twitter to complain about 'grasping Beckham' and branded him a fraud. Months later he was still harping on about it, saying that the public had forgiven Beckham too quickly.

I understand a degree of disappointment, but is it really that surprising to find out that your hero has a very human desire to be seen – and recognized – as a decent person? Or that he might have over-egged his selflessness a little in order to conform to the altruistic narrative? I can definitely see how we might trust him a bit less now, and be more suspicious of the ulterior motives that could explain his actions in other aspects of his life. I suspect he is seen as a little less authentic, and that matters to how we judge people.

But the exposé also made clear just how much Beckham had done for charity. He has raised millions of pounds as a Goodwill Ambassador for UNICEF and through his David Beckham 7 fund. He donated his entire salary from his time at Paris St-Germain to the charity. He has supported a number of causes, from poverty reduction to wildlife protection. It seems absurd to me that in so many people's eyes all this good had somehow been rendered worthless by the fact that he wanted some recognition for it. That, to me, is a 'fucking joke'. If you could trace all of the vulnerable children that have been helped by the money that he's raised over the years, I bet that none of them would give a toss that he now expected a knighthood for his efforts and was pissed off when it didn't arrive.

There is a good deal of evidence showing that we tend to behave more altruistically when we can be recognized for our good deeds. In a study which sought to assess the degree to which we believe our motivations for acting altruistically are related to status, researchers found that individuals underestimated the effect that making a donation public, as compared to keeping it private, would have on their effort in a task.[5] Participants were asked to engage in the mind-numbing task of counting os and 1s in a series of tables and earned money for charity for every correctly solved table. They alternated between engaging in this task while their performance was made public and when it was kept private, following which they were given feedback on how much they had earned in one condition and asked to guess how they got on under the opposite condition. The results showed that the participants performed significantly better when their performance was made public, but that they lacked self-awareness about the extent to which a public performance influenced the amount of effort they put in and the money they earned. We seem to be unaware of the degree to which our own good deeds are usefully motivated by status.

A recent lab-based study has neatly demonstrated the effectiveness of celebrating high donors and shaming low ones.[6] Groups of between five and eight participants were given the opportunity to donate part of their $10 payment for taking part in the study to the American Red Cross. There were three groups. All of those in the first group had their names and donations publicized. In the second group, only the names and donations of the highest donors were publicized, while in the third group, the names of both the highest and lowest donors were publicized. Donations were highest in the third group where naming and shaming created a tournament-like experience in which participants competed to be the highest, but also not to be the lowest, donor.

With altruism in mind, the suggestions in Part One about making good social outcomes a sign of social status (e.g. through publishing lists of the highest taxpayers) is directly relevant here. The wealthy are lauded in the *Sunday Times* Rich List and the Forbes 500, creating a rarefied hierarchy before our eyes. In comparison, 'The Philanthropy 50' hardly gets a look in. I had the privilege of being on the *Sunday Times* Alternative Rich List judging panel this year, which was a supplement in the middle of the Rich List. The juxtaposition of different measures of success and their economic value could not have been starker. Take Alisher Usmanov, the Russian business magnate, as just one example. His fortune was made through his metal and mining operations and many of his charities of choice are related to his favourite hobby of fencing. Contrast Usmanov with Daniel Broadhead, a twenty-one-year-old from Sheffield, who was the first living person to donate part of his liver to an unknown recipient.

Which reminds me, I donated my fee for that gig to charity. I discussed it with my kids and we decided to split the £2,000 equally between a charity helping homeless people and one that supports the children of addicts. Alongside my kids being a little more socially aware now, I'm hoping for some external recognition for that – or maybe I now just look like a dick. Oh well, the charities benefited and I feel even better about it, which gives me further incentive to donate again. So I'll willingly take some flak for those benefits.

I appreciate that not looking like a dick is a pretty strong motivation for not showing off too much. But be warned: toning down your positive pursuits (otherwise known as 'humblebragging') can backfire.[7] In one experiment, people were asked to look at different Twitter posts and answer a series of questions relating to the person who wrote the Tweet. Some people read Tweets that were outright brags, such as 'I just received an award for my teaching', and some read Tweets that were humblebrags, such as 'I just received an award for my teaching. #Whaaaaaat?' Researchers found that humblebragging reduced likeability and perceived competence relative to outright bragging.

HAPPY INSIDE

So Jack gains from external recognition. But where's the self-interest in Jill who hides her charitable light under a bushel? Before we can jump to the conclusion that she is a pure altruist, we need to consider the second possible motivation for her generosity: the internal benefit she might get from giving. The same consideration applies to Jack by the way: just because he seeks and potentially gains from external recognition does not necessarily diminish the degree to which he might seek and gain internal reward from his generosity.

Strictly speaking, we would need to know whether giving 2 per cent of her income to charity makes Jill happier than if she used that money in other ways. We obviously can't know whether or not she is maximizing her happiness from using her money in this way but we do know quite a bit about how helping others brings considerable personal happiness. It's partly why I spent half a chapter in

Happiness by Design talking about the benefits of pro-social behaviour. One study from the US found that givers were 43 per cent more likely to report being 'very happy' than were non-givers.[8] Volunteers have been shown to be less depressed, have lower mortality rates and higher life satisfaction than non-volunteers.[9] The term 'warm glow' has most famously been used by the economist James Andreoni since the 1980s to refer to the quiet pleasure we get from giving.[10]

This is also one of the few areas where researchers have established reliable causal data, so that we can be confident that there is a relationship from helping others to personal happiness. In a study conducted in the US, individuals who were randomly assigned to spend a windfall of money on another person or donate it to charity reported being happier afterwards than those who were instructed to spend it on themselves.[11] Neuroscientific evidence also seems to support this; areas linked to reward-processing in the brain have been shown to be activated when individuals make voluntary donations, including when they are made anonymously.[12] And a recent study in the Netherlands found that students who were given information (via a carbon-footprint calculator) that their carbon footprint was less than the average student reported feeling physically warmer afterwards than those who had been told their carbon footprint was higher than the average student. It seems that feeling as if we are doing good makes us happy.[13]

A study that asked students from the University of British Columbia to remember either the last time they spent money on themselves or on someone else, found that those that recalled spending on someone else were in a better mood.[14] Moreover, being in this good mood led them to be more likely to choose to engage in another pro-social act at a later point that day. There is considerable personal gain from doing good – even if you don't shout about it from the rooftops.

MISTAKEN MARTYRS

So even though Jill doesn't need any external recognition she does receive internal benefit. And so does Jack. And David Beckham. And all of us who engage in any pro-social behaviour. We might not all need external recognition, and some of you might judge Jack and David Beckham harshly for seeking it, but don't delude yourselves into believing that there is never any self-interest in your acts of kindness. We could just leave it at that but the narrative of pure altruism is not just wrong; it causes harm when it is used to judge the value of pro-social acts.

The idea that we should strive to be martyrs is as ludicrous as the neo-classical idea that we are purely self-interested beings. While religion might have us fixated on the idea that people are either sacrificial saints or self-interested sinners, a modicum of introspection or observation of the world around us will tell us that, by and large, we are reasonable people somewhere in between the two. We frequently and quite comfortably engage in activities that yield good both for us and for others.

In one study in the US which looked at volunteering, people with more self-oriented motives for getting involved (e.g. self-esteem, enhancing personal development) stuck at volunteering for longer than those who claimed to be doing it for community and social-issue reasons.[15] When the Zambian government recruited community healthcare workers, it found that the workers who were recruited via posters that emphasized career incentives (compared to those who responded to ads about the community benefits of their work) conducted 29 per cent more household visits and held twice as many community mobilization visits.[16] These were still good people: they were applying to be community healthcare workers after all. But they were also interested in their career progression. The recruits swayed by the career incentives made many more healthcare visits and their patients had better health outcomes.

If we demand that individuals receive no benefit whatsoever in order to be considered true altruists, then we are communicating the idea that doing good requires that you reduce your own happiness. This clearly isn't enticing. In the presence of the self-sacrificing narrative of pure altruism, it follows that we would see levels of pro-social behaviour that lie below the levels that would maximize the happiness of donors as well as recipients.

Moreover, encouraging individuals to view their good deeds as being morally virtuous could backfire, and lead to even fewer good deeds. The basic idea is that viewing yourself as 'nice' gives you licence to be 'naughty'. Licensing effects follow from the recognition that we are neither purely nice nor purely naughty; rather, that each of us acts in ways that balance a range of competing motivations and objectives. A nice illustration of licensing comes from work carried out prior to the US presidential election in 2008.[17] Some participants were initially asked who they were planning to vote for and were then faced with a hiring task. They were told to imagine themselves as a police chief in a small, predominantly white and racially prejudiced town and to state whether they felt a black or white officer was more suitable as a hire. Those who had been given the opportunity to establish their 'non-racist credentials' by endorsing Barack Obama were found to be more likely to express a preference for a white police officer in the hiring task than were those that weren't asked about their plans to vote.

We can think of licensing effects as working along the lines of a moral bank account in our minds: the charitable giving earns moral credits which can be withdrawn to purchase the right to fiddle our expenses. In a study exploring moral credits, researchers in Canada found that people who were assigned to purchase products in a green online store rather than a conventional one were more likely to lie in a later task.[18] Another study, conducted in the US, found that participants who were asked and committed themselves to take part in a fundraiser for the Red Cross a few weeks into the future were more likely to express a preference for the white police officer in the same hiring task discussed above than those who were never asked in the first place. In follow-up work, researchers found that, after committing to the same Red Cross fundraiser, individuals were more likely to negatively stereotype black people as violent, lazy, aggressive, criminal and hostile.[19]

Sometimes licensing effects could be perceived rather than real. There is some suggestion from US data that liberals are less pro-social than conservatives, although this is largely explained by income effects.[20] But it might also be that liberals think of themselves as being more intellectually concerned about inequalities in society and so do not feel compelled to back up their concerns with real action.

Perhaps it's not surprising, therefore, that in a study which included children from the US, Canada, China, Jordan, Turkey and

South Africa children in religious families were found to give less.[21] A group of children were given ten stickers and asked how many they would like to anonymously donate to another child in their school who hadn't been given any so that they could join in the game. The scenario did not allow for any reputational gains from giving. The kids with religious parents gave away fewer stickers than the kids of non-religious parents. The study also asked the parents about how generous they considered their kids to be and the religious parents thought their kids were more generous than the non-religious parents. It seems that being religious means that you perceive yourself (or your kids) as better people.

But this doesn't mean that these children will do fewer good acts overall in their lives. If they turn out anything like those Americans who report 'feeling God's love more than once a day', they'll be more than twice as likely to volunteer, and give more than $5,000 annually, to help those in need than their non-religious counterparts.[22] What's important, then, is that we recognize the knock-on effects of our good deeds, since some contexts may give us licence to behave less well without us ever realizing. If you find yourself patting yourself on the back for a good deed, stop for a moment to consider its subsequent impact on the other things you do that day.

EMPATHY AS AN ENEMY

So while Jack shouts about it and Jill keeps quiet, they both derive a happiness hit from giving to charity. As I have suggested in *Happiness by Design*, one important way to encourage more pro-social behaviour is to make the internal benefit of helping others more salient to people. If I was in charge of running a campaign to increase donations and volunteering, I would use the slogan 'Do good and feel good'. (It's odd that advertising agencies aren't clamouring to hire me.)

But so much depends on how we feel when helping others. And how we feel about helping others largely determines our judgements about what causes are the most worthy of our support. The trap here is that feelings of empathy don't do as much good as we'd expect. On the face of it, it is a good thing to experience the world as you think someone else does. When you feel someone's pain, you are motivated to alleviate it. But in his book *Against Empathy*, Paul Bloom describes empathy's 'spotlight effect' that means we naturally focus on what we care about and relate to, given our limited ability to think far beyond our immediate circumstances.[23] The spotlight illuminates the problem we have in focus but casts all other issues into shadow, some of which may be much more worthy causes. The spotlight is innumerate, parochial and short-sighted and is, therefore, a poor guide to how we should target our efforts to do good.

Stalin was on to the innumeracy of empathy long before Bloom, famously declaring: 'A single death is a tragedy; a million deaths is a statistic.' This innumeracy may in large part be due to the identifiable-victim effect.[24] This is the tendency for people to offer more support to a specific victim who has been personalized in some way than to a vaguely defined group of victims. Bloom demonstrates this effect in a study from Sweden, where he finds that people donated more to Save the Children when they were shown a picture of a single starving child named Rokia in Mali than when they were provided with a list of staggering statistics about starvation throughout Africa.[25]

This would not matter so much if we could put Rokia front and centre in order to help more of the other starving children in Africa. Some evidence from Daniel Batson, an American social psychologist, suggests that getting individuals to empathize with a member of a stigmatized group, such as homeless people or people with AIDS, can actually lead people to have more positive attitudes towards the whole population.[26] Batson cautions, however, that this approach is only likely to be helpful if the whole group shares the same needs as the individual that people feel empathy for. If a charity campaign garners support for homeless people, for example, by telling the story of a person who has fallen on tough times and is on the street because they lost their job, they may receive donations towards a job training programme, but the campaign is unlikely to do much for homeless people who have wound up on the streets through, for example, addiction, and who require a different kind of help altogether.

Other research finds that creating a sense of empathy for a single victim can also lead people to take decisions that have worse outcomes overall. In another study by Batson, participants were told about a young girl, Sherri, who was terminally ill and on a waiting list for pain-relief medicine alongside other ill children.[27] Those higher up the waiting list were in the greatest pain. The researchers then asked half the participants to imagine how Sherri was feeling in order to induce a sense of empathy towards her. All participants were then asked if they wanted to bump Sherri up the list, even though the children ahead of her were in more pain. Those that had been made to feel more empathy towards Sherri were much more willing to do so, disadvantaging the group of children in greater pain.

Empathy is also characteristically parochial. When you empathize with someone you imagine being in their shoes. This is easier if their feet are the same size. Our empathy is often most easily elicited for others who are somehow like us, or those near us, and as such it can distort our efforts for good in the same way prejudice might. One fascinating study from Switzerland investigates participants' willingness to help reduce another's pain when the individual in pain was represented as a fan of their own soccer team, and compared to a rival team's supporter.[28] The results indicated that individuals were less likely to help supporters of the rival team and that the neural activity signalling empathetic concern in the brain was inhibited when they were watching their rivals.

Finally, we are also less empathetic to those who are distant in time from us. Our inaction on climate change is just one example of our failure to empathize with future generations. Some of the costs of our current lifestyles will be borne by future generations. If we are serious about reducing suffering, experienced near and far, now and later, then the empathy that we feel most easily for members of our current in-group might not be the best way to change behaviours in ways to mitigate the harmful effects of climate change.

LOOK AT JACK ON TOP OF THE HILL

Rather than empathy, we need to show some cold, calculating compassion towards future generations. For us to help others as much as possible, we need to weigh the personal gain we get from our efforts against the benefits we can generate from our actions. Looking after

Poppy and Stanley when they are ill, or lending a mate some money to help tide them over until payday, is made both more likely and more enjoyable if I feel empathy towards them. When it comes to helping other people that are more distant to me, however, a case can be made for seeking to cleanse our pro-social behaviour of empathy and to instead show a more detached compassion.

The Effective Altruism movement applies evidence and reason to determine the most efficient ways of reducing suffering in the world.[29] It's not always possible to properly establish what works, or if what works in one place will work as well in another, and we cannot always be sure that our donations will go to where they are intended. But the movement does the important job of reminding us to be less parochial when thinking about worthy causes for our donations. Peter Singer, a professor of bioethics at Princeton University, is a leading advocate of effective altruism, arguing that the most effective ways to reduce suffering involve reducing global poverty. I had the privilege of meeting Peter when I was a visiting scholar at Princeton. He has donated 20 per cent of his salary to charity his whole working life and is one of the best examples of just how much better the world would be if we all lived according to his utilitarian logic.

What of the respective benefits from Jack's and Jill's (similarly sized) donations? Jack gives to charities working on deworming and combating malaria. He chose these charities based on their ranking on the website GiveWell, which carries out extensive research and ranks charities by the benefits they generate. (If you're reading this and thinking about donating, the process is quick and easy.) Jill's money goes towards breast cancer patient support and will contribute to maintaining a helpline for patients to call about their concerns. Jill lost her mum to breast cancer a few years ago and she feels very strongly about the work of the charities she donates to.

The overall impact generated by Jack's compassion and impartiality outweighs that resulting from Jill's empathy and partiality. When discussing consequentialism in the Introduction, I argued that partiality is reasonable when those that we care about are affected by our decisions. I care more about my family and friends than I do yours, and you care more about those close to you. Sadly, at this point, Jill's mum doesn't benefit, though it is better that she gives to breast cancer charities than not to give at all. Empathy has no doubt encouraged lots of people to raise money for charity who wouldn't otherwise have done before, and we must never forget that it is a lot better than doing nothing. But Jack's choice of charity has had a greater net effect in reducing misery than has Jill's. Therefore, on one compelling measure of who is a 'better person', Jack comes out on top. When we look at their reasons for giving and the results of their altruism, there's a strong case for celebrating Jack's approach, even if some people think he is a bit of a pain in the arse.

What of my kids' choice of charities for my donation that I trumpeted earlier? Well, they were obviously nudged a little bit into making their choices. I did this in a way that sought to highlight that sometimes people are judged harshly for what is taken to be behaviour that they have some control over (in the case of homelessness) or bear the brunt of judgements made about the behaviour of those they are affected by (in the case of children of addicts). So the exercise was as much about instilling in them the kinds of values I want them to grow up with, which will hopefully have a range of long-term benefits, as it was about an appraisal of the immediate benefits from my two-grand donations. But, on reflection, Bloom's charge of parochialism lingers in the back of my mind. A lesson for another day perhaps.

One obvious way to focus on results (consequences) over reasons (motivation) is to provide people with information about the effectiveness of the charity they are solicited by. But this doesn't always change people's likelihood of donation. In a study carried out with the US charity Freedom from Hunger, potential donors who were told that 'rigorous scientific methodologies' had shown the positive impact of the organization's work were no more likely to donate than those who were solicited with their standard fundraising email.[30]

A different approach may be warranted – one that initially grabs people's attention with emotionally arousing stories but then directs them towards harder facts. The approach of websites such as the one Jack uses, which allow for different charities to be jointly compared, may provide a fruitful way forward in the presentation of data. Being able to see the various benefits generated from a given donation side by side, along with how many people are giving to that charity at any one time, can provide a better sense of how well each one is doing and we can more easily use this information to maximize impact. Another option is to give people the information that their initial judgements can bias giving in ways that are less beneficial overall, and then offer them the chance to give this task to a charity expert who can ensure their money goes to where it will do the most good.

CONCLUSIONS

We normally see self-interest and altruism as being opposed to one another, with the latter being the more virtuous. A lot has been written about virtue, as distinct from self-interest, in the literature on ethics. Being virtuous makes people feel good. Sure, we are capable of making huge personal sacrifices for the benefit of others but these acts also give us an elevated sense of self. They might not always make us smile more or cry less but they can serve to help us walk a little taller. That we might benefit personally from helping others should be celebrated, not undermined. By misdirecting our attention to altruistic motivations, we are distracted from what is important – the consequences of the act.

We would do well to challenge the narrative that charity and volunteering should be kept magnanimously silent. We feel fine about broadcasting our foreign holidays and cute babies, but we are often much more squeamish when it comes to talking about the good that we do. In addition to the status we might get from making our good deeds known, which might spur us to do more of them, speaking up will also likely have a positive influence on the behaviour of those around us. Contributing to a generosity norm by being vocal can lead to positive knock-on effects that simply won't happen if we keep quiet. If you really don't want to shout about your own generosity, then at least broadcast the good deeds of other people you know (and get them to broadcast yours in turn).

In our roles as parents, friends, employees and policy-makers, we need to celebrate the selfishness of 'selflessness'. Social media provides a public channel through which altruistic acts can be shared, promoted and encouraged. We need to keep in mind that we should care about the results of doing good, and should only consider the reasons for feeling good that lie behind those actions when we can use them (or downplay them) to bring about even better results. With altruism, as with everything, our goal should be to reduce suffering by as much as possible.

When we judge David Beckham for wanting a knighthood in recognition of the huge benefit he has brought to thousands of children through his work for UNICEF more harshly than if he hadn't bothered in the first place, we have fallen straight into the narrative trap. There is no doubt the world is a better place for his charity work. And if anyone has the ear of anyone on the Honours Committee, tell them to give Goldenballs his fucking knighthood.

8

Healthy

Before we get going with this narrative, here are two questions for you to answer. Please make a note of your answers, and we'll come back to the questions at the end of Part Three.

Please read the following statements and indicate whether you would choose Life A or Life B *for yourself*:

Life A: You are physically healthy. You often feel miserable.
Life B: You are not physically healthy. You hardly ever feel miserable.

Please read the following statements and indicate whether you would choose Life A or Life B *for a friend*:

Life A: Your friend is physically healthy. Your friend often feels miserable.
Life B: Your friend is not physically healthy. Your friend hardly ever feels miserable.

The social narrative considered here is that you have a responsibility to maximize your health, and the health of those on whose behalf you make decisions. When I discuss health, I primarily have in mind physical health. I am not referring to mental health, where there is considerable overlap with misery. Indeed, we might use measures of mental illness, such as depression, as measures of precisely the kind of suffering that I think policy-makers should devote most of their effort to alleviating. So I don't consider a focus on mental health to be a harmful social narrative at all. The social story of health is one of us each being responsible for living as healthily as possible for as long as possible. So I will also consider longevity under the umbrella of health. How healthy you are will often affect how long you live, and so it makes sense to discuss one alongside the other.

You might ask why I consider expecting people to be responsible for their health as falling into a narrative trap at all. Surely being unhealthy and dying prematurely causes misery (or at the very least is highly correlated with it)? It is certainly true that longitudinal studies show that health conditions such as heart attacks and strokes have a clear, detrimental impact on happiness, and reporting having a disability is one of the factors that is strongly associated with being in the most miserable 1 per cent of the ONS data. Such adverse health conditions will also impact negatively on the happiness of those that care about us. There are also stark inequalities in health and life expectancy by social class that require urgent attention.

It does not follow, however, that we should each be expected to reduce our risks of all adverse health effects unremittingly, and to be judged harshly if we are unwilling or unable to conform to this ideal. We care about health, but also about happiness. My health greatly contributes towards my happiness, of course, but there have been plenty of times in my life when I have willingly sacrificed my health for my happiness: every time I have partied hard, for example. We each have different opportunities, constraints and preferences, and yet the healthy narrative judges me harshly for doing this. There is no good reason to if, given my opportunities, constraints and preferences, I am happier overall from my actions.

Moreover, it does not follow that we should seek to preserve and prolong life at all costs. The healthy narrative means that considerable state resources are devoted to end-of-life care and away from where they could do more good in alleviating suffering. About 25 per cent of healthcare costs are incurred caring for people in their last year of life, regardless of whether that care is publicly or privately funded.[1] I would like to see an end to these kinds of wasteful decisions.

THE NEW HEALTHISM

An emphasis on being healthy assumes a high level of personal responsibility over the state of our health. Taking responsibility for our health is considered virtuous, and health has become an integral part of our social identities. As such, people are more likely to attribute their own or others' poor health to personal agency rather than to more important structural and biological reasons.[2]

'Healthism' was a term first coined by the American political scientist Richard Crawford in 1980 to describe an ideological shift towards situating 'the problem of health and disease at the level of the individual'.[3] Those with available resources to optimize their chances of good health can be celebrated for their success at ageing slowly. At the same time, those with fewer resources are looked down upon for the early deterioration of their bodies.

Technological developments such as wearable electronics, sensory detectors and advances in mobile-phone data collection are shifting the ability to track the details of our own health from the hands of healthcare providers to our own pockets. As a result, good physical health has been catapulted to the forefront of our social narratives as the onus of healthism at the individual level is made even more salient. We have become ever more judgemental of those who do not fit the healthy ideal, either because they are unable to or because they do not value diet and fitness as highly as we feel they should.

Just because your physique is slim and toned and you only eat organic produce, however, does not mean that you can judge others for not prioritizing their health in the same way you do. The real danger here is that we risk further glamourizing the idea that we should all be held responsible for maintaining our physical health. I'm sure that many people find the social sharing aspect of health a great motivation for living a more active and often fulfilling life. I suspect there are also many more of us who want to throw our phones out of the window if we see one more photo of avocado pulp on sourdough with poached eggs eaten by a wanker in patterned Lycra leggings.

A lot of how we judge people's health-related behaviours has to do with social class. As I've mentioned, I spend a lot of time around working-class bodybuilders. Many of the people I know take part in amateur competitions. Despite the health benefits of lean muscle, I have heard lots of disparaging comments about bodybuilding. Some academics I know have labelled it 'ridiculous' and for 'stupid people'. OK, so getting down to 3 per cent body fat, covering yourself in fake tan and posing like Bruce Forsyth on stage is pretty ridiculous. But not any more ridiculous than training for a marathon, which some of my middle-class colleagues not only seem to enjoy but also consider to be more commendable than bodybuilding.

We judge people badly who engage in health-related behaviours that are much more prominent among working-class people, such as heavy drinking, smoking and illegal drug use. My own research suggests that we are more circumspect about judging these kinds of behaviours so harshly when we have an opportunity to discuss some of the social determinants of behaviour.[4] It remains an open question whether or not the relatively harsh judgement is quick to recur when people leave a researcher-led focus group and return to the real world.

The important point from the perspective of the healthy narrative trap is that we often moralize about the rightness and wrongness of certain health behaviours, when instead we should be focusing on the consequences for misery of those actions. There is no doubt that an unhealthy lifestyle can cause considerable misery for the person affected and those close to them. It is very difficult, though, for any of us to know in advance the best path to follow for ourselves. I think my nights out have been worth it but I cannot be certain. It is simply impossible for us to know what other people, with different preferences and facing different sets of opportunities and constraints, should do. So there can be no one-size-fits-all approach to what constitutes responsible action pertaining to the trade-off between health and other determinants of happiness.

JUDGING WEIGHT

To further illustrate our rush to judgement based on the healthy narrative, consider obesity in adults (I will not refer to childhood obesity, for which a very different discussion would be required). Obesity is the most widespread manifestation of unhealthiness in developed countries. It is assumed to involve a considerable degree of personal responsibility (it is a moot point, for the purposes of this discussion, that this assumption is erroneous and that obesity has a number of genetic, social and environmental antecedents that are outside an individual's control).[5] In a nutshell, we don't like fat people very much.

We crudely categorize how fat someone is according to their body mass index (BMI), which is calculated by dividing their weight in kilograms by the square of their height in metres. A BMI of under 18.5 is defined as underweight; between 18.5 and 25 as normal weight; 25.1 to 29.9 as overweight; 30 to 39.9 as obese; and over 40 is defined as morbidly obese. The BMI says nothing about body composition (muscle is denser than fat) but obesity and morbid obesity are linked to poorer health and premature death.[6] There do not appear to be any adverse consequences for health from being overweight, at least not up to a BMI of 27. This was the overweight cut-off until 1998 when it was lowered, thus categorizing many more people as having 'a weight problem' (about 30 million in the US), and thus increasing the market for weight-loss drugs and interventions.[7]

The association between BMI and happiness is actually quite weak. There appears to be no happiness hit at all to being overweight, and only morbid obesity really seems to affect experiences of happiness.[8] So being fat does not generally make people miserable. Obese people report lower levels of life satisfaction than those who are not obese, but mostly when they are surrounded by people of 'normal weight'.[9] To illustrate the stigma associated with obesity, much of the hit in happiness comes from perceptions of being discriminated against.[10]

In the labour market, weight doesn't seem to matter too much for men but many studies have shown that obese women earn significantly less than their non-obese counterparts, especially in jobs that require social interaction.[11] Either employers don't like fat women, or customers don't, or the former assume that the latter won't. Some of the discrimination might be statistical in that obese people tend to take more time off sick or be less productive overall, though this seems only to be the case for jobs that involve physical tasks.[12] Wages are therefore determined as much by persuasion as they are by productivity. In support of this, one Swedish study created fake CVs, with photos attached, and sent them out to prospective employers.[13] The researchers duplicated all the CVs, changing only the photos so that candidates were made to appear fatter in one set. Applicants with seemingly obese faces were about 8 per cent less likely to be called for interview than applicants who appeared to have thin faces.

Given that we appear to behave in a prejudicial way against fat people, we need to find good reasons for not liking them. Ah, I know, they cost a lot of money. Yes, that's it, they are a drain on public resources and that's a bad thing. We have all heard how obesity is costing the healthcare system a fortune. It seems that there are almost daily news reports about how obesity is one of the main reasons for a funding crisis in the UK National Health Service. The costs to the UK NHS from treating obesity is currently around £6 billion.[14]

Implicit in these headlines is a moral judgement of all those obese people who are draining the public purse of money that could otherwise be put to better use. I say this because the claims about the costs of obesity are spurious unless we know what health conditions we would otherwise be spending public money on if people were not obese. We also have a funding crisis in social care for an ageing population. The premature deaths experienced as a result of obesity limit the numbers of people going on to live with dementia in older age. So obesity saves money too. Moreover, obese people save the taxpayer huge amounts in pension costs by dying earlier, in much the same way as smokers do. This is to say nothing of the money that they put into the economy from buying more food. So it is just as likely, compared to the alternative of living thinner for longer, that fat people save the welfare system a fortune. Depending on the assumptions made, and how we value costs incurred now compared to those incurred in the future, obesity could cost more or less than the alternative of treating those same people for something else later in life.

In any case, just think how silly the cost argument is anyway. Leaving to one side the impact of passive smoking, if we only cared about the public purse, we would be *encouraging* people to take up smoking. Long-term smokers die ten years earlier than non-smokers on average, and therefore reduce the burden on healthcare services at an expensive time of life.[15] They also die relatively quickly and cheaply from lung cancer. But it is the savings on pension costs that are the real exchequer windfall from smoking. One great way to sort out the 'black hole' in pension provision would be to encourage secondary-school kids to start smoking forty a day. We don't do this because we care about early coffins as well as full coffers.

Given all of this, I can only conclude that the cost escalation arguments about obesity are driven by the strength of the healthy narrative, and the harsh moral judgement of those who are unhealthy. It also helps the narrative that obesity rates are much higher among the working class than the middle class:[16] it's all those fat, lazy working-class folk that are crippling our beloved NHS.

OK, let's move on from cost, and look for another reason why we don't like obesity. Let's say we care about people's health. This is the view taken by many doctors, especially those working in public health, and it fits the social narrative that it is our responsibility to live as healthily as possible for as long as possible. Many doctors will tell their patients to adopt a healthy lifestyle, not necessarily (or even) because it will make them happy but because they have a responsibility to themselves, to their families and to society to be healthy.

As a behavioural scientist, I am aware that many of our decisions about health, as with so many domains of life, are misinformed and mistaken. But it is not always mistaken to put our health at risk because we care about more than just health. There were 137 deaths at work in the UK in 2016, with the majority occurring in construction, agriculture and manufacturing. Many more people were injured. Far greater multiples of people are in employment, of course, and so the death and injury rates are relatively low: the current risk of death at work is about 1 in 250,000. Nonetheless, many of us are making trade-offs between health and income. While average salaries in the higher-risk industries are below the national average, workers in these sectors are paid more than they would earn in other jobs. (It is noteworthy that 133 of the 137 deaths were men and, given the industries within which they worked, we can be pretty sure that most of them would have been working class. The absolute numbers may be too small for policy-makers and journalists to care about, but if 97 per cent of the mortality in a specific area were concentrated among middle-class women, I'm pretty sure there would be more interest and concern.)

We are also justifiably willing to trade off our health for direct happiness benefits. Of course there are many people who take extreme risks with their lives and who over-indulge in food, and these are serious problems that I am not trivializing. Many people are heavily constrained in the choices they make and we must do much more than we are doing currently to tackle the economic and social determinants of health. But notwithstanding these systemic challenges, there are many people who simply enjoy eating pizza and chocolate, and it is simply not our place to judge them without knowing more about their opportunities, constraints and preferences.

The fundamental question is whether or not what we give up in terms of health is compensated for by increases in other determinants of happiness (such as income) or by increases in happiness itself. And the only way to know this would be to know our lifetime happiness conditional upon all the possible choices and trade-offs we might make. This is impossible to calculate in practice but it is the benchmark by which it is, in principle, possible to judge all that we do. Your lifetime happiness, properly accounting for how you affect other people's happiness, is the final arbiter of the rightness of any action, including over-eating and bodybuilding and running marathons and . . .

I HOPE I DIE BEFORE I GET OLD

The healthy narrative in terms of longevity is best encapsulated by the vast amounts of money devoted to end-of-life care. These costs might be justified if they were driven by well-thought-through decisions on the part of patients, families, clinicians and policy-makers. Patients may quite reasonably become more risk-seeking in their treatment decisions as their health declines. For example, studies have shown that most cancer patients will decide to undergo aggressive and expensive treatment despite marginal potential benefits.[17]

The narrative of hope on behalf of the dying person will play a critical role in driving these decisions and justifying their accompanying costs. Hope is characterized by an anticipation of tomorrow being better – or least not worse – than today; and where this anticipation does not have to be evidence-based. Hope is considered to be a positive motivational state that drives a sense of goal-directed agency and careful planning to meet those goals.[18] Many of the studies showing the benefits of hope have been conducted using populations in poor health, where lower levels of hope have been shown to predict poorer quality of life.[19] Hopeful narratives in end-of-life care are tied to ideas of perseverance, resilience and bravery.[20] In contrast, when hope is taken away, such as when people know for certain that they have Huntington's disease (as opposed to it being a high likelihood), they work less and generally invest less in their life.[21]

The benefits that people get from anticipating their future survival are therefore used to justify the high value placed on the life of someone near the end of their life and/or facing a high risk of death. If hope raises the perceived value of life, it is likely to encourage people to engage in, promote and also be willing to fund costly life-extending treatments. It follows that somebody who values their own life or somebody else's life highly will invest more resources into prolonging it and be judgemental of others that don't. Some studies have shown that patients with unrealistically positive expectations about their prognosis are more likely to engage in invasive treatments than those without these expectations.[22] This has been referred to as the 'action component of hope'. Hope can be particularly important to carers of sick relatives, particularly to parents of children with terminal illnesses.[23]

But all of this can sometimes result in an inability to accept the reality of the situation, and to instead promote treatment that only reduces the quality of life remaining.[24] Employing a narrative of hope may also alter someone's point of reference about what to expect during their lifetime. Specifically, it creates a greater discrepancy between their desired (hoped for) state and the actual realized state, which we know results in a disproportionately negative emotional reaction. There is also a strong tendency to link hope with greater certainty of a cure, which further discourages patients from accepting their actual odds of survival. Hope is the enemy of acceptance. In contrast to hope, which focuses on the preservation of future life, acceptance aims to promote an appreciation of life as it is currently. It follows that people who accept their condition would be less likely to engage in life-prolonging treatment.

Part of a patient's tendency to associate hope with a cure comes from the medical advice they receive. Doctors often express a conflict between telling a patient the truth and sugar-coating facts about the severity of the illness to preserve hope (and because, well, you never really know).[25] In a large postal survey of doctors from Europe, South America and Canada carried out by researchers in the US, average responses of doctors from each group fell within the 'strongly agree' category when asked whether they would like to be told the truth about their own terminal illness.[26] Yet only 26 per cent of European doctors thought that their own patients would like to know. The doctors might be right about their patients' preferences, but I suspect that they would help them more if they told them the truth about their condition and helped them focus on adaptation rather than prolonging hope.

It is easy to see how hope can be a very manipulative concept, used by healthcare practitioners to justify a course of action they might be professionally committed to proving works. End-of-life care provision in Western culture is typically based on 'medical' considerations, since disease is often perceived as something that is curable with human intervention; thus focus is often placed on treatment in the first instance, which can quickly become costly and aggressive.[27] Doctors may also gain, financially as well as egotistically, from continuing expensive therapies and drug treatments. It looks good to be doing something risky and complex, even if it might not do good.

The pressure to preserve life is often compounded by family members who need to feel that they have done everything they can to maximize the chances of survival, but, here too, such preferences may not be in their own long-term interests. Family members will often have to live with the memory of their loved one's painful decline rather than peacefully accepting their death at an earlier stage. Our deceased family and friends live on in our memories, and it is good for our happiness that we remember them well. It is good for our own legacies (insofar as these matter to us) that we live on well in the memories of those we leave behind. Since many of those memories will be formed in the last few weeks, days or hours of life, it makes a lot of sense for all concerned to ensure those memories are not tarnished.

On top of all of this, there is a complex interaction between the patient and family members, all of whom are trying to second guess what everyone else is thinking. They might try to do what everyone else wants, which might not be what they actually want. There could come a time when everyone would agree on a peaceful death, for example – if only they could articulate that to each other. Instead, they all go on wrongly believing that everyone else (apart from them) wants to preserve life, and so they continue with treatment for the patient long after the point they would have all agreed to stop.

With all of this in mind, I have to ask whether investing in expensive, invasive medical treatment at the end of someone's life, with the often-false hope of beating unfavourable odds, is worth it. It would seem that I am not alone in this doubt. In a recent survey of nearly 10,000 households in seven European countries, roughly 75 per cent of people opted for 'improve quality of life for the time they had left', with only 2 per cent of people in England saying that they thought extending life was most important.[28] According to results from the Health and Retirement Study in the US, the vast majority of people completing advance directives elect for limited or comfort care, rather than all care possible.[29] All of this suggests that comfort does seem to play an important role in framing people's choices at the end of life. However, this assumes that people know when they have reached the end, which might not always be the case since hope also distorts our ability to recognize how far away into the future that point is.

Note that these are preferences elicited in detached circumstances, as compared to the emotional states people are in when faced with decisions about which treatment path to select 'on the spot', where, in addition to their own emotional reactions to being ill, they may also be under pressure from family members and medical practitioners. My own work as a health economist shows a clear preference among older people for improvements in quality of life over extensions in length of life.[30] And yet healthcare professionals continue to prioritize life extension. To overcome this bias, patients will have to actively request alternative options. But, as we know from classic experiments in behavioural science, opposing authority is very difficult.[31]

There is also a discrepancy between where people want to die and where they actually die. According to the latest evidence from the

National Survey of Bereaved People in England, four out of five respondents said that they would prefer to die at home.[32] It is worth noting, however, that these preferences can change over time. As a patient's health declines, they may seek more medical attention, for example. Another study has shown that about one in five changed their preference as they neared their end of life, usually shifting from preferring a death at home to one in hospital (due to such factors as uncontrolled pain and to reduce caregiver burden, and because of an inability of carers to safely care for the person at home).[33]

The 'medicalization' of dying means that over half of people die in hospital and it is predicted that just one in ten will die at home by 2030 in the UK.[34] The medicalization of dying is a relatively recent phenomenon: fifty years ago the majority of people died at home. The change has come about largely because of the improvements in modern scientific capabilities, which have also brought with them an air of arrogance among some medical professionals who believe that it is possible and preferable to prolong a life whatever the circumstances.

Living better and living longer are not the same thing, however. The social narrative of hope can completely blinker decision-makers in the midst of despair, precisely when they need the soundest advice. Sometimes it is good for us to hope for the best, but sometimes we must get our heads around preparing for the worst. Perhaps a bit of self-delusion is good for us at times, but we cannot forget the basic principle that life does, ultimately, end. Some 'false hope' can help us in times of crisis, such as upon diagnosis of a terminal illness, but there comes a point at which hope becomes denial and denial becomes a sort of wilful negligence of inherently limited time and resources.

Facing up to the facts can be very upsetting for both the dying and the families of those facing death. But we need to reframe the loss of hope not as despair but as a kind of healthy acceptance. Stories of hope sound heroic. We celebrate people who 'fight cancer right to the end', for example. But those who confront their own mortality often experience positive consequences in the life they live.[35] There is also evidence that patients have better symptom control, lower psychological distress and improved quality of life when palliative care is integrated into their treatment.[36]

So, if we are to reduce the overall suffering associated with the end of our lives, we need to create a heroic narrative for dying well as well as for prolonging life, and recognize when it's time to bow out. Death is inevitable, and by adhering to the heroic narrative of fighting death we all become losers.

DEATH DENIED

This brings us neatly to the fiercely debated topic of euthanasia: the ability to end someone's life prematurely to relieve suffering. This is clearly a complex, political and far-reaching topic, with entrenched deontological positions and a general absence of good evidence on the consequences of adopting a particular policy. My discussion will focus on voluntary euthanasia, whereby patients give their consent for a doctor to assist them in dying (either indirectly by preparing the medication for the patient or directly by administering the medication to the patient). This is to be contrasted with non-voluntary euthanasia, whereby a patient is unable to give consent, e.g. in the case of someone in an irreversible coma, and involuntary euthanasia, whereby the patient has explicitly stated that they do not want to die. In most jurisdictions, non-voluntary euthanasia is legal, most often under conditions whereby it requires no action on the part of doctors, such as a notice 'do not resuscitate' in the event that an already very ill patient has a further adverse health event, and involuntary euthanasia is illegal.

The most interesting discussion therefore relates to voluntary euthanasia, or 'assisted dying'. In many countries around the world, including the UK, assisted dying is illegal. There are some notable exceptions. In the US, state law allows assisted dying in Oregon, Vermont, New Mexico, California, Colorado, Washington DC and Montana. In all states except Montana, two dying requests must be made by the patient, at least fifteen days apart, and the patient's illness must be terminal with a prognosis of less than six months; in Montana assisted dying is allowed but only after a court ruling. There is a tentative legal framework under which assisted dying is allowed in Japan. This framework contends that the patient must be suffering from an incurable and unbearable physical condition, whereby imminent death is inevitable.

In Germany, a lethal drug cocktail can be taken by the patient so long as nobody is assisting (e.g. supporting the hand). This right is only granted to patients with serious, incurable illnesses who have decided to end their lives freely and it must be approved by the German Federal Institute for Drugs. The positions in Canada, Switzerland, Belgium, Luxembourg and the Netherlands also only require that the condition is incurable (rather than terminal). In all cases, the request must be made by the patient while they are fully conscious and of sound mind. In all cases except for the Netherlands, you must be over the age of eighteen to qualify for assisted death. In the Netherlands, a person between the ages of sixteen and eighteen must have their guardian consulted, even though the guardian does not have final veto on the decision, and between the ages of twelve and sixteen guardian consent is mandatory. Importantly, all of these countries recognize suffering over and above the prospect of imminent death.

There can be a lot of misery associated with dying. In approaching death, people can experience extreme and prolonged discomfort, physical pain and mental suffering. Despite this, many countries do not allow assisted dying. This means that there are some potentially strong arguments against it. The restrictions in the countries that do allow assisted dying shed light on some of these concerns. Note that in all cases the condition must at least be incurable, so death does not take away any realistic prospect of improvement. Note also that the patient must be deemed to have the capacity to make a coherent and considered decision. We change our minds a lot and most decisions are reversible to some large extent. We cannot reverse death, and so we need to be damn sure that the decision is the right one.

If we adopt the perspective of negative utilitarianism and take misery reduction as our objective, then there are other concerns to be alert to. The first is the substantive rationality of the decision, which I define in terms of reducing experiences of misery. It is not enough to make a coherent and considered decision: for death to be the better decision (and not just the preferred one), the future prospects of staying alive must be worse than not existing at all and not just in theory.

While we can never know what might have been, there are data suggesting that we underestimate our ability to adapt to negative changes.[37] Without any experience of an adverse health state, many people say they would rather be dead than to live through it.[38] In reality, we cope much better than we expect. We make the most serious kinds of prediction errors about future happiness when there is a large amount of time between choosing and experiencing: I can predict with greater accuracy the impact of breaking my leg this week as compared to doing so next year.[39] We are also pretty hopeless at forecasting future happiness when we are feeling at our worst because we take our current feelings and project them into the future.[40]

It follows that we can be more confident that a preference to die is more likely to be substantively rational if three conditions are met:

1. the patient has sufficient experience of their illness to be able to make a reasonable assessment of what the future impact might be;
2. the decision is made as close to the desired time of death as possible so that the impact of poor health can be better predicted; and
3. wherever possible, the decision to die is consistent across mood states.

Patient interviews have shown that one in four people requesting assisted dying are clinically depressed.[41] Unfortunately we do not have comparable data on depression rates for those with similar health conditions who do not request assisted dying. Nonetheless, the high rate of depression among those who want to die has led some people to argue that, in such circumstances, the desire to die cannot be considered a coherent and considered preference.[42] Belgium, Luxembourg and the Netherlands are the only countries that accept assisted-dying requests from individuals with intolerable mental suffering where there is no related physical component.

In most jurisdictions that allow assisted dying, then, those suffering from incurable mental illnesses are not afforded the same right to die as those with incurable physical illnesses. Notwithstanding whether such patients can make the decision to die with a 'sound mind', the main reason for this restriction is that there is more uncertainty surrounding incurable in the context of mental as compared to physical health: a depressed person might recover in the way a severely physically disabled person stands no chance of doing. But does this justify telling somebody whose life has been unbearable for the last twenty years that they must live on in the hope that their mental health might one day improve?

In one extraordinary recent case in Belgium, Emily, a twenty-four-year-old woman with persistent depression and mental health problems, requested the right to die.[43] Emily had been suffering with severe mental health complications from childhood. She recalled expressing a desire to die at the age of just three, and found life a living hell. She engaged in regular self-harm and had attempted suicide on many occasions. It took a number of qualified health professionals as well as testimonies from her family and friends before Emily was finally granted permission to end her life. It was a long-drawn-out process in which her death had been very carefully considered alongside her potential to one day live a happy life.

What's remarkable about this case is that once Emily's permission to die had been granted, her mental health improved. She felt feelings of worthiness and a lessening of despair that she could barely remember ever feeling. Others' acceptance of her wish to die appears to have served as validation that her struggle was being listened to, and she may also have benefited from feeling as if she was in control for the first time. The acceptance of others was such a powerful factor that, in fact, she decided not to die. It seems that being allowed to die had, quite literally, saved her life. Emily's case serves as a powerful reminder of just how significant a role acceptance (by oneself and from other people) plays in behaviour change.

All in all, we need to be as confident as possible that we would really be better off from being allowed to die than from living on. In most cases, the patient will consider the impact on their family when making this decision. It is for us to decide how much we wish to account for the preferences of other people. Yet many loved ones will put great pressure on us to go on living while others might push us to end our life early. Many more concerns have been expressed about the latter pressure in the literature on assisted dying, but the former also persuades people who are dying to act against their own best interests.

We saw in Part Two that love is often used in a controlling way, and there will surely be many people who will implicitly suggest (and probably sometimes explicitly state) that their close relative should carry on living 'if you love me'. If love were instead expressed in a liberating way, we would support those close to us in making the right decision for them. Just as a parent should try and keep their nose out of a child's decision about whether or not to have children, a child or a spouse should try and keep their noses out of their parent's or partner's decision about assisted dying.

In the case of a patient being bullied into dying sooner than they would choose freely, safeguards need to be in place to ensure that the patient is not unduly influenced by the preferences of family members. The Swiss laws on assisted dying stress that those assisting death can only do so if there is no personal gain to that person.[44] There is nothing in what I have read, however, that strictly precludes family members from intervening strategically. So to safeguard patients, in most jurisdictions, more than one medical practitioner has to sign off on the decision, and this is what the Commission on Assisted Dying suggests should happen in the UK if we were to allow assisted dying.[45]

Beyond the possibility of an individual being persuaded to act against their best interests, those who oppose assisted dying argue that sanctioning it would create a 'slippery slope' whereby society begins to judge more and more states as being worse than dead, thus corroding the 'sanctity of life'. There is no evidence that I am aware of, however, which suggests that there has been any change in how vulnerable patients are treated in those places that have allowed assisted dying. This is not to say that it does not happen, only that we don't know about it if it does.

There have been a couple of studies that have looked at the impact of assisted dying on the experiences of the relatives after the death of their family member. One was carried out in Oregon and sampled three groups: families of patients who received lethal prescriptions; those who received prescriptions but did not use them; and those who did not pursue assisted dying. The results suggested similar experiences in terms of connectedness and the overall quality of death by families of patients in all three groups.[46] Those in the first group reported greater preparedness for death relative to the other two groups, however. This group also reported better perceived quality of dying in the moment of death. The other study was carried out in the Netherlands and found that 92 per cent of families thought that assisted dying had a positive effect on the quality of the end of their loved one's life, primarily by preventing or ending suffering.[47]

For quite some time, my own instincts have been against assisted dying. I know enough about how good we are at adapting to adversity – and how bad we are at predicting it – to have serious doubts about the substantive rationality of a decision in any moment to end our life. I have also been concerned that family members might hurry along the death of a relative they wanted to see the back of. But having looked into assisted dying in a bit more detail, I am satisfied that the safeguards in place where it does exist are, by and large, sufficiently robust so as to reduce misery in highly controlled and limited circumstances. But there are some instances we need to be alert to. It has recently been reported, for example, that 7 per cent of those successfully euthanized in the Netherlands were categorized as 'tired of living'.[48] This loose categorization potentially puts vulnerable individuals at risk in circumstances where their symptoms might be better dealt with through some other means. It is essential, therefore, that stringent and detailed rules are put in place if we are to avoid sliding on to that slippery slope.

CONCLUSIONS

Healthism is in its ascendancy. We are ever more obsessed with physical health and life expectancy, and we look scornfully at those who put their health at risk, even though we may know nothing of their opportunities, constraints or preferences. We also look admiringly at people who fight death right up until the bitter end, even though we may know nothing of the costs incurred in doing so. These judgements come from a social narrative about certain (usually middle-class defined) types of good health being good for us, longer lives always being better than shorter ones – and each individual being responsible and held to account for maximizing their health.

The healthy narrative continues to place physical health up on a pedestal to the detriment of its psychological counterpart – mental health. Only one in three people with mental health problems receives treatment for their condition, while almost everyone receives treatment for a physical health condition. People with anorexia nervosa (the mental health problem with the highest mortality rate) are often turned away because their weight is not 'low enough' to receive treatment. This results in many patients resorting to yet further weight loss in order to qualify themselves for more immediate treatment, and greater weight loss means diminished odds of recovery. This is a disgrace in a developed country.

Lifetime happiness is determined by the amount of happiness and also by the duration over which that happiness is experienced. When it comes to life expectancy, the social narrative of hope as it applies to end-of-life care is likely to damage individuals and lead to an inefficient and unfair allocation of scarce resources. Assuming that patients are responsible for pursuing life at all costs places undue pressure on them to sacrifice their happiness and the happiness of those around them. When deciding for others, we need to make a shift from quantity of life to quality, so that we can better provide the palliative care and treatment for patients that improves their happiness and, importantly, that of those affected by their eventual and inevitable death. We should also, under highly regulated conditions, allow people to request that those close to them assist in ending their lives without the fear of prosecution for those who do assist.

I am actually quite optimistic about our ability to rein in the healthy narrative, if we present the general public with the opportunity costs of alternative funding choices. Alan Williams was a professor of health economics at the University of York and a huge influence on my early academic life. He was a great advocate of the 'fair innings' argument: that people's entitlement to healthcare resources should diminish as they get older.[49] Most of the empirical work conducted in this area broadly supports this idea, and people are especially keen to prioritize children who face limited life expectancies.[50] Alan wrote that the 'vain pursuit of immortality is dangerous for elderly people'. I agree, and even more so as I get older.

9

Volitional

Before we get going with this narrative, here are two questions for you to answer. Please make a note of your answers, and we'll come back to the questions at the end of Part Three.

Please read the following statements and indicate whether you would choose Life A or Life B *for yourself*:

Life A: You believe that you freely choose all that you do. You often feel miserable.

Life B: You do not believe that you have much control over what you do. You hardly ever feel miserable.

Please read the following statements and indicate whether you would choose Life A or Life B *for a friend*:

Life A: Your friend believes that they freely choose all that they do. Your friend often feels miserable.

Life B: Your friend does not believe that they have much control over what they do. Your friend hardly ever feels miserable.

The final yet perhaps most wide-reaching social narrative I will consider is that we act volitionally; that is, with a considerable degree of free will over what we do. To some large extent, each of us is assumed to be free to choose how to live. It follows that we can judge other people (and ourselves too) on the basis of those choices. We can treat them (or ourselves) with respect or contempt according to whether or not they (or we) behave in the ways we expect, usually framed around other social narratives. All of the judgements we make about how people behave, including (but not limited to) the extent to which they follow a particular narrative, are underpinned by this notion of volition.

As we understand more about human behaviour, however, we are increasingly able to resort to one or a combination of four determining factors:

1. genetic influences;
2. social environments;
3. decision contexts; and
4. randomness.

To be clear, when I use randomness here I am referring to outcomes that are genuinely the result of chance, as distinct from outcomes that could be attributable to one of the other three causes if only we had more information. In the context of the narrative trap, the influence of factors outside our control means easing off on those who do not live according to the rules we would like them to follow (or even according to the rules they set for themselves and fall short of). But it does not mean easing off on dealing with the consequences of actions. In fact, quite the contrary: the only things that needs our attention are the consequences of our behaviour – and any motivation behind our actions should be viewed in terms of how it affects these outcomes.

For ease of exposition, I will consider the four factors in turn, as the main determinants, but the interaction among them will be where much of the explanation of human behaviour can be found. Epigenetics, for example, shows how different environments can activate certain genes. Having a predisposition to act in a certain way is not enough for you to act in that way: the environment needs to activate the genes in a way that brings about a behavioural response. But you should find the evidence on main effects compelling enough in itself to show just how tiny the role is for free will.

IT'S ALL IN THE GENES

The Human Genome Project, an international scientific project set up to map . . . you guessed it, the human genome, estimates that each of us has between 20,000 and 25,000 genes.[1] We all have two copies of each type of gene, one inherited from each parent, and so our parents affect how we look, as well as think, feel and act. There is so much that could be discussed here as the evidence base is constantly expanding, but let me say a few words about education, which is an important component of the Reaching narrative. A recent study of 354,224 people from 102 cohorts found strong positive associations between genetic diversity and higher levels of cognitive ability and educational attainment.[2]

In fact, genes present the most significant influence on academic achievement. Robert Plomin, Professor of Behavioural Genetics at King's College London, has been able to demonstrate this using the largest longitudinal twin study in the world, with 10,000 pairs of twins.[3] He found that at least half of the difference in children's performance at both GCSE and A-level exams in the UK can be attributed to the differences in their DNA. Contrary to what we might expect, particularly given the excessive amount of time and money that goes into selecting the best schools for our children, differences between the schools that children attend account for, at most, 20 per cent of the variation in academic achievement. One finding that especially interests me is that the average difference in IQ between siblings is thirteen points, which is not a whole lot lower than the seventeen-point difference that exists between two randomly chosen people.[4]

Genes affect happiness too. In an interesting study looking at the link between happiness, mastery, optimism and parental factors, adolescent well-being was found to be positively associated with parents' well-being, and particularly with that of fathers.[5] It is unclear, however, how much of this is related to genetic factors or factors in their shared environment. A longitudinal study looking at 615 adoptive and non-adoptive families suggests that the happiness transfer from parents to children is, in fact, largely the result of genetic factors and not contagion or environmental effects.[6] This study found that happiness levels within families were more highly correlated in non-adoptive families, therefore suggesting that the happiness levels being detected were more likely to be a result of genes rather than environment.

SOCIAL ENVIRONMENTS

Since we have no control over our genes, we quickly forget them as a major determinant of life outcomes. One determinant that we are a little more willing to accept (but often not so willing to act upon) is the role of socio-economic status. The social status and income of our parents matter greatly. In the US, if your parents move up the distribution of family income scale by 1 per cent, you are 0.7 per cent more likely to enrol in college.[7] Intriguingly, this effect is constant (i.e. linear) across the whole income distribution. So whether you're a poor kid getting marginally less poor or rich kid getting marginally richer, the chances of you enrolling in college increase by the same amount for each increase in your parents' place in the income distribution.

I'm sure you won't be surprised to find that there is a strong correlation between a parent's and a child's height. But perhaps you would be a little more surprised that exactly the same strong correlation exists between a parent's and a child's income. The likelihood that somebody who starts off in the lowest decile of the income distribution will reach the highest decile is the same as the likelihood that a father who is 5′6″ will have a son who grows up to be 6′1″. It can happen, but not that often. If you want to be tall, be born to tall parents; if you want to be rich, be born to rich ones.

As if being born into disadvantage was not enough, there is now evidence to suggest that the stresses associated with poverty can also adversely affect our biology. Among other things, poverty can reduce the surface area of your brain and increase your chances of obesity.[8] Those born into poverty are also more likely to experience trauma, which affects biological and psychological development by disrupting important neural regulatory processes, resulting in problematic behavioural responses, including criminality.[9] There is new evidence showing that 90 per cent of juvenile offenders in the US have experienced childhood trauma of some kind.[10]

It is completely beyond me that any sensible person, armed with the benefit of introspection – let alone any of the available evidence – could delude themselves into believing that anyone can make it if they work hard enough no matter what background they come from.

CONTEXT MATTERS

In 1999, two psychologists, Dan Wegner and Thalia Wheatley, conducted a series of experiments to see how the brain made decisions.[11]
They found that there is a lag of a quarter of a second between the time
we make a choice and when we become consciously aware of it. Many
of you will be familiar with the distinction in the brain between system 1, the 'automatic' bit, and system 2, the 'deliberative' part. Now, it
is worth saying that there aren't really two systems in the brain – it is
obviously much more complex than that – but it is a useful distinction
for illustrating the different influences of context and cognition. System 1 has evolved to respond to situational stimuli, often in ways that
we are unaware of.[12] It is always present, active and engaged. It is effort-
less, fast and automatic. It operates in the background below conscious
awareness. We make thousands of big and small decisions every day,
and system 1 ensures that most are made quite effortlessly and in ways
that, by and large, make life a lot more manageable for us.

But it can also make associations that system 2 would find quite
baffling if only it was aware of them. Consider the effects on behaviour of the brightness of light, for example. Dim environments have
been found to increase creativity and even to reduce calorie intake.[13]
In contrast, bright environments have been shown to improve honesty. In one experiment, university students in Taiwan were randomly
assigned to one of three lighting conditions: low, medium and high.[14]
At the end of the experiment, participants were given extra money,
as if by mistake, and asked to make sure they had received the
amount 'they deserved'. While only 50 per cent of students returned
the extra money under low lights, 85 per cent did so in the high light
condition. In real world settings, more street lighting has been exten-
sively linked to crime reduction. Crucially, in these and other
'priming' studies, participants are typically completely unaware that
the context of their decision has influenced them.

There are serious questions in the literature about the (lack of) rep-
licability of these sorts of priming studies, and these should not be
understated. But neither can the fact that we are influenced by unconscious cues in our environment, even if we can't always fully nail

down when, where, on whom and for how long. What matters is recognizing just how much of what we do is influenced by these unconscious
environmental cues. No one would say that how honest they are depends
on how bright the lights are. As a result, we readily, but spuriously,
find system 2 reasons for our actions. These post-hoc rationalizations
provide a coherent story for our behaviour but they typically bear very
little relation to what really drove our actions in the first place. We like
to think of ourselves as acting in spite of context, yet so much of our
behaviour can be explained precisely because of it.

And a good job too. We simply have to make too many decisions
and your head would explode if you had to think about each and every
one of them. In contrast, I find this quite liberating and encouraging,
because it offers us real hope to change behaviour by changing contextual stimuli. We only have so much attentional energy, and where we
really do need to think hard is in relation to how best to allocate it. I've
previously used the analogy of taking your dog to the park. You can't
consciously dictate how your dog runs around once it is in a park. But
you can choose which park you take it to. Analogously, you can't
decide on how you will respond to situational triggers, but you do
have some say over which triggers you are exposed to.

Sometimes the number of parks we have available to us is limited,
and the control we have over where and how to allocate our attention is restricted. People who do not have much spare cognitive
capacity because they are burdened by thinking about how to pay
the bills, for example, score worse on intelligence tests than when
their minds are free to think more clearly. This has been shown in
two very different populations: in a New Jersey shopping mall and
with sugar cane farmers in rural India.[15] In the mall study, shoppers
completed a number of different tests to measure their IQ and ability
to control their impulses. Before doing so, half of the group were
asked to think about what they would do if their car broke down and
the repair cost was $150. The other half were asked the same ques-
tion but this time the repair cost was a whopping $1,500. The scores
on each test were compared for those with incomes above or below
$70,000 per year. For the $150 condition, there was no difference
between income groups on the IQ and impulse-control measures. But
for the $1,500 condition, the lower-income participants performed

significantly worse than their richer counterparts. The knock-on effects on performance of the stressful and cognitively demanding task of finding a lot of money for a repair bill when you don't have very much was equivalent to missing a night's sleep.

The implications of results like this for how we attribute responsibility are really quite profound. We might no longer see differences between the behaviours of rich and poor people as related to differences in 'trait' that define who they are but rather as differences in 'state' related to the abundance or scarcity of resources. Indeed, this is a much better working assumption since it has been shown that rich people will behave just like poor people when they are faced with scarcity.

While we might sometimes ascribe our own behaviour to context – I fiddled my taxes because I was short of cash and not because I'm a cheat – we explain other people's behaviour nearly entirely in terms of their (assumed) underlying disposition – you fiddled your taxes because you are fundamentally the type of person who cheats. The tendency for us to place more importance on internal characteristics compared to external factors in explaining the behaviour of other people is known as the fundamental attribution error.[16] This bias is a central concept in psychological research and it lies at the heart of how we judge other people. We can only ever observe what people do and not what drove them to act in that way. Because we prefer an ordered world to a chaotic one, we extrapolate from what someone does to the kind of person we think they are in the narrative of our lives.[17]

Understanding the contextual drivers of behaviour is especially important in public-policy settings, where those making decisions on behalf of others will often be ill-informed about the environments and contexts within which those other people live. If we are rich and someone else is poor, we might not have any real sense that their behaviour is driven by scarcity in the ways described above.

RANDOMNESS

One determinant of life outcomes that introduces considerable noise (and which we are really reluctant to embrace) is randomness. From the moment each of us is randomly born into poverty or privilege, so much of what happens to us continues to be the result of chance. Luck matters in all sorts of ways, and in ways that policy-makers and parents often choose to ignore.

In the UK and the US, pupils born later in the school year (the 'summer babies') are at an unfair academic disadvantage.[18] They receive the same schooling while their brains are at a less developed stage than their peers, making it difficult for them to process the information with the same levels of competency. This difference in ability is particularly marked at the early stages of a child's life when the brain is undergoing rapid development. The effect decreases over time but is still significant at age sixteen when pupils are making important life choices. Summer babies are also much less likely to excel at sport given that they are smaller than their classmates.

Much has been written about the effects of class size on learning (it actually has a small effect) but much less has been written about the huge disadvantage being born in August in the UK brings – and even less (i.e. nothing) done about it. This is particularly galling for me as Poppy was born in April and, worse still, Stanley in late July. Stanley is actually pretty good at most sports and he would be bloody amazing among his peer group if my wife had had the foresight to delay getting pregnant by six weeks.

DELUDE YOURSELF

Despite its influence, we really hate the idea of luck because it takes control out of our hands, and humans love to feel like they are in control. Luck is ambiguous and indiscriminate, it strips us of agency, it smashes through the idea that we have influence over what happens, or that we can at least explain it. We feel cheated by luck as an explanation. It is a very unsatisfactory story because it is not really a story at all. As a consequence, we fail to attribute our successes to luck, even when our good fortune is made resoundingly obvious.

One interesting study carried out at the University of California, Berkeley has shown that people happily attribute their winning position in a game of monopoly to their individual talent even when the game has obviously been rigged in their favour.[19] In this study, individuals were told that the flip of a coin would determine whether they had access to certain privileges during the game, including additional dice, twice the amount of money and a higher bonus for passing Go. After the game they were asked why they thought they had (unsurprisingly) won the game. Participants responded by going into detail about their personal contribution to earning their successes throughout the game; they were far more attuned to what it was that had made them responsible for their inevitable victory than they were to the notion that chance had a big role to play.

If we went back a hundred years, we would think that free will played a much greater part in behaviour than we do now. It is an open question where we will be in another hundred years but my prediction is that behaviour influenced by the 'noise' of real volition will have all but disappeared. Free will is left to rearrange the deck chairs on the *Titanic* while factors outside our control steer the ship. (Not that your life is necessarily anything like a ship hitting an iceberg but you get the analogy.) But we like to think that we have control over the direction of the ship. In an experiment that has been replicated in various ways, people were told to try to control random flashing lights using a dummy button. Although the lights were flashing at random, people came away from the study thinking that they had played a key part in the appearance of the flashing lights.

It is often good for us, however, to believe we are in control even though we might not be. In a stark example, Bruno Bettelheim observed this while analysing survival tactics employed by individuals held in Nazi concentration camps. He found that the individuals most likely to survive were those who had managed to preserve areas in which they could carry out activities independently, away from Nazi control. Subsequent studies have shown that perceived lack of control is linked to increased stress, disease onset and a number of mental health conditions. The story of Emily in the last chapter is a powerful reminder of this.

Believing that we are in control of our actions also makes it more likely that we will be motivated to achieve good outcomes. When our motivation to achieve is higher we become more action oriented, which brings about better consequences. Belief in free will has been shown to be associated with better job performance, as measured by workplace performance evaluations. And through promoting feelings of belongingness, studies have also suggested that free will contributes to people's sense of purpose. While these studies are not causal they are suggestive of important links between perceived agency and happiness.

Roy Baumeister of Florida State University has conducted a number of studies into the importance of free will. He and his colleagues have found that students with a weaker belief in free will were less likely to volunteer their time to help a classmate than were those whose belief in free will was stronger. Similarly, those primed to hold a deterministic view by reading statements such as 'Science has demonstrated that free will is an illusion' were less likely to give money to a homeless person or to lend someone a mobile phone. People induced to believe less in free will were also more likely to take a sneak look at the answers on a test, or steal from a money pot when given opportunity to, than those who were not primed in this way.[20]

Neuroscientific studies have shown that undermining beliefs in free will also affect lower-level brain processes. For example, people who read passages denying the existence of free will experience less activation of neural networks associated with task preparation when completing simple tasks such as pressing a button. In this study, undermining free will did not change people's estimations of when the intention to move entered their awareness, suggesting that the impact of denying free will takes place outside conscious awareness.

DON'T DELUDE YOURSELF ABOUT OTHER PEOPLE

While feeling like we have free will can often be beneficial to us as individuals, believing that others act volitionally is usually harmful to social justice. The idea that anyone can succeed if only they work hard enough, for example, is borne out of wilful ignorance of systemic inequalities in the modern world. Rather than trying to achieve equal chances, which will never happen, let's look instead at how best to redistribute resources in ways that bring about outcomes that are judged to be fair (accounting for the fact that we have very little control over those outcomes). This is a far more tractable problem.

As a society, though, we certainly remain wedded to the idea that talent and effort should, and most often do, determine success. It has long seemed odd to me why so many people seem to think that it's OK for society to richly reward talent when it is determined almost entirely by genes, environment, context and luck and not at all by free will. Perhaps it is because we consider talent to be more highly correlated with good outcomes than luck alone and those good outcomes are a legitimate basis for reward. I could probably live with that explanation if the reward was somehow proportional to the good outcomes, and if we adequately compensated the talentless for losing out in life's lottery. But the gross inequalities we observe in society show just how much we over-reward the talented and under-compensate the talentless.

It would be intuitive to most people that we have more control over how much effort we put in as compared to how much talent we have. We are seen to have a considerable amount of choice over how hard we work. Part of our attraction to effort in the West comes from the 'American dream' ideology that you can be whoever you want to be if you work hard at it. This idea permeates liberal democracies and has come to dominate our understanding of success. Not only is effort freely chosen, it has also become seen as the major determinant of success (perhaps directly as a result of the perception of free will associated with it).

It might be intuitive that we have more free will in relation to effort than to talent, and it lends support to the idea of social mobility: if you choose to work hard, you can make it. But can we really choose how hard we work? The answer is that we simply do not know. It could well be that your desire to work hard and to act upon that desire are both determined largely (and perhaps even entirely) by genes, environment, context and luck.

Supporting this idea, associations have been found between children and their parents' work ethic. A recent Dutch study investigating this link found that men's work ethic was correlated with their past relationship quality with their parents, but that women's work ethic was not.[21] The same study also found associations between teenagers' approach to work and the quality of their relationship with their fathers (but not with their mothers), perhaps because of the traditional onus on men to be the breadwinners. While further research is needed to clarify these links and assess causality it does seem that genetic influence and/or early socialization may be playing a role here.

So just because you think you are choosing to work hard does not mean that you have chosen that desire or the ability to act upon it. This is not to say that you can't do anything to change your life: I wouldn't have bothered writing my last book if I thought that was true. It's just that you have a lot less control over what you do than you think (and, from *Happiness by Design*, that changing your context is the most effective way to change your behaviour).

A major part of the motivation for continuing to tell the 'successful striving' narrative in the face of better evidence is our desire to see the world as just. A belief in a just world is crucial for containing anxiety and uncertainty. In a rapidly changing world, this narrative serves as a warm, fuzzy security blanket that shields us from the frosty truth of gross inequality and injustice. But if we believe that life outcomes are largely the result of effort, then we will have much less concern for inequalities than if we believe those inequalities to be the result of chance. The hard-work narrative causes considerable harm to the unluckiest people in society.

Ironically, perhaps, it is the upwardly mobile folk who are the least likely to attribute success to luck.[22] This is because those who go from rags to riches are keen to put their own success down to hard work and perseverance, and to therefore assume that others can make it just as they did. Similarly, ex-smokers are often the most judgemental of smokers. The logic is quite simple: 'I have given up; so can they.' It is also simply wrong. There will be significant differences between those who are able to quit and those who are not, which are due to unobservable factors and randomness.

Moreover, those who have made the transition from rags to riches probably notice the more obvious privilege that most other successful people around them have had, thus making it even less likely that they will notice their own, less obvious, good fortune. I have often explained my own success in terms of being a bit clever and quite a lot lucky, yet this explanation does not go down very well with many people, including those who were previously from working-class backgrounds themselves. So we can't even rely on those who were once poor to fight for redistribution.

Only when we accept that most of life's outcomes are determined mostly by factors outside our control will we be able to properly judge many of life's inequalities as being unfair. Critically, the fact that there is very little volition in what we do means that we can relax our judgements about the extent to which others do or don't fulfil the narratives laid out in this book. Many of us are wired in ways that make wealth, success and education more appealing. We should all be alert, however, to the fact that our idealized view of these desires is shaped in large part by social construction. By accepting that much of what happens in life is out of your control, you free yourself from the dangers of the Reaching narratives and the 'I really should have achieved more' mentality.

When it comes to the Related narrative, each of us has important individual (and largely predetermined) preferences that need to be satisfied. You can be more accepting of the fact that you might never live up to how you are expected to 'relate' to other people. You might just not be cut out for marriage, for example. And even if you are the marrying type, you can now accept that many people aren't, and avoid judging them for being different.

When it comes to responsibility, we can all learn to show a little more humility in our judgements of why and in what ways people help other people, and why and in what ways they trade off their health for other concerns, including happiness itself. Ultimately, a less-delusional understanding of volition gives us greater freedom to embrace the choices others make in their pursuit of happiness.

IT'S ABOUT IMPACT, RIGHT?

We have seen how belief in free will can be helpful at the individual level but less so when it comes to judging others. So you might now be wondering how it is possible to balance two seemingly discordant beliefs about volition. A focus on impact can potentially do this. Even if all of our behaviour might eventually be traced back to genetic and environmental influence, we can still be held accountable for the impact we have on those around us. This holds irrespective of your views about how much free will we have. It would be interesting to see whether those who had their beliefs in free will undermined in the aforementioned studies still act as badly when reminded that they can still be held to account for the impact of their actions.

One important place where the debate between impact and accountability is slowly unfolding is the courtroom. Once neuroscience has advanced to the point where every behaviour has a neural marker, it is easy to imagine how we might begin to see ever fewer people placed on the bad side of the law. If we can prove that 'my brain made me do it', then the difference between those who do good and bad things becomes a matter of simple biology.

You might be surprised to find that this is already happening. A recent study has reported 204 cases since 2015 in which neuroscientific evidence has been used in courts in England and Wales.[23] It has been limited to appeals against conviction or against sentencing, but has covered a range of crimes: murder, crimes of violence, crimes of dishonesty, sexual offences and driving offences. Most of the appeals against conviction were unsuccessful, but appeals against the length of sentence were successful in over half of the cases considered. It seems that courts in the US are even more open to the idea that criminal behaviour can be understood as a medical condition. A recent US study reported that 5 per cent of murder trials, and 25 per cent of death row cases, have used evidence from neuroscience and behavioural genetics.[24] Although such evidence has never determined a verdict, it has affected sentencing.

This shows that we can still choose to punish consequences even if the causes were not freely chosen. The legal system takes into consideration the action (the crime committed) and the intention (the guilty mind) when determining suitable punishment. Both must be present in order for the defendant to be proven guilty. The impact will be affected by the intent, of course: the feelings I have about my broken nose will be affected by whether you accidentally elbowed me in the face or punched me for being annoying. But it's still a broken nose. And the impact of your actions, even the accidental elbow, needs to be acknowledged by you, and my nose still needs to be fixed.

Our fixation on why a crime occurred is explicable if it helps us to prevent further crime and thus reduce future impact. It is nonetheless noteworthy that criminologists spend so much time focusing their research on the perpetrators of crime and so little time on the impact on the victims of crime. There are some exceptions, such as Joanna Shapland, with whom I used to work in Sheffield, who continues to rightly argue that we need to do much more to understand the impact of crime and the judicial process on victims. When victims are asked about their preferences and feelings, they universally desire that 'justice is seen to be done', which always means that they want the impact of the crimes to be appreciated by the perpetrator and the judicial system, and only sometimes requires an explanation from the perpetrator of the intention behind the crime.

Now, I suspect that some of you might feel a little more comfortable with intentions being largely irrelevant when judging good actions, such as charitable giving, but be more troubled by downplaying motivation when it comes to bad deeds, such as criminal actions. This would be consistent with the Knobe effect, named after a contemporary American philosopher called Joshua Knobe.[25] He constructed the following thought experiment in which a CEO who only cares about maximizing profits decided to adopt a new programme because it is expected to be good for profits.[26] Imagine that the CEO knows that the programme would benefit the environment. Do you think he intended to benefit the environment? Only about one in four people think so. But what if the programme would harm the environment. Do you think that the CEO intended to harm the environment now? More than four out of five people think so.

Intriguingly, this suggests that it might not be clear to us whether or not an action was intentional (and, by extension, an action for which we can hold someone to account) until we have judged the consequences of that action to be good or bad. Knobe's work makes an important contribution to our understanding of how we judge intentions and impact. Yet again, context matters. But we should not conflate what is descriptively relevant with the normative importance of impact. The CEO should be held to account for his impact on the environment – and irrespective of whether he had any free will to behave as he did.

Very few of us behave badly with intent to harm, yet we often do cause others great harm. To say 'I didn't mean it' is therefore probably true – but so is the harm caused. As perpetrators of harm, we need to take responsibility for ameliorating the harm we cause rather than seeking to absolve ourselves by recourse to the lack of intent to harm. This 'I didn't mean it' mentality is a product of our egos: our selfish need to maintain a commendable self-image in the face of criticism. There is a certain irony in trying to make someone else feel better by redirecting self-assuring attention back at ourselves.

CONCLUSIONS

We like to think we are free to choose and that we can judge others for their choices. But the belief in free will can trigger a damaging emotional response. When we believe that someone has freely chosen to cause harm, the normal response is upset, anger and blame. We will often act in accordance with these emotions without full consideration of their impact. Opening our eyes to free will as an illusion gives us more scope to act in ways that really influence the root causes of good and bad behaviour.[27]

Behaving and misbehaving, achieving and falling short, are really all about design power and hardly at all about willpower. By disentangling judgements of free will from assessments of impact, we can more effectively deal with the consequences of our actions, and the actions of others. We are constantly reminding our children that they need to be alert to the impact that their actions have, irrespective of their intentions. At least, that is our intention. We remind them too that their academic and sporting successes, and their happiness, are down to luck as well as their own effort and talents. Oh, and also due in no small part to their parents, who are ruthless with bedtimes.

Not everything can be done at home. The school system could do better to counteract disadvantage by simply changing when exams are held. Research conducted in the UK shows that working-class boys do less well in GCSE exams when World Cup and European Championship matches are on at the same time, i.e. every two years.[28] Working-class kids like football more and the excitement distracts them from their schoolwork, leaving them at a significant disadvantage to their middle-class peers. I know only too well how this feels: I did my A-levels in 1986 when England were playing at the World Cup in Mexico. I'm sure I did less well in my maths exam because of the pain of losing to Argentina in the quarter-finals (courtesy of Diego Maradona's 'Hand of God' and Goal of the Century). Once we focus directly on consequences, the solution is simple: change when the exams take place.

Companies could try to reduce implicit bias when hiring by relying on more objective criteria, such as skills tests or completing job-relevant tasks, instead of interviews. If you must use interviews, make them structured; and setting out the key objectives beforehand can reduce your susceptibility to bias throughout.[29] Employees wishing to focus on work can eliminate potential distractions such as text messages and calls by switching off their phones for designated periods of time, or – better still – leaving them in another room.[30]

Once policy-makers accept that much of what happens is out of other people's control, they will become increasingly intolerant of inequalities in happiness. People do not choose to be miserable, and many of the supposed bad choices that led them to be so weren't really choices at all. Viewed in this way, inequalities in happiness are mostly also unfair differences. My mantra for public policy is thus: 'From each according to his luck, to each according to his happiness.'

Wrapping Up Responsible

The benefits of adopting a negative utilitarian perspective are nowhere more obvious than when addressing the harm caused by the Responsible meta-narrative. We could all probably be a little more altruistic towards those we care about, and especially towards those we have no obvious affinity with. But only if we get something from it as well. We should judge the goodness of an act much more by the goodness of its consequences, and hardly at all by the alleged goodness of its motivation. If we belittle rather than celebrate good actions when they are motivated by anything other than selflessness, we not only shame the reasonable pro-social people among us, but we also set up unrealistic expectations about what should motivate us. And this results in more suffering in the world. The narrative of pure altruism is counterproductive.

The Responsible narrative as it applies to health creates and prolongs misery. Reconsidering being healthy as a constrained choice rather than as an unrestricted responsibility would help to lessen the harsh judgement associated with those who aren't willing or able to be walking shrines to fitness and longevity. It would allow us to properly consider the trade-offs people make over health and other determinants of happiness and calmly evaluate whether these maximize happiness, rather than rushing to judgement based on their failure to maximize health. And it would remove the unnecessary pressure placed on those living with and treating terminal illness, allowing real choice over a dignified death and freeing resources to be used where they reduce misery most.

I have no doubt that those who suffer the most would be treated much better if we accepted the fact that our desires and our willingness and ability to act upon them are determined by factors that lie almost entirely outside our control. While we each may gain individually from deluding ourselves that we act volitionally, we allow society to inflict unacceptable levels of harm on the worst off by deluding ourselves that they are responsible for their suffering, and also for their likelihood of alleviating it.

Your place in society is almost entirely determined for you and not by you. And so is mine. None of us should ever forget that when we heap praise on those who succeed and scorn on those who do not. The randomness of life's lottery means that we all need to do what we can to reduce inequalities between the winners and losers. It is a source of some discomfort to me that people like me who have jumped up several rungs of the social ladder are often the most critical of those who have failed to do so.

OK, so, results time again. Please see the graph below. Taken together, the Responsible meta-narrative is the one that our respondents are most willing to trade their happiness for. At least one third of people say they would actively make themselves miserable to pursue one of these narratives. For health, the figure is around two thirds for the whole sample. The importance of health is confirmed in a much bigger and more rigorous study I conducted with my colleagues

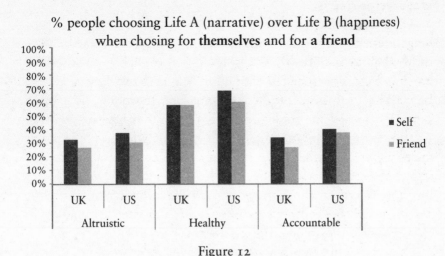

% people choosing Life A (narrative) over Life B (happiness) when chosing for **themselves** and for **a friend**

Figure 12

Matt Adler and Georgios Kavetsos. We asked 13,000 members of the general public in the UK and the US whether they would choose to live a life where they felt happy or to live a life high in either income, physical health, family, career success or education. Happiness was the overwhelming choice for most of the narratives, but when it comes to the healthy narrative, well over half chose physical health over happiness.[1] Just as with Reaching (and in contrast to Related), all three Responsible narratives appear to be slightly more important in the US than in the UK. As with all the narratives, happiness trumps the narrative when choosing for others as compared to for themselves.

Conclusion

Social narratives can trap us, and those around us. We will often fail to notice them, and even when we do we will find it really hard to accept that the narratives we've heard since childhood can be the source of widespread misery. Most stories can be initially alluring. But just because something feels good at first is no guarantee that it will stay that way. And just because something floats your boat does not mean that it will prevent someone else's from sinking. To live our lives by stringent rules and guidelines is to take away the modicum of volition we might just about possess. We need to look past our preconceived ideas about what a good life should look like and consider how these ideas play out in practice – for ourselves and for those whose lives we influence. The crucial point is that there is no one-size-fits-all prescription for how to live and we need to free ourselves from the idea that there is.

GETTING OVER OURSELVES

A focus on happiness is the key to overcoming misguided biases driven by social stories. Our experiences are what matter, and not the stories we tell about them. Constantly monitoring happiness will be very effortful, and so you will need to adopt some rules of thumb. Sometimes following the social narratives discussed in this book will be consistent with reducing misery, at other times it will not, and at yet other times it will be hard to know. I am not suggesting that you ditch the narratives as a matter of principle. That would be just as silly as suggesting that you follow them blindly. When to hold and when to fold on a narrative will differ across people, time, place and context.

I tell myself that working at the LSE brings me more happiness overall than working at a less prestigious university closer to my home in Hove because the misery of the commute is more than offset by the benefits that come from teaching bright students, working with smart colleagues, with better opportunities for collaborative research, policy impact and public engagement. I do think I'm happier at the LSE, but I could be wrong and I might instead be trapped by the narrative of success that makes me more miserable overall.

The narratives discussed here have often required me to focus on big decisions, such as what job to take, and whether or not to marry. But we must not forget that happiness is experienced moment-to-moment. *Don't Sweat the Small Stuff* was a bestseller for Richard Carlson a couple of decades ago, and many people still use the saying as a way to remind themselves or others that they should not let the little annoyances in life drive them crazy.[1] But happiness (and misery) *are* found in the small stuff: in the moments of laughter (or tears) with a friend, in the breath of fresh air (or smog), in the funny (or nasty) exchange with a stranger. 'Don't sweat the big stuff' would actually be a more helpful piece of advice. So rather than thinking about how to get rich, for example, you might instead focus on how you can ensure you get enough sleep every night. Working out how to be happy is not easy but, as I point out in *Happiness by Design*, it is made a little more tractable by focusing on the daily activities of life.

It is also worth keeping in mind the results of our study on the trade-off between the narratives and happiness, where people are more narrative driven when it comes to their own decisions than they are when deciding for a friend. So your own grip on a narrative might be relaxed if you consider what advice you would give to a friend. Take their advice from time to time, and give them yours. You will each become a little freer from the narratives as a result. The old adage 'Do unto others as you would have them do unto you' should instead be 'Do unto yourself as you would do unto others.' Jesus Christ updated by behavioural science.

DECIDING FOR OTHERS

When making decisions on behalf of others, we will obviously be informed by the Reaching, Related and Responsible narratives. Arguably parents have the greatest impact on the behaviour of other people and are also perhaps the most committed to the idea that their children should live according to the stories discussed in this book. I reckon the majority of parents would want their children to be successful and educated, to marry and to have children of their own. And not just (and sometimes not even) because they think these narratives will make their kids happy, but because they will make them (the parents) happy. Many more parents than would ever let on are living their own lives through their children, and many get great pleasure out of showing off about what great jobs their kids have.

I encourage all you parents out there to allow your kids to pursue lives that are good for them, whether or not this means them following a narrative, and whether or not it would make you happier if they did conform. Whatever implicit pressures I might exert on Poppy and Stanley, I certainly won't be one of those selfish parents who puts pressure on their kids to have their own kids just so that they can be a grandparent. I'm thankful that I never felt any pressure from my own parents to have children. This may indeed go some way towards explaining why I didn't have kids until I was forty. By this age I was much better placed psychologically to not fuck them up anywhere near as much as I would have done if I had become a dad a decade earlier.

I am proud and very lucky that my mum brought me up to be open- and fair-minded. She was ahead of the times on all sorts of social issues: her tolerance of the very simple idea that two men could love one another is especially memorable to me at a time when this attitude was not accepted in our social circles. That her social attitudes were so different to her parents gives me faith that prevailing narratives can be broken. Poppy and Stanley have hopefully been instilled with the same core values, and they might even be more proactive in espousing them than I have been.

Those of you with the ability to influence more children than just your own, such as those working within the education sector, can also speak up for social class and other bases upon which people are subject to discrimination by helping to ensure that the curricula in schools, colleges and universities are genuinely inclusive of different values and ways of learning. We have seen how this is not only fair; it is efficient too.

Those of you who are in positions of authority in organizations should also engage in regular and critical assessments of performance metrics and consider how a broader scope of judgement that takes into account different backgrounds might improve the outcomes they produce. Genuinely embracing diversity can enhance personal experiences and broaden professional gains. This requires more than simply wider demographic representation in decision-making, which is where most of the discussions of diversity are focused.[2] It requires diversity in attitude and opinion too, and an inclusive approach to properly allow for difference.

If you are a researcher, you might like to pay a little more attention to the influence of narratives on human behaviour and happiness. Stories are the invisible cornerstone of academic research. Academics take their own stories into their research, under the cloak of objectivity. So here is a call to arms for researchers to ask whether and to what extent narratives interfere with the broader purpose of their research agenda. All those happiness researchers who use life-satisfaction measures are implicitly assuming that social stories should form part of happiness. They might agree with this, but I would like to see them more explicitly defend that position. In order to break free from a one-size-fits-all approach to how to live, the research community also needs to move away from its fixation on averages. There are important lessons to be learned from what makes the average person happy, of course, but none of us is average and we certainly don't see ourselves as such.

I am not immune to falling into narrative traps as a researcher. Indeed, I have had some of my own preconceptions challenged during the course of writing this book. I was particularly surprised about what little benefit higher education provides for individuals and society. Some of my academic colleagues have really struggled with this idea too; those who have not been to university are not at all surprised or troubled. I have also changed my mind on euthanasia. My fears about the 'slippery slope' have been satisfied by the safeguards that would have to be put in place.

As a policy-maker, you could also consider using reductions in misery as the lens through which to appraise interventions, rather than outcomes associated with the narratives such as income. Along with people such as Richard Layard at the LSE and Gus O'Donnell, former Cabinet Secretary in the UK, I now take every opportunity when advising policy-makers to ask them what they would do differently if they focused on misery reduction as a policy goal. The simple answer to this question is that mental health would matter more than it does. As it stands, only one in three people with common mental health problems receive treatment for their condition (compared to pretty much everyone, in one way or another, who has a physical health problem) – and even then only after a long wait.[3]

As a politician, you might consider alerting the public to the narratives used by other politicians and political parties and provide a more compelling social narrative based on minimizing misery. I appreciate that swimming against the tide of social narratives is a hard sell but I'm optimistic that policy proposals based on reining ourselves in from over-reaching, more acceptance of different ways of relating to one another, and a clear focus on being responsible for the consequences of our actions can form the basis of a new populist movement.

I have a lot of respect for ordinary people. I grew up in the East End of London and was fascinated by events such as the Battle of Cable Street, where an assorted group of communists, anarchists, Jews and Irish confronted Oswald Mosley and his Blackshirts as they sought to march through the East End in October 1936, supported by a police presence.[4] The anti-fascists fought hard and Mosley retreated. The fascists' popularity diminished as a direct result of the public protest (at least that's what I was told as a kid many times, so it must be true). This is the kind of populism I hope we will see again. A populism that will avoid some of the narrative traps I have discussed.

Breaking free from our addiction to the Reaching narrative will lead us to be more challenging of the assumption that globalization and neoliberalism must benefit society. There are good reasons why they do not, irrespective of the degree to which you personally benefit: the few who become very wealthy, successful and educated do not appear to gain much happiness; the many more who remain poor, in a low-status job and uneducated are made miserable by their conditions; and those in the middle are not as happy as they could be because they are expected to be reaching for more. By adopting a 'just enough' approach, the rich would more willingly transfer resources to the poor, at hardly any happiness costs to themselves and with huge happiness benefits to others, and those in the middle would be happier with what they already have.

Breaking from the Related meta-narrative liberates us from social conservatism. Now, you will obviously resist this if you are a social conservative, but you are still free to pursue a life of marriage and monogamy with children of your own. The data discussed in this book, however, simply do not allow you to make a strong enough case to impose your values on other people, any more than they allow others to impose their values on you. Each to their own, or, if you prefer, just get on with your life.

And breaking free from the Responsible meta-narrative will mean that we can tackle those, usually on the political right according to a rather outdated spectrum, who claim that anyone can 'make it' if they really want to and if they work really hard. Notwithstanding the importance of personal feedback, the Responsible narrative probably does more than others to prevent any political party that is serious about winning power from taking misery reduction as seriously as it should.

We must not get caught out by the allure of considering intentions over impact. The moral case for focusing on causes is questionable, while for consequences it is compelling. If we want to tackle injustice, we must focus on the harm that injustice causes. Sure, we can attribute blame for poverty, etc., but only if this does not end up in victim blaming, which it nearly always does to some large degree. Blaming those adversely affected compounds the impact instead of alleviating it. The suggestion that the poor are lazy and undeserving does not exactly help them in dealing with the financial challenges they face on a daily basis. Few people choose a life of misery.

Reflecting on the three meta-narratives, I found that reaching-based stories most strongly constrain the working class and that related-based stories most strongly control the behaviour of women. And, perhaps a little ironically, although perhaps directly as a result, it is the working class who probably have most to gain from not being judged harshly if, beyond basic levels, they eschew wealth, success and wisdom. And women certainly have the most to gain from at least questioning the idea that they should be married, monogamous and have children. For the Responsible narrative, women are judged more harshly than men for acting selfishly, and the working class are looked down upon for trading off their health against other pleasures in life. The least well off in society, which will include Black, Asian and minority ethnic people, are generally assumed to have much more control over changing the conditions of their own lives than any evidence would support.

So while the narratives always serve the interests of those in power, the groups they serve best will depend on the context. This means that we need to be more nuanced in our discussions about where the 'real' challenges of 'discrimination by narrative' lie. It is not surprising that class matters most when it comes to money, and gender is the key issue when we talk about sex. But it reminds us that we need to know something about the specific context of the discrimination in order to determine whose cause needs fighting for the strongest. Being alert to context in this way stops us getting into distracting and divisive debates about whether class, race or gender matters most. Each is important in its own right and each can be relatively more or less important in specific contexts.

THIS IS THE MODERN WORLD

Going against the grain of social narratives can be challenging. It is likely that the task is being made harder by the powerful role played by social media. I have referred to social media at various points in the book where it is changing the nature of a narrative, e.g. in relation to what being successful looks like. Overall, it seems to me that social media has made visible, and consequently magnified, the importance of having achieved according to the main narratives. When a behaviour that is judged to be good is noticed by more people, the behaviour becomes more prevalent. Social media has made it possible that literally millions of people can witness, appreciate and envy your successes. There are also now huge economic returns to being recognized: compare the reach and marketing potential of Cristiano Ronaldo with that of Johan Cruyff.

Social media also makes it easier for all of us to construct identities for ourselves that hide who we really are and instead portray the person we would like to be. We can regulate which images people see of us and which ones they don't. We can decide what particular style we would like to brand ourselves with and communicate carefully constructed opinions that bolster our self-image. In addition to this (and very much unlike real life), we can airbrush our faces and bodies and navigate our social success by deleting and editing posts in response to the feedback gained from other people's reactions. All of this allows us to craft a particular image of ourselves as protagonists of popular social stories.

That social media can act as a digital veil is not new. It can encourage nasty behaviour that might otherwise be chastised in the real world. The increased distance and anonymity we get from being behind a screen detaches us from the consequences of our actions: we don't get punished and we can't see how much we are hurting people. This environment is bound to make bad behaviour more likely. It is also hard to know how to react to it. We should not curtail free speech, and none of us has the right not to be offended, so perhaps better enforcement of existing laws on, for example, the incitement to commit criminal acts is what is required.

I have some, admittedly correlational, data to support the case that online engagement makes people miserable. Our analysis of data from 7,000 Germans shows that a significantly larger proportion of the miserable group use Facebook, Instagram and Twitter more often than do the happy group. This group is also more likely than the happy folk to engage in online activities such as uploading pictures and posting updates on social media while on or after a holiday.

It's not all doom and gloom, though. Social media might also lead to the formation and reinforcement of groups that are anti-narrative.

You can find 'becoming minimalist', a group with over 800,000 members, which actively celebrates spending less money with an emphasis on sustainable living. And then there's a 'Childfree Choice' group on Facebook with a following of over 20,000, which allows people who decide against having kids to share experiences and promote the benefits. This can act as a nice counterbalance to the prevailing narratives but runs the risk of creating tensions between groups who each think that they are living a better life: witness the vitriolic debate between working and stay-at-home mums.

It seems glib yet still important to say that social media is not the problem, it's just that we don't know how to control our consumption of it. We simply don't have any cues that signal us to stop scrolling. We have licensing laws for alcohol because of its addictive nature and it could be argued that we require some regulation of social media use. I was working at the University of York in the early 1990s when alcohol was removed from the list of drinks you could have at a lunch event. (I recall that my mentor, Alan Williams, was not at all happy about this.) It's a trickier thing to implement practically but we should now try to do the same with social media.

A FINAL WORD FROM THE WORKING-CLASS HERO

The guy I spoke about in the Introduction who accosted me at that festival was very clear that I had a duty to act in a certain way. As far as he was concerned I was 'playing the working-class hero' in a rather distasteful way. Judging by some of the comments that have been written about me online, he is not alone. One of my favourites, for what it's worth, was 'Maybe happiness can be found in the wearing of unpleasant spectacles? And chavvy watches' in response to a photo of me in the gym, wearing my white specs and a sports watch, for a piece I wrote for the *Guardian*. The *Guardian* quite rightly moderates comments for racist and sexist content but clearly not for classist insults.

When I stated that I do not like to read fiction, I was judged very harshly for this by other academics as well as in the press. So not only am I expected to conform to stories about how LSE professors ought to behave when I am working, I am expected to use my leisure time in ways that conform with the stereotype, too. I have often felt obliged to rein in who I am because I do not conform to what is expected of me in my career, or at least to hide who I am. This sometimes makes me miserable. But I have also had many people thank me for being a breath of fresh air and sometimes an inspiration; and so I will continue to go, authentically, against the grain. I am not so sanctimonious as to say that I only stand out because it inspires others to question convention. There is no such thing as pure altruism and I do get personal benefit from being different. It rarely feels pleasurable to go against the grain but it often feels purposeful. But it shouldn't always feel so bloody hard.

I would like those of you who feel more of an obligation to fit in, at work or elsewhere, to not be chastised if you really would like to behave in ways that are not consistent with the prevailing social stories. Ultimately, insofar as we have any choice over such matters, each of us has to decide for ourselves when we conform and the circumstances under which we want to stand out. We can each live our lives in ways that reduce our own misery by as much as possible, properly accounting for the impact that our actions have on other people.

We can make decisions on behalf of others according to the same misery-minimizing rules. For some of us, some of the time, this will mean acting in ways that are consistent with elements of the Reaching, Related and Responsible meta-narratives. But certainly not for all of us all of the time. There is stigma associated with trying to conform to a narrative and falling short and there is a separate stigma from not trying to conform in the first place. We should have more respect than we currently do for those who forsake social narratives that simply aren't for them.

Thank you so much for making it this far with me. I hope this book has made a small contribution towards allowing you to live the way you choose a little more, and to judge others who behave differently a little less. Here's to us all escaping the myth of the perfect life, and to being Happy Ever After.

Notes

INTRODUCTION

1 Dolan, P. (2015), *Happiness by Design: Finding Pleasure and Purpose in Everyday Life*. London: Penguin.

2 Jay, K. L. and Jay, T. B. (2015), Taboo word fluency and knowledge of slurs and general pejoratives: deconstructing the poverty-of-vocabulary myth. *Language Sciences*, 52, 251–9; Giordano, F. (2016), The relationship between profanity and intelligence. *Yale Review of Undergraduate Research in Psychology*, 16.

3 Jay, K. L. and Jay, T. B. (2015), Taboo word fluency and knowledge of slurs and general pejoratives: deconstructing the poverty-of-vocabulary myth. *Language Sciences*, 52, 251–9.

4 Generous, M. A., Frei, S. S. and Houser, M. L. (2015), When an instructor swears in class: functions and targets of instructor swearing from college students' retrospective accounts. *Communication Reports*, 28 (2), 128–40.

5 Cordova, J. V. (2001), Acceptance in behavior therapy: understanding the process of change. *The Behavior Analyst*, 24 (2), 213–26.

6 Hechter, M. and Opp, K. (2005), *Social Norms*. New York: Russell Sage Foundation.

7 Fiske, S. T. (2009), *Social Beings: Core Motives in Social Psychology*. Hoboken, NJ: John Wiley & Sons Inc.

8 Dominique, J. F., Fischbacher, U., Treyer, V., Schellhammer, M., Schnyder, U., Buck, A. and Fehr, E. (2004), The neural basis of altruistic punishment. *Science*, 305 (5688), 1254–8; Raine, A. and Yang, Y. (2006), Neural foundations to moral reasoning and antisocial behavior. *Social Cognitive and Affective Neuroscience*, 1 (3), 203–13.

9 Pratto, F., Sidanius, J., Stallworth, L. M. and Malle, B. F. (1994), Social dominance orientation: a personality variable predicting social and political attitudes. *Journal of Personality and Social Psychology*, 67 (4), 741.

10 Atkinson, A. B. and Brandolini, A. (2013), On the identification of the middle class. In J. C. Gornick and M. Jäntti, eds., *Income Inequality: Economic Disparities and the Middle Class in Affluent Countries.* Stanford, Calif.: Stanford University Press, 77–100.

11 Natcen Social Research. *British Social Attitudes* (2015). Retrieved from http://www.bsa.natcen.ac.uk/latest-report/british-social-attitudes-33/social-class.aspx.

12 Dolan, P. and Kudrna, L. (2016), Sentimental hedonism: pleasure, purpose, and public policy. In Joar Vittersø, ed., *Handbook of Eudaimonic Well-Being.* Switzerland: Springer International Publishing, 437–52.

13 Gamst, F. C. (1991), Foundations of social theory. *Anthropology of Work Review*, 12 (3), 19–25.

14 Walker, A. D. M. (1974), Negative utilitarianism. *Mind*, 83 (331), 424–8.

15 Darwall, S. (2007), *Consequentialism.* Malden, Mass.: Blackwell.

16 Scanlon, T. M. (2003), *Rights, Goals, and Fairness.* Cambridge: Cambridge University Press.

17 Nickerson, R. S. (1998), Confirmation bias: a ubiquitous phenomenon in many guises. *Review of General Psychology*, 2 (2), 175.

18 Adams, H. E., Wright, L. W. and Lohr, B. A. (1996), Is homophobia associated with homosexual arousal? *Journal of Abnormal Psychology*, 105 (3), 440–45.

I. WEALTHY

1 Pilling, D. (2018), *The Growth Delusion.* New York: Tim Duggan Books, 19.

2 Pew Research Center (2008), Social demographics and trends. Retrieved from http://www.pewsocialtrends.org/2008/04/30/who-wants-to-be-rich/.

3 Allstate National Journal Heartland Monitor XXI Key Findings (2014). Retrieved from http://heartlandmonitor.com/wp-content/uploads/2015/03/FTI-Allstate-NJ-Heartland-Poll-Findings-Memo-11-5-14.pdf.

4 Stiglitz, J. (2013), *The Price of Inequality.* New York: W.W. Norton & Company.

5 Pfeffer, F. T. and Killewald, A. (2015), How rigid is the wealth structure and why? Inter- and multigenerational associations in family wealth. *Population Studies Center Research Report*, 15-845.

6 Layard, R., Mayraz, G. and Nickell, S. (2008), The marginal utility of income. *Journal of Public Economics*, 92 (8–9), 1846–57.

7   Dolan, P., Peasgood, T. and White, M. (2008), Do we really know what makes us happy? A review of the economic literature on the factors associated with subjective well-being. *Journal of Economic Psychology*, 29 (1), 94–122; Layard, R. and Clark, D. M. (2014), *Thrive: The Power of Evidence-Based Psychological Therapies*. London: Penguin.

8   Smith, S. C. (2015), *Ending Global Poverty: A Guide to What Works*. New York: St. Martin's Press.

9   Kahneman, D. and Deaton, A. (2010), High income improves evaluation of life but not emotional well-being. *Proceedings of the National Academy of Sciences*, 107 (38), 16489–93.

10 Suls, J. and Wheeler, L., eds., (2013), *Handbook of Social Comparison: Theory and Research*. New York: Springer Science & Business Media.

11 Boyce, C. J., Brown, G. D. and Moore, S. C. (2010), Money and happiness: rank of income, not income, affects life satisfaction. *Psychological Science*, 21 (4), 471–5; Luttmer, E. F. (2005), Neighbors as negatives: relative earnings and well-being. *Quarterly Journal of Economics*, 120 (3), 963–1002.

12 Diener, E., Sandvik, E., Seidlitz, L. and Diener, M. (1993), The relationship between income and subjective well-being: relative or absolute? *Social Indicators Research*, 28 (3), 195–223.

13 Knight, J., Song, L. and Gunatilaka, R. (2009), Subjective well-being and its determinants in rural China. *China Economic Review*, 20 (4), 635–49; Graham, C. and Felton, A. (2006), Inequality and happiness: insights from Latin America. *Journal of Economic Inequality*, 4 (1), 107–22.

14 Cheung, F. and Lucas, R. E. (2016), Income inequality is associated with stronger social comparison effects: the effect of relative income on life satisfaction. *Journal of Personality and Social Psychology*, 110 (2), 332; Layard, R., Mayraz, G. and Nickell, S. (2010), Does relative income matter? Are the critics right? In E. Diener., J. F. Helliwell and D. Kahneman, eds., *International Differences in Well-Being*. New York: Oxford University Press, 139–65.

15 Luttmer, E. F. (2005), Neighbors as negatives: relative earnings and well-being. *Quarterly Journal of Economics*, 120 (3), 963–1002.

16 Prati, A. (2017), Hedonic recall bias. Why you should not ask people how much they earn. *Journal of Economic Behavior & Organization*, 143, 78–97.

17 Agarwal, S., Mikhed, V. and Scholnick, B. (2016), Does Inequality Cause Financial Distress? Evidence from Lottery Winners and Neighboring Bankruptcies. Federal Reserve Bank of Philadelphia Working Paper No. 16-4.

18 Winkelmann, R. (2012), Conspicuous consumption and satisfaction. *Journal of Economic Psychology*, 33 (1), 183–91.

19 O'Brien, E., Kristal, A. C., Ellsworth, P. C. and Schwarz, N. (2018), (Mis)imagining the good life and the bad life: envy and pity as a function of the focusing illusion. *Journal of Experimental Social Psychology*, 75, 41–53.

20 Veblen, T. (1899), *The Theory of the Leisure Class: An Economic Study of Institutions*. London: Unwin Books.

21 Perez-Truglia, R. (2013), A test of the conspicuous-consumption model using subjective well-being data. *Journal of Socio-Economics*, 45, 146–54.

22 Ibid.

23 Linssen, R., van Kempen, L. and Kraaykamp, G. (2011), Subjective well-being in rural India: the curse of conspicuous consumption. *Social Indicators Research*, 101 (1), 57–72.

24 Walasek, L. and Brown, G. D. (2015), Income inequality and status seeking: searching for positional goods in unequal US states. *Psychological Science*, 26 (4), 527–33.

25 Association for Consumer Research (2014), Conspicuous Consumption of Time: When Busyness and Lack of Leisure Time Become a Status Symbol. Retrieved from http://www.acrwebsite.org/volumes/v42/acr_v42_16843.pdf.

26 British Social Attitudes 28. Retrieved from http://www.bsa.natcen.ac.uk/media/38952/bsa28_8housing.pdf.

27 Allstate National Journal Heartland Monitor XXI Key Findings (2014). Retrieved from http://heartlandmonitor.com/wp-content/uploads/2015/03/FTI-Allstate-NJ-Heartland-Poll-Findings-Memo-11-5-14.pdf.

28 Foye, C., Clapham, D. and Gabrieli, T. (2017), Home-ownership as a social norm and positional good: subjective wellbeing evidence from panel data. *Urban Studies*, 1–22.

29 United Kingdom Home Ownership Rate (2005–2018). Retrieved from https://tradingeconomics.com/united-states/home-ownership-rate.

30 Foye, C. (2016), The relationship between size of living space and subjective well-being. *Journal of Happiness Studies*, 18 (2), 427–61.

31 Frank, R. (2007), *Falling Behind: How Rising Inequality Harms the Middle Class* (Vol. 4). Oakland, Calif.: University of California Press.

32 Alpizar, F., Carlsson, F. and Johansson-Stenman, O. (2005), How much do we care about absolute versus relative income and consumption? *Journal of Economic Behavior & Organization*, 56 (3), 405–21.

2. SUCCESSFUL

1 Cook, E. (1997), Capitalism and 'friends' make you miserable. *Independent*, 31 August. Retrieved from https://www.independent.co.uk/news/capitalism-and-friends-make-you-miserable-1248156.html.

2 Pew Research Center (2012), Young Women Surpass Young Men in Career Aspirations. Retrieved from www.pewresearch.org/fact-tank/2012/05/03/young-women-surpass-young-men-in-career-aspirations/.

3 Clark, A. E. and Oswald, A. J. (1994), Unhappiness and unemployment. *Economic Journal*, 104 (424), 648–59.

4 Lucas, R. E., Clark, A. E., Georgellis, Y. and Diener, E. (2004), Unemployment alters the set point for life satisfaction. *Psychological Science*, 15 (1), 8–13.

5 Oesch, D. and Lipps, O. (2012), Does unemployment hurt less if there is more of it around? A panel analysis of life satisfaction in Germany and Switzerland. *European Sociological Review*, 29 (5), 955–67; Clark, A., Knabe, A. and Rätzel, S. (2010), Boon or bane? Others' unemployment, well-being and job insecurity. *Labour Economics*, 17 (1), 52–61.

6 Knabe, A., Rätzel, S., Schöb, R. and Weimann, J. (2010), Dissatisfied with life but having a good day: time-use and well-being of the unemployed. *Economic Journal*, 120 (547), 867–89.

7 Chadi, A. and Hetschko, C. (2017), Income or Leisure? On the Hidden Benefits of (Un-)Employment. IAAEU Discussion Paper Series in Economics, No. 06/2017.

8 White, M. P. and Dolan, P. (2009), Accounting for the richness of daily activities. *Psychological Science*, 20 (8), 1000–1008; Christodoulou, C., Schneider, S. and Stone, A. A. (2014), Validation of a brief yesterday measure of hedonic well-being and daily activities: comparison with the day reconstruction method. *Social Indicators Research*, 115 (3), 907–17.

9 Dolan, P., Kudrna, L. and Stone, A. (2017), The measure matters: an investigation of evaluative and experience-based measures of wellbeing in time use data. *Social Indicators Research*, 134 (1), 57–73.

10 Krueger, A. B. (2017), Where Have All the Workers Gone? An Inquiry into the Decline of the US Labor Force Participation Rate. Brookings Papers on Economic Activity Conference Draft.

11 City and Guilds' Career Happiness Index (2012). Retrieved from https://www.cityandguilds.com/news/November-2012/careers-happiness-index-2012#.Wg0ob7acagQ.

12 Legatum Report on Wellbeing and Policy (2014), p. 72. Retrieved from https://li.com/docs/default-source/commission-on-wellbeing-and-policy/commission-on-wellbeing-and-policy-report-march-2014-pdf.pdf.

13 eFinancialCareers. White paper (2014). Retrieved from http://finance.efinancialcareers.com/rs/dice/images/eFC-US-Retention-2014.pdf.

14 Doherty, L. (2004), Work-life balance initiatives: implications for women. *Employee Relations*, 26 (4), 433–52.

15 Walker, E., Wang, C. and Redmond, J. (2008), Women and work-life balance: is home-based business ownership the solution? *Equal Opportunities International*, 27 (3), 258–75.

16 Roberts, J., Hodgson, R. and Dolan, P. (2011), 'It's driving her mad': gender differences in the effects of commuting on psychological health. *Journal of Health Economics*, 30 (5), 1064–76.

17 Social Mobility and Child Poverty Commission (2015), Non-educational Barriers to the Elite Professions Evaluation. Retrieved from https://www.gov.uk/government/publications/non-educational-barriers-to-the-elite-professions-evaluation.

18 Laurison, D. and Friedman, S. (2016), The class pay gap in higher professional and managerial occupations. *American Sociological Review*, 81 (4), 668–95.

19 Fiske, S. and Markus, H. (2012), *Facing Social Class*. New York: Russell Sage Foundation (pp. 88–90).

20 Rucker, D. D. and Galinsky, A. D. (2017), Social power and social class: conceptualization, consequences, and current challenges. *Current Opinion in Psychology*, 18, 26–30.

21 Kraus, M. W. and Keltner, D. (2009), Signs of socioeconomic status: a thin-slicing approach. *Psychological Science*, 20 (1), 99–106.

22 Dietze, P. and Knowles, E. D. (2016), Social class and the motivational relevance of other human beings: evidence from visual attention. *Psychological Science*, 27 (11), 1517–27.

23 Stellar, J. E., Manzo, V. M., Kraus, M. W. and Keltner, D. (2012), Class and compassion: socioeconomic factors predict responses to suffering. *Emotion*, 12 (3), 449.

24 George, J. M. (2000), Emotions and leadership: the role of emotional intelligence. *Human Relations*, 53, 1027–55; Alon, I. and Higgins, J. M. (2005), Global leadership success through emotional and cultural intelligences. *Business Horizons*, 48, 501–12.

25 Chen, E. and Matthews, K. A. (2001), Cognitive appraisal biases: an approach to understanding the relation between socioeconomic status

and cardiovascular reactivity in children. *Annals of Behavioral Medicine*, 23 (2), 101–11.

26 Pettigrew, T. F. and Tropp, L. R. (2006), A meta-analytic test of intergroup contact theory. *Journal of Personality and Social Psychology*, 90 (5), 751.

27 The Organization for Economic Co-operation and Development (OECD). Regulations in force on 1 January 2013. Retrieved from https://www.oecd.org/els/emp/United%20States.pdf.

28 Ariely, D., Kamenica, E. and Prelec, D. (2008), Man's search for meaning: the case of Legos. *Journal of Economic Behavior & Organization*, 67 (3), 671–7.

29 Hackman, J. R. and Oldham, G. R. (1976), Motivation through the design of work: test of a theory. *Organizational Behavior and Human Performance*, 16 (2), 250–79.

3. EDUCATED

1 Willets, D. (2017), *A University Education*. New York: Oxford University Press, Introduction.

2 United States Census Bureau (February 2017 report). Retrieved from https://www.census.gov.

3 O'Leary, N. C. and Sloane, P. J. (2005), The return to a university education in Great Britain. *National Institute Economic Review*, 193 (1), 75–89.

4 Fisher, S. D. and Hillman, N. (2014), *Do Students Swing Elections? Registration, Turnout and Voting Behaviour among Full-Time Students*. Oxford: Higher Education Policy Institute.

5 Department for Business, Innovation and Skills (2013), The Impact of University Degrees on the Lifecycle of Earnings. Table 16, p. 54, shows a graduate premium for medicine of £429k for men and £454k for women. Retrieved from https://www.gov.uk/government/uploads/system/uploads/attachment_data/file/229498/bis-13-899-the-impact-of-university-degrees-on-the-lifecycle-of-earnings-further-analysis.pdf.

6 Oreopoulos, P. and Salvanes, K. G. (2011), Priceless: the nonpecuniary benefits of schooling. *Journal of Economic Perspectives*, 25 (1), 159–84.

7 Binder, M. and Coad, A. (2011), From Average Joe's happiness to Miserable Jane and Cheerful John: using quantile regressions to analyze the full subjective well-being distribution. *Journal of Economic Behavior & Organization*, 79 (3), 275–90.

8   Gonzalez-Mulé, E., Carter, K. M. and Mount, M. K. (2017), Are smarter people happier? Meta-analyses of the relationships between general mental ability and job and life satisfaction. *Journal of Vocational Behavior*, 99, 146–64.

9   Veenhoven, R. and Choi, Y. (2012), Does intelligence boost happiness? Smartness of all pays more than being smarter than others. *International Journal of Happiness and Development*, 1 (1), 5–27.

10 Koenen, K. C., Moffitt, T. E., Roberts, A. L., Martin, L. T., Kubzansky, L., Harrington, H., . . . and Caspi, A. (2009), Childhood IQ and adult mental disorders: a test of the cognitive reserve hypothesis. *American Journal of Psychiatry*, 166 (1), 50–57.

11 Smith, D. J., Anderson, J., Zammit, S., Meyer, T. D., Pell, J. P. and Mackay, D. (2015), Childhood IQ and risk of bipolar disorder in adulthood: prospective birth cohort study. *British Journal of Psychiatry (Open Access)*, 1 (1), 74–80.

12 MacCabe, J. H., Lambe, M. P., Cnattingius, S., Sham, P. C., David, A. S., Reichenberg, A., Murray, R. M. and Hultman, C. M. (2010), Excellent school performance at age 16 and risk of adult bipolar disorder: national cohort study. *British Journal of Psychiatry*, 196 (2), 109–15.

13 Friedman, S. (2016), Habitus clivé and the emotional imprint of social mobility. *Sociological Review*, 64 (1), 129–47.

14 Berlant, L. (2011), *Cruel Optimism*. Durham, NC: Duke University Press.

15 Akerlof, G. A. (1997), Social distance and social decisions. *Econometrica: Journal of the Econometric Society*, 65 (5), 1005–27.

16 Christie, H., Tett, L., Cree, V. E., Hounsell, J. and McCune, V. (2008), 'A real rollercoaster of confidence and emotions': learning to be a university student. *Studies in Higher Education*, 33 (5), 567–81; Aries, E. and Seider, M. (2005), The interactive relationship between class identity and the college experience: the case of lower income students. *Qualitative Sociology*, 28 (4), 419–43.

17 Johnson, S. E., Richeson, J. A. and Finkel, E. J. (2011), Middle class and marginal? Socioeconomic status, stigma, and self-regulation at an elite university. *Journal of Personality and Social Psychology*, 100 (5), 838.

18 O'Keeffe, P. (2013), A sense of belonging: improving student retention. *College Student Journal*, 47 (4), 605–13.

19 Pratto, F., Sidanius, J. and Levin, S. (2006), Social dominance theory and the dynamics of intergroup relations: taking stock and looking forward. *European Review of Social Psychology*, 17 (1), 271–320.

20 Friedman, S. (2014), The price of the ticket: rethinking the experience of social mobility. *Sociology*, 48 (2), 352–68.

21 Lehmann, W. (2014), Habitus transformation and hidden injuries: successful working-class university students. *Sociology of Education*, 87 (1), 1–15.

22 Kyndt, E., Raes, E., Lismont, B., Timmers, F., Cascallar, E. and Dochy, F. (2013), A meta-analysis of the effects of face-to-face cooperative learning. Do recent studies falsify or verify earlier findings? *Educational Research Review*, 10, 133–49.

23 Stephens, N. M., Fryberg, S. A., Markus, H. R., Johnson, C. S. and Covarrubias, R. (2012), Unseen disadvantage: how American universities' focus on independence undermines the academic performance of first-generation college students. *Journal of Personality and Social Psychology*, 102 (6), 1178.

24 Croizet, J. C. and Claire, T. (1998), Extending the concept of stereotype threat to social class: the intellectual underperformance of students from low socioeconomic backgrounds. *Personality and Social Psychology Bulletin*, 24 (6), 588–94.

25 Spencer, B. and Castano, E. (2007), Social class is dead. Long live social class! Stereotype threat among low socioeconomic status individuals. *Social Justice Research*, 20 (4), 418–32.

26 Department for Education. GCSE and equivalent attainment by pupil characteristics: 2013 to 2014 (revised 2015). Retrieved from https://www.gov.uk/government/statistics/gcse-and-equivalent-attainment-by-pupil-characteristics-2014.

27 Valero, A. and Van Reenen, J. (2016), *The Economic Impact of Universities: Evidence from across the Globe* (No. w22501). National Bureau of Economic Research.

28 Sabates, R. (2008), Educational attainment and juvenile crime: area-level evidence using three cohorts of young people. *British Journal of Criminology*, 48 (3), 395–409.

29 Vezzali, L., Gocłowska, M. A., Crisp, R. J. and Stathi, S. (2016), On the relationship between cultural diversity and creativity in education: the moderating role of communal versus divisional mindset. *Thinking Skills and Creativity*, 21, 152–7; Scacco, A. and Warren, S. S. (2016), Can Social Contact Reduce Prejudice and Discrimination? Evidence from a Field Experiment in Nigeria. Unpublished working paper.

30 Dee, T. S. (2004), Are there civic returns to education? *Journal of Public Economics*, 88 (9), 1697–720.

31 Wolf, A. (2002), *Does Education Matter? Myths about Education and Economic Growth*. London: Penguin.

32 Purcell, K., Elias, P., Atfield, G., Behle, H., Ellison, R., Luchinskaya, D., ... and Tzanakou, C. (2012), *Futuretrack Stage 4: transitions into employment, further study and other outcomes*. Warwick Institute for Employment Research, Warwick.

33 Lochner, L. (2004), Education, work, and crime: a human capital approach. *International Economic Review*, 45 (3), 811–43.

34 Pilling, D. (2018), *The Growth Delusion*. New York: Tim Duggan Books (p. 19).

35 Willets, D. (2017), *A University Education*. New York: Oxford University Press (p. 86).

36 Reay, D. (2017), *Miseducation: Inequality, Education and the Working Classes*. Bristol: Policy Press (p. 118).

37 Burger, K. (2010), How does early childhood care and education affect cognitive development? An international review of the effects of early interventions for children from different social backgrounds. *Early Childhood Research Quarterly*, 25 (2), 140–65.

38 Anderson, L. M., Shinn, C., Fullilove, M. T., Scrimshaw, S. C., Fielding, J. E., Normand, J., ... and Task Force on Community Preventive Services (2003), The effectiveness of early childhood development programs: a systematic review. *American Journal of Preventive Medicine*, 24 (3), 32–46.

39 Heckman, J. J. and Carneiro, P. (2003), Human Capital Policy. National Bureau of Economic Research Working Paper No. 9495; Heckman, J. J. and Masterov, D. V. (2007), The productivity argument for investing in young children. *Applied Economic Perspectives and Policy*, 29 (3), 446–93.

40 Nesta, The future of UK skills: employment in 2030. Retrieved from http://data-viz.nesta.org.uk/future-skills/.

41 Stahl, G. (2015), *Identity, Neoliberalism and Aspiration: Educating White Working-Class Boys*. London: Routledge.

WRAPPING UP REACHING

1 Case, A. and Deaton, A. (2017), Mortality and morbidity in the 21st century. *Brookings Papers on Economic Activity*, 397.

2 Kolbert, E. (2014), *The Sixth Extinction: An Unnatural History*. London: Bloomsbury.

4. MARRIED

1 Schwartz, B. (2004), *The Paradox of Choice: Why More is Less*. New York: Ecco.

2 Gilbert, D. T. and Ebert, J. E. (2002), Decisions and revisions: the affective forecasting of changeable outcomes. *Journal of Personality and Social Psychology*, 82 (4), 503.

3 Cacioppo, J. T., Cacioppo, S., Gonzaga, G. C., Ogburn, E. L. and Vanderweele, T. J. (2013), Marital satisfaction and break-ups differ across on-line and off-line meeting venues. *Proceedings of the National Academy of Sciences*, 110 (25), 10135–40.

4 Davison, M. L. (2014), Brave new world: the social impact of hooking up in the internet age. *Kill Your Darlings*, (17), 26.

5 Knee, C. R., Patrick, H., Vietor, N. A. and Neighbors, C. (2004), Implicit theories of relationships: moderators of the link between conflict and commitment. *Personality and Social Psychology Bulletin*, 30 (5), 617–28.

6 Finkel, E. J., Burnette, J. L. and Scissors, L. E. (2007), Vengefully ever after: destiny beliefs, state attachment anxiety, and forgiveness. *Journal of Personality and Social Psychology*, 92(5), 871–86.

7 Aron, A., Fisher, H., Mashek, D. J., Strong, G., Li, H. and Brown, L. L. (2005), Reward, motivation, and emotion systems associated with early-stage intense romantic love. *Journal of Neurophysiology*, 94 (1), 327–37.

8 Younger, J., Aron, A., Parke, S., Chatterjee, N. and Mackey, S. (2010), Viewing pictures of a romantic partner reduces experimental pain: involvement of neural reward systems. *PLoS One*, 5(10), e13309.

9 Fisher, H., Xu, X., Aron, A. and Brown, L. (2016), Intense, passionate, romantic love: a natural addiction? How the fields that investigate romance and substance abuse can inform each other. *Frontiers in Psychology*, 7.

10 Brand, S., Luethi, M., von Planta, A., Hatzinger, M. and Holsboer-Trachsler, E. (2007), Romantic love, hypomania, and sleep pattern in adolescents. *Journal of Adolescent Health*, 41 (1), 69–76.

11 Marazziti, D. and Canale, D. (2004), Hormonal changes when falling in love. *Psychoneuroendocrinology*, 29 (7), 931–6.

12 Song, H., Zou, Z., Kou, J., Liu, Y., Yang, L., Zilverstand, A., . . . and Zhang, X. (2015), Love-related changes in the brain: a resting-state functional magnetic resonance imaging study. *Frontiers in Human Neuroscience*, 9.

13 Reis, H. T. and Aron, A. (2008), Love: what is it, why does it matter, and how does it operate? *Perspectives on Psychological Science*, 3, 80–86.

14 Mansson, D. H. and Myers, S. A. (2011), An initial examination of college students' expressions of affection through Facebook. *Southern Communication Journal*, 76 (2), 155–68.

15 Marshall, T. C., Lefringhausen, K. and Ferenczi, N. (2015), The Big Five, self-esteem, and narcissism as predictors of the topics people write about in Facebook status updates. *Personality and Individual Differences*, 85, 35–40.

16 Academia. Murder, Gender and the Media. Narratives of Dangerous Love. Retrieved from https://www.academia.edu/218932/Murder_Gender_and_the_Media._Narratives_of_Dangerous_Love.

17 Francis-Tan, A. and Mialon, H. M. (2015), 'A diamond is forever' and other fairy tales: the relationship between wedding expenses and marriage duration. *Economic Inquiry*, 53 (4), 1919–30.

18 Clark, A. E., Diener, E., Georgellis, Y. and Lucas, R. E. (2008), Lags and leads in life satisfaction: a test of the baseline hypothesis. *Economic Journal*, 118 (529).

19 Stutzer, A. and Frey, B. S. (2006), Does marriage make people happy, or do happy people get married? *Journal of Socio-Economics*, 35 (2), 326–47.

20 Kaplan, R. M. and Kronick, R. G. (2006), Marital status and longevity in the United States population. *Journal of Epidemiology & Community Health*, 60 (9), 760–65; Painter, M., Frech, A. and Williams, K. (2015), Nonmarital fertility, union history, and women's wealth. *Demography*, 52 (1), 153–82.

21 Thoits, P. A. (1992), Identity structures and psychological well-being: gender and marital status comparisons. *Social Psychology Quarterly*, 55 (3), 236–56.

22 Wanic, R. and Kulik, J. (2011), Toward an understanding of gender differences in the impact of marital conflict on health. *Sex Roles*, 65 (5–6), 297–312.

23 Troxel, W. M., Robles, T. F., Hall, M. and Buysse, D. J. (2007), Marital quality and the marital bed: examining the covariation between relationship quality and sleep. *Sleep Medicine Reviews*, 11 (5), 389–404.

24 Troxel, W. M. (2010), It's more than sex: exploring the dyadic nature of sleep and implications for health. *Psychosomatic Medicine*, 72 (6), 578.

25 Office for National Statistics. Retrieved from https://www.ons.gov.uk/peoplepopulationandcommunity/birthsdeathsandmarriages/divorce.

26 Eastwick, P. W., Finkel, E. J., Krishnamurti, T. and Loewenstein, G. (2008), Mispredicting distress following romantic breakup: revealing the time course of the affective forecasting error. *Journal of Experimental Social Psychology*, 44 (3), 800–807.

27 Spielmann, S. S., MacDonald, G., Maxwell, J. A., Joel, S., Peragine, D., Muise, A. and Impett, E. A. (2013), Settling for less out of fear of being single. *Journal of Personality and Social Psychology*, 105 (6), 1049.

28 National Center for Health Statistics. Retrieved from https://www.cdc.gov/nchs/.

29 Rosenfeld, M. J. (2017), Who wants the Breakup? Gender and Breakup in Heterosexual Couples. Draft paper.

30 Kposowa, A. J. (2003), Divorce and suicide risk. *Journal of Epidemiology & Community Health*, 57 (12), 993–5.

31 Ross, C. E. and Mirowsky, J. (2013), The sense of personal control: social structural causes and emotional consequences. In C. S. Aneshensel, J. C. Phelan and A. Bierman, eds., *Handbooks of Sociology and Social Research. Handbook of the Sociology of Mental Health*. New York: Springer Science & Business Media, 379–402.

32 Hetherington, E. M. and Stanley-Hagan, M. (2002), Parenting in divorced and remarried families. In M. H. Bornstein, ed., *Handbook of Parenting: Being and Becoming a Parent*. Mahwah, NJ: Lawrence Erlbaum Associates, 287–315.

33 Amato, P. R. (2003), Reconciling divergent perspectives: Judith Wallerstein, quantitative family research, and children of divorce. *Family Relations*, 52 (4), 332–9.

34 Hetherington, E. M. and Kelly, J. (2002), *For Better or For Worse: Divorce Reconsidered*. New York: W. W. Norton & Company.

35 Emery, R. E. and Coiro, M. J. (1995), Divorce: consequences for children. *Pediatrics in Review*, 16, 306–10; Brock, R. and Kochanska, G. (2015), Interparental conflict, children's security with parents, and long-term risk of internalizing problems: a longitudinal study from ages 2 to 10. *Development and Psychopathology*, 28 (1), 45–54.

36 Slonim, G., Gur-Yaish, N. and Katz, R. (2015), By choice or by circumstance? Stereotypes of and feelings about single people. *Studia Psychologica*, 57 (1), 35.

37 DePaulo, B. and Morris, W. (2005), Singles in society and in science. *Psychological Inquiry*, 16 (2), 57–83.

38 Lau, G. P., Kay, A. C. and Spencer, S. J. (2008), Loving those who justify inequality: the effects of system threat on attraction to women who embody benevolent sexist ideals. *Psychological Science*, 19 (1), 20–21.

39 Day, M., Kay, A., Holmes, J. and Napier, J. (2011), System justification and the defense of committed relationship ideology. *Journal of Personality and Social Psychology*, 101 (2), 291–306.

40 Cross, S. E., Bacon, P. L. and Morris, M. L. (2000), The relational-interdependent self-construal and relationships. *Journal of Personality and Social Psychology*, 78, 791–808.

41 Surra, C. A. (1985), Courtship types: variations in interdependence between partners and social networks. *Journal of Personality and Social Psychology*, 49 (2), 357.

42 Bureau of Labor Statistics (2015). Table 4. Volunteers by type of main organization for which volunteer activities were performed and selected characteristics. Retrieved from https://www.bls.gov/news.release/volun.t04.htm.

43 DePaulo, B. and Morris, W. (2005), Singles in society and in science. *Psychological Inquiry*, 16 (2), 57–83.

44 A Rosenfeld longitudinal study cited in the *Washington Post*, 18 March 2016. Retrieved from https://www.washingtonpost.com/news/wonk/wp/2016/03/18/how-the-likelihood-of-breaking-up-changes-as-time-goes-by/?utm_term=.cc251af459d1.

45 Perel, E. (2006), *Mating in Captivity*. New York: HarperCollins.

46 Chambers, C. (2013), The marriage-free state. *Proceedings of the Aristotelian Society*, 113 (2), pt. 2, 123–43.

5. MONOGAMOUS

1 British Social Attitudes, Moral Issues: Sex, Gender and Identity. Retrieved from http://www.bsa.natcen.ac.uk/media/39147/bsa34_moral_issues_final.pdf; Norc (2013), Trends in Public Attitudes about Sexuality and Morality. Retrieved from http://www.norc.org/PDFs/sexmoralfinal_06-21_FINAL.PDF.

2 The National Survey of Sexual Attitudes and Lifestyles (2013). Retrieved from http://www.natsal.ac.uk/home.aspx.

3 The Pew Research Center (2014), French more accepting of infidelity than people in other countries. Retrieved from http://www.pewresearch.org/fact-tank/2014/01/14/french-more-accepting-of-infidelity-than-people-in-other-countries/.

4 Maykovich, M. K. (1976), Attitudes versus behavior in extramarital sexual relations. *Journal of Marriage and Family*, 38, 693–9.

5 Stephens-Davidowitz, S. (2017), *Everybody Lies*. London: Bloomsbury.

6　University of Michigan (2006), Lovers and Liars: How Many Sex Partners Have You Really Had? Retrieved from http://www.ur.umich.edu/0506/Feb20_06/04.shtml.

7　Alexander, M. and Fisher, T. (2003), Truth and consequences: using the bogus pipeline to examine sex differences in self-reported sexuality. *Journal of Sex Research*, 40 (1), 27–35.

8　Muise, A., Schimmack, U. and Impett, E. A. (2016), Sexual frequency predicts greater well-being, but more is not always better. *Social Psychological and Personality Science*, 7 (4), 295–302.

9　Hicks, L. L., McNulty, J. K., Meltzer, A. L. and Olson, M. A. (2016), Capturing the interpersonal implications of evolved preferences? Frequency of sex shapes automatic, but not explicit, partner evaluations. *Psychological Science*, 27 (6), 836–47.

10　Graham, C. A., Mercer, C. H., Tanton, C., Jones, K. G., Johnson, A. M., Wellings, K. and Mitchell, K. R. (2017), What factors are associated with reporting lacking interest in sex and how do these vary by gender? Findings from the third British national survey of sexual attitudes and lifestyles. *British Medical Journal*, 7 (9), e016942.

11　Loewenstein, G., Krishnamurti, T., Kopsic, J. and McDonald, D. (2015), Does increased sexual frequency enhance happiness? *Journal of Economic Behavior & Organization*, 116, 206–18.

12　Fan, C. (2014), *Vanity Economics*. Cheltenham: Edward Elgar Publishing Limited.

13　Kleiman, D. G. (1977), Monogamy in mammals. *Quarterly Review of Biology*, 52 (1), 39–69.

14　Bloomberg (2010), More US women report cheating on their spouse. Retrieved from https://www.bloomberg.com/graphics/infographics/more-us-women-report-cheating-on-their-spouse.html.

15　Lippa, R. A. (2009), Sex differences in sex drive, sociosexuality, and height across 53 nations: testing evolutionary and social structural theories. *Archives of Sexual Behavior*, 38 (5), 631–51.

16　Armstrong, E. A., Hamilton, L. T., Armstrong, E. M. and Seeley, J. L. (2014), 'Good girls': gender, social class, and slut discourse on campus. *Social Psychology Quarterly*, 77 (2), 100–122.

17　Wlodarski, R., Manning, J. and Dunbar, R. I. M. (2015), Stay or stray? Evidence for alternative mating strategy phenotypes in both men and women. *Biology Letters*, 11 (2), 20140977.

18　National Survey of Sexual Attitudes and Lifestyles (2000–2001). Retrieved from https://discover.ukdataservice.ac.uk/catalogue/?sn=5223.

19 Henrich, J., Boyd, R. and Richerson, P. J. (2012), The puzzle of monogamous marriage. *Philosophical Transactions of the Royal Society B*, 367 (1589), 657–69.

20 Costa, M., Braun, C. and Birbaumer, N. (2003), Gender differences in response to pictures of nudes: a magnetoencephalographic study. *Biological Psychology*, 63 (2), 129–47.

21 Chivers, M. L., Rieger, G., Latty, E. and Bailey, J. M. (2004), A sex difference in the specificity of sexual arousal. *Psychological Science*, 15 (11), 736–44.

22 Omarzu, J., Miller, A. N., Schultz, C. and Timmerman, A. (2012), Motivations and emotional consequences related to engaging in extramarital relationships. *International Journal of Sexual Health*, 24 (2), 154–62.

23 Blow, A. and Hartnett, K. (2005), Infidelity in committed relationships II: a substantive review. *Journal of Marital and Family Therapy*, 31(2), 217–33.

24 Banfield, S. and McCabe, M. P. (2001), Extra relationship involvement among women: are they different from men? *Archives of Sexual Behavior*, 30 (2), 119–42.

25 Cross, C. P., Cyrenne, D. L. M. and Brown, G. R. (2013), Sex differences in sensation-seeking: a meta-analysis. *Scientific Reports*, 3, 2486.

26 Rosenfeld, M. J. (2017), Who wants the Breakup? Gender and Breakup in Heterosexual Couples. Draft paper.

27 Forste, R. and Tanfer, K. (1996), Sexual exclusivity among dating, cohabiting, and married women. *Journal of Marriage and Family*, 58, 33–47.

28 Tsapelas, I., Fisher, H. E. and Aron, A. (2011), Infidelity: when, where, why. In W. R. Cupach and B. H. Spitzberg, eds., *The Dark Side of Close Relationships II*. New York: Routledge, 175–96.

29 Blow, A. and Hartnett, K. (2005), Infidelity in committed relationships II: a substantive review. *Journal of Marital and Family Therapy*, 31 (2), 217–33.

30 Munsch, C. L. (2015), Her support, his support: money, masculinity, and marital infidelity. *American Sociological Review*, 80 (3), 469–95.

31 Lammers, J., Stoker, J. I., Jordan, J., Pollmann, M. and Stapel, D. A. (2011), Power increases infidelity among men and women. *Psychological Science*, 22 (9), 1191–7.

32 Lammers, J. and Maner, J. (2016), Power and attraction to the counternormative aspects of infidelity. *Journal of Sex Research*, 53 (1), 54–63.

33 Blackwell, D. (2014), Digital Disruption: An Exploratory Study of Trust, Infidelity, and Relational Transgressions in the Digital Age.

Ph.D. Thesis, University of Pennsylvania. https://repository.upenn. edu/dissertations/AAI3635471.

34 Charny, I. W. and Parnass, S. (1995), The impact of extramarital relationships on the continuation of marriages. *Journal of Sex and Marital Therapy*, 21, 100–115.

35 Blow, A. and Hartnett, K. (2005), Infidelity in committed relationships II: a substantive review. *Journal of Marital and Family Therapy*, 31 (2), 217–33.

36 Amato, P, R. and Rogers, S. J. (1997), A longitudinal study of marital problems and subsequent divorce. *Journal of Marriage and Family*, 59 (3), 612–24; Grant Thornton (2016), Matrimonial Survey. Retrieved from http://www.grantthornton.co.uk/globalassets/1.-member-firms/united-kingdom/pdf/publication/2016/matrimonial-survey-2016.pdf.

37 Buunk, B. (1987), Conditions that promote breakups as a consequence of extradyadic involvements. *Journal of Social and Clinical Psychology*, 5, 271–84.

38 Schneider, J. P., Irons, R. R. and Corley, M. D. (1999), Disclosure of extramarital sexual activities by sexually exploitative professionals and other persons with addictive or compulsive sexual disorders. *Journal of Sex Education and Therapy*, 24, 277–87.

39 Foster, J. D. and Misra, T. A. (2013), It did not mean anything (about me). Cognitive dissonance theory and the cognitive and affective consequences of romantic infidelity. *Journal of Social and Personal Relationships*, 30 (7), 835–57.

40 DePaulo, B. M., Kashy, D. A., Kirkendol, S. E., Wyer, M. M. and Epstein, J. A. (1996), Lying in everyday life. *Journal of Personality and Social-Psychology*, 70 (5), 979.

41 Van't Veer, A., Stel, M. and van Beest, I. (2014), Limited capacity to lie: cognitive load interferes with being dishonest. *Judgment and Decision Making*, 9 (3), 199–206.

42 Rubin, J. D., Moors, A. C., Matsick, J. L., Ziegler, A. and Conley, T. D. (2014), On the margins: considering diversity among consensually non-monogamous relationships. *Journal für Psychologie*, 22 (1), 1–23.

43 Moors, A. C., Conley, T. D., Edelstein, R. S. and Chopik, W. J. (2015), Attached to monogamy? Avoidance predicts willingness to engage (but not actual engagement) in consensual non-monogamy. *Journal of Social and Personal Relationships*, 32 (2), 222–40.

44 Conley, T. D., Moors, A. C., Matsick, J. L. and Ziegler, A. (2013), The fewer the merrier? Assessing stigma surrounding consensually non-monogamous romantic relationships. *Analyses of Social Issues and Public Policy*, 13, 1–30.

45 Moors, A. C., Matsick, J. L. and Schechinger, H. A. (2017), Unique and shared relationship benefits of consensually non-monogamous and monogamous relationships. *European Psychologist*, 22 (1), 55–71.

46 Grunt-Mejer, K. and Campbell, C. (2016), Around consensual nonmonogamies: assessing attitudes toward nonexclusive relationships. *Journal of Sex Research*, 53, 45–53.

47 Sheff, E. (2010), Strategies in polyamorous parenting. In M. Barker and D. Langdridge, eds., *Understanding Non-Monogamies*. London: Routledge, 169–81.

48 Topping, K., Dekhinet, R. and Zeedyk, S. (2013), Parent–infant interaction and children's language development. *Educational Psychology*, 33 (4), 391–426.

49 Conley, T. D., Ziegler, A., Moors, A. C., Matsick, J. L. and Valentine, B. (2013), A critical examination of popular assumptions about the benefits and outcomes of monogamous relationships. *Personality and Social Psychology Review*, 17, 124–41.

50 Conley, T. D., Moors, A. C., Matsick, J. L. and Ziegler, A. (2013), The fewer the merrier? Assessing stigma surrounding consensually non-monogamous romantic relationships. *Analyses of Social Issues and Public Policy*, 13 (1), 1–30.

51 Moors, A. C., Selterman, D. and Conley, T. D. (2016), Personality correlates of attitudes and desire to engage in consensual non-monogamy among sexual minorities. Unpublished paper.

6. CHILDREN

1 The Parent Zone (2015), *Parenting in the Digital Age: How are We Doing?* Retrieved from https://parentzone.org.uk/trending/research-reports.

2 Vicedo Castello, M. (2005), *The Maternal Instinct*. Cambridge, Mass.: Harvard University Press.

3 Taket, A., Crisp, B. R., Nevill, A., Lamaro, G., Graham, M. and Barter-Godfrey, S., eds., (2009), *Theorising Social Exclusion*. London: Routledge, 187–92.

4 Chancey, L. and Dumais, S. A. (2009), Voluntary childlessness in marriage and family textbooks, 1950–2000. *Journal of Family History*, 34 (2), 206–23.

5 Shapiro, G. (2014), Voluntary childlessness: a critical review of the literature. *Studies in the Maternal*, 6 (1), 1–15.

6 Rich, S., Taket, A., Graham, M. and Shelley, J. (2011), 'Unnatural', 'unwomanly', 'uncreditable' and 'undervalued': the significance of being a childless woman in Australian society. *Gender Issues*, 28 (4), 226–47.

7 Gallup News (2013), Desire for Children Still Norm in US. Retrieved from http://news.gallup.com/poll/164618/desire-children-norm.aspx.

8 Taket, A., Crisp, B. R., Nevill, A., Lamaro, G., Graham, M. and Barter-Godfrey, S., eds., (2009), *Theorising Social Exclusion*. London: Routledge, 187–92.

9 Dolan, P. and Rudisill, C. (2015), Babies in waiting: why increasing the IVF age cut-off might lead to fewer wanted pregnancies in the presence of procrastination. *Health Policy*, 119 (2), 174–9.

10 Arpino, B., Balbo, N. and Bordone, V. (2016), Life satisfaction of older Europeans: the role of grandchildren. Retrieved from http://docplayer.net/53786442-Life-satisfaction-of-older-europeans-the-role-of-grand-children.html.

11 Blackstone, A. and Stewart, M. D. (2016), 'There's more thinking to decide': how the childfree decide not to parent. *Family Journal*, 24 (3), 296–303.

12 Adloff, F. (2009), What encourages charitable giving and philanthropy? *Ageing and Society*, 29 (8), 1185–205.

13 Survey of Health, Ageing and Retirement in Europe. Retrieved from http://www.share-project.org.

14 Chi Kuan Mak, M., Bond, M. H., Simpson, J. A. and Rholes, W. S. (2010), Adult attachment, perceived support, and depressive symptoms in Chinese and American cultures. *Journal of Social and Clinical Psychology*, 29 (2), 144–65.

15 Blackstone, A. and Stewart, M. D. (2016), 'There's more thinking to decide': how the childfree decide not to parent. *Family Journal*, 24 (3), 296–303.

16 Herbst, C. M. and Ifcher, J. (2016), The increasing happiness of US parents. *Review of Economics of the Household*, 14 (3), 529–51.

17 Nomaguchi, K. and Milkie, M. (2003), Costs and rewards of children: the effects of becoming a parent on adults' lives. *Journal of Marriage and Family*, 65, 356–74.

18 Murtaugh, P. A. and Schlax, M. G. (2009), Reproduction and the carbon legacies of individuals. *Global Environmental Change*, 19 (1), 14–20.

19 Hansen, T. (2012), Parenthood and happiness: a review of folk theories versus empirical evidence. *Social Indicators Research*, 108, 26–64.

20 Pollmann-Schult, M. (2014), Parenthood and life satisfaction: why don't children make people happy? *Journal of Marriage and Family*, 76 (2), 319–36.

21 Myrskylä, M. and Margolis, R. (2014), Happiness: before and after the kids. *Demography*, 51 (5), 1843–66.

22 Margolis, R. and Myrskylä, M. (2018), A global perspective on happiness and fertility. *Population and Development Review* (in press).

23 Hamoudi, A. and Nobles, J. (2014), Do daughters really cause divorce? Stress, pregnancy, and family composition. *Demography*, 51 (4), 1423–49.

24 Kabatek, J. and Ribar, D. (2017), Teenage daughters as a cause of divorce. *SSRN Electronic Journal*.

25 Mind. Postnatal depression and prenatal mental health. Retrieved from https://mind.org.uk/information-support/types-of-mental-health-problems/postnatal-depression-and-perinatal-mental-health/.

26 Herbst, C. and Ifcher, J. (2015), The increasing happiness of US parents. *Review of Economics of the Household*, 14 (3), 529–51.

27 van Scheppingen, M. A., Denissen, J., Chung, J., Tambs, K. and Bleidorn, W. (2017), Self-esteem and relationship satisfaction during the transition to motherhood. Unpublished paper.

28 Gorchoff, S. M., John, O. P. and Helson, R. (2008), Contextualizing change in marital satisfaction during middle age. *Psychological Science*, 19, 1194–200.

29 Bouchard, G. (2013), How do parents react when their children leave home? An integrative review. *Journal of Adult Development*, 21 (2), 69–79.

30 Kahneman, D., Krueger, A. B., Schkade, D. A., Schwarz, N. and Stone, A. A. (2004), A survey method for characterizing daily life experience: the day reconstruction method. *Science*, 306 (5702), 1776–80.

31 White, M. P. and Dolan, P. (2009), Accounting for the richness of daily activities. *Psychological Science*, 20 (8), 1000–1008.

32 Fingerman, K. L., Cheng, Y. P., Birditt, K. and Zarit, S. (2011), Only as happy as the least happy child: multiple grown children's problems and successes and middle-aged parents' well-being. *Journals of Gerontology Series B: Psychological Sciences and Social Sciences*, 67 (2), 184–93.

33 Pillemer, K., Suitor, J. J., Riffin, C. and Gilligan, M. (2017), Adult children's problems and mothers' well-being: does parental favoritism matter? *Research on Aging*, 39 (3), 375–95.

34 Fingerman, K. L., Cheng, Y. P., Birditt, K. and Zarit, S. (2011), Only as happy as the least happy child: multiple grown children's problems and successes and middle-aged parents' well-being. *Journals of Gerontology Series B: Psychological Sciences and Social Sciences*, 67 (2), 184–93.

35 Howard, K., Martin, A., Berlin, L. J. and Brooks-Gunn, J. (2011), Early mother–child separation, parenting, and child well-being in

Early Head Start families. *Attachment & Human Development*, 13 (1), 5–26.

36 Sarkadi, A., Kristiansson, R., Oberklaid, F. and Bremberg, S. (2008), Fathers' involvement and children's developmental outcomes: a systematic review of longitudinal studies. *Acta Paediatrica*, 97 (2), 153–8; Flouri, E. and Buchanan, A. (2003), The role of father involvement in children's later mental health. *Journal of Adolescence*, 26 (1), 63–78.

37 Delatycki, M. B., Jones, C. A., Little, M. H., Patton, G. C., Sawyer, S. M., Skinner, S. R., . . . and Oberklaid, F. (2017), The kids are OK: it is discrimination, not same-sex parents, that harms children. *Medical Journal of Australia*, 207 (9), 1.

38 Topping, K., Dekhinet, R. and Zeedyk, S. (2013), Parent–infant interaction and children's language development. *Educational Psychology*, 33 (4), 391–426.

39 De Bellis, M. D. and Zisk, A. (2014), The biological effects of childhood trauma. *Child and Adolescent Psychiatric Clinics of North America*, 23 (2), 185–222.

40 Berglund, K. J., Balldin, J., Berggren, U., Gerdner, A. and Fahlke, C. (2013), Childhood maltreatment affects the serotonergic system in male alcohol-dependent individuals. *Alcoholism: Clinical and Experimental Research*, 37 (5), 757–62.

41 Bravo, J. A., Dinan, T. G. and Cryan, J. F. (2014), Early-life stress induces persistent alterations in 5-HT1A receptor and serotonin transporter mRNA expression in the adult rat brain. *Frontiers in Molecular Neuroscience*, 7, 24; Matsunaga, M., Ishii, K., Ohtsubo, Y., Noguchi, Y., Ochi, M. and Yamasue, H. (2017), Association between salivary serotonin and the social sharing of happiness. *PLoS One*, 12 (7), e0180391.

42 Bowlby, J. and Ainsworth, M., The origins of attachment theory. In S. Goldberg, R. Muir and J. Kerr, eds. (2000), *Attachment Theory: Social, Developmental, and Clinical Perspectives*. New York: Routledge, 45ff.

43 Hazan, C. and Shaver, P. (1987), Romantic love conceptualized as an attachment process. *Journal of Personality and Social Psychology*, 52 (3), 511.

44 Sheinbaum, T., Kwapil, T. R., Ballespí, S., Mitjavila, M., Chun, C. A., Silvia, P. J. and Barrantes-Vidal, N. (2015), Attachment style predicts affect, cognitive appraisals, and social functioning in daily life. *Frontiers in Psychology*, 6, 296.

45 Moriceau, S., Wilson, D. A., Levine, S. and Sullivan, R. M. (2006), Corticosterone serves as a switch between love and hate in infancy:

dual circuitry for odor-shock conditioning during development. *Journal of Neuroscience*, 26, 6737–48.

WRAPPING UP RELATED

1 Gilbert, D. (2009), *Stumbling on Happiness*. Toronto: Vintage Canada.

7. ALTRUISTIC

1 Farrelly, D., Clemson, P. and Guthrie, M. (2016), Are women's mate preferences for altruism also influenced by physical attractiveness? *Evolutionary Psychology*, 14 (1), doi. 10.1177/1474704915623698.

2 Raihani, N. J. and Smith, S. (2015), Competitive helping in online giving. *Current Biology*, 25 (9), 1183–6.

3 Arnocky, S., Piché, T., Albert, G., Ouellette, D. and Barclay, P. (2017), Altruism predicts mating success in humans. *British Journal of Psychology*, 108 (2), 416–35.

4 Rand, D. G., Brescoll, V. L., Everett, J. A., Capraro, V. and Barcelo, H. (2016), Social heuristics and social roles: intuition favors altruism for women but not for men. *Journal of Experimental Psychology: General*, 145 (4), 389.

5 Kataria, M. and Regner, T. (2015), Honestly, why are you donating money to charity? An experimental study about self-awareness in status-seeking behavior. *Theory and Decision*, 79 (3), 493–515.

6 Samek, A. and Sheremeta, R. M. (2017), Selective recognition: how to recognize donors to increase charitable giving. *Economic Inquiry*, 55 (3), 1489–96.

7 Sezer, O., Gino, F. and Norton, M. I. (2018), Humblebragging: a distinct – and ineffective – self-presentation strategy. *Journal of Personality and Social Psychology*, 114 (1), 52.

8 Gordon College (2006), Who Really Cares: The Surprising Truth about Compassionate Conservatism – America's Charity Divide – Who Gives, Who Doesn't, and Why it Matters. Retrieved from https://www.gordon.edu/ace/pdf/Spro7BRGrinols.pdf.

9 Meier, S. and Stutzer, A. (2008), Is volunteering rewarding in itself? *Economica*, 75 (297), 39–59; Thoits, P. A. and Hewitt, L. N. (2001), Volunteer work and well-being. *Journal of Health and Social Behavior*, 115–31.

10 Andreoni, J. (1990), Impure altruism and donations to public goods: a theory of warm-glow giving. *Economic Journal*, 100 (401), 464–77.

11 Dunn, E. W., Aknin, L. B. and Norton, M. I. (2008), Spending money on others promotes happiness. *Science*, 319 (5870), 1687–8.

12 Harbaugh, W. T., Mayr, U. and Burghart, D. R. (2007), Neural responses to taxation and voluntary giving reveal motives for charitable donations. *Science*, 316 (5831), 1622–5; Moll, J., Oliveira-Souza, D. and Zahn, R. (2008), The neural basis of moral cognition. *Annals of the New York Academy of Sciences*, 1124 (1), 161–80.

13 Taufik, D., Bolderdijk, J. W. and Steg, L. (2015), Acting green elicits a literal warm glow. *Nature Climate Change*, 5 (1), 37.

14 Aknin, L. B., Dunn, E. W. and Norton, M. I. (2012), Happiness runs in a circular motion: evidence for a positive feedback loop between prosocial spending and happiness. *Journal of Happiness Studies*, 13 (2), 347–55.

15 Omoto, A. M. and Snyder, M. (1995), Sustained helping without obligation: motivation, longevity of service, and perceived attitude change among AIDS volunteers. *Journal of Personality and Social Psychology*, 68 (4), 671.

16 Ashraf, N., Bandiera, O. and Lee, S. S. (2014), Do-gooders and go-getters: career incentives, selection, and performance in public service delivery. *STICERD-Economic Organisation and Public Policy Discussion Papers Series*, 27, 54.

17 Effron, D. A., Cameron, J. S. and Monin, B. (2009), Endorsing Obama licenses favoring whites. *Journal of Experimental Social Psychology*, 45 (3), 590–93.

18 Mazar, N. and Zhong, C. B. (2010), Do green products make us better people? *Psychological Science*, 21 (4), 494–8.

19 Cascio, J. and Plant, E. A. (2015), Prospective moral licensing: does anticipating doing good later allow you to be bad now? *Journal of Experimental Social Psychology*, 56, 110–16.

20 Gordon College (2006), Who Really Cares: The Surprising Truth about Compassionate Conservatism – America's Charity Divide – Who Gives, Who Doesn't, and Why it Matters. Retrieved from https://www.gordon.edu/ace/pdf/Spr07BRGrinols.pdf.

21 Decety, J., Cowell, J. M., Lee, K., Mahasneh, R., Malcolm-Smith, S., Selcuk, B. and Zhou, X. (2015), The negative association between religiousness and children's altruism across the world. *Current Biology*, 25 (22), 2951–5.

22 Post, S. G. (2014), Six sources of altruism: springs of morality and solidarity. In V. Jeffries, ed., *The Palgrave Handbook of Altruism, Morality,
and Social Solidarity.* New York: Palgrave Macmillan, 179–93.

23 Bloom, P. (2016), *Against Empathy.* London: The Bodley Head.

24 Jenni, K. and Loewenstein, G. (1997), Explaining the identifiable victim effect. *Journal of Risk and Uncertainty,* 14 (3), 235–57.

25 Small, D. A. and Loewenstein, G. (2003), Helping a victim or helping the victim: altruism and identifiability. *Journal of Risk and Uncertainty,* 26 (1), 5–16.

26 Batson, C. D., Chang, J., Orr, R. and Rowland, J. (2002), Empathy,
attitudes, and action: can feeling for a member of a stigmatized group
motivate one to help the group? *Personality and Social Psychology
Bulletin,* 28 (12), 1656–66.

27 Batson, C. D., Klein, T. R., Highberger, L. and Shaw, L. L. (1995), Im-
morality from empathy-induced altruism: when compassion and justice
conflict. *Journal of Personality and Social Psychology,* 68 (6), 1042.

28 Singer, T. and Klimecki, O. M. (2014), Empathy and compassion. *Current Biology,* 24 (18), R875–R878.

29 Arikha, N. (2015), The most good you can do: how effective altruism
is changing ideas about living ethically. *Jewish Quarterly,* 62 (2), 85.

30 Karlan, D. and Wood, D. H. (2017), The effect of effectiveness: donor
response to aid effectiveness in a direct mail fundraising experiment.
Journal of Behavioral and Experimental Economics, 66, 1–8.

8. HEALTHY

1 Hogan, C., Lunney, J., Gabel, J. and Lynn, J. (2001), Medicare beneficiaries' costs of care in the last year of life. *Health Affairs,* 20 (4),
188–95; Becker, G., Murphy, K. and Philipson, T. (2007), The Value of
Life Near its End and Terminal Care. National Bureau of Economic
Research, Working Paper. No. 13333.

2 Steinbrook, R. (2006), Imposing personal responsibility for health.
New England Journal of Medicine, 355 (8), 753–6.

3 Crawford, R. (1980), Healthism and the medicalization of everyday
life. *International Journal of Health Services,* 10 (3), 365–88.

4 Dolan, P., Cookson, R. and Ferguson, B. (1999), Effect of discussion
and deliberation on the public's views of priority setting in health care:
focus group study. *British Medical Journal,* 318 (7188), 916–19.

5 Reidpath, D. D., Burns, C., Garrard, J., Mahoney, M. and Townsend,
M. (2002), An ecological study of the relationship between social and

environmental determinants of obesity. *Health & Place*, 8 (2), 141–5; Loos, R. J. (2012), Genetic determinants of common obesity and their value in prediction. *Best Practice & Research: Clinical Endocrinology & Metabolism*, 26 (2), 211–26.

6 Borrell, L. N. and Samuel, L. (2014), Body mass index categories and mortality risk in US adults: the effect of overweight and obesity on advancing death. *American Journal of Public Health*, 104 (3), 512–19.

7 Nuttall, F. Q. (2015), Body mass index: obesity, BMI, and health: a critical review. *Nutrition Today*, 50 (3), 117.

8 Bradford, W. D. and Dolan, P. (2010), Getting used to it: the adaptive global utility model. *Journal of Health Economics*, 29 (6), 811–20.

9 Wadsworth, T. and Pendergast, P. M. (2014), Obesity (sometimes) matters: the importance of context in the relationship between obesity and life satisfaction. *Journal of Health and Social Behavior*, 55 (2), 196–214.

10 Jackson, S. E., Beeken, R. J. and Wardle, J. (2015), Obesity, perceived weight discrimination, and psychological well-being in older adults in England. *Obesity*, 23 (5), 1105–11.

11 Cawley, J. (2004), The impact of obesity on wages. *Journal of Human Resources*, 39 (2), 451–74.

12 Finkelstein, E. A., daCosta DiBonaventura, M., Burgess, S. M. and Hale, B. C. (2010), The costs of obesity in the workplace. *Journal of Occupational and Environmental Medicine*, 52 (10), 971–6; Gates, D. M., Succop, P., Brehm, B. J., Gillespie, G. L. and Sommers, B. D. (2008), Obesity and presenteeism: the impact of body mass index on workplace productivity. *Journal of Occupational and Environmental Medicine*, 50 (1), 39–45.

13 Rooth, D. O. (2009), Obesity, attractiveness, and differential treatment in hiring: a field experiment. *Journal of Human Resources*, 44 (3), 710–35.

14 IEA Discussion Paper (2017), Obesity and the Public Purse: Weighing Up the True Cost to the Taxpayer. Retrieved from https://iea.org.uk/wp-content/uploads/2017/01/Obesity-and-the-Public-Purse-PDF.pdf.

15 Medical News Daily (2013), Smokers Die Ten Years Sooner than Non-smokers. Retrieved from https://www.medicalnewstoday.com/articles/261091.php.

16 Pampel, F. C., Denney, J. T. and Krueger, P. M. (2012), Obesity, SES, and economic development: a test of the reversal hypothesis. *Social Science & Medicine*, 74 (7), 1073–81.

17 Slevin, M. L., Stubbs, L., Plant, H. J., Wilson, P., Gregory, W. M., Armes, P. J. and Downer, S. M. (1990), Attitudes to chemotherapy:

comparing views of patients with cancer with those of doctors, nurses, and general public. *British Medical Journal*, 300 (6737), 1458–60.

18 Snyder, C. R. (2002), Hope theory: rainbows in the mind. *Psychological Inquiry*, 13 (4), 249–75.

19 Griggs, S. and Walker, R. K. (2016), The role of hope for adolescents with a chronic illness: an integrative review. *Journal of Pediatric Nursing*, 31 (4), 404–21.

20 MacArtney, J. I., Broom, A., Kirby, E., Good, P., Wootton, J., Yates, P. M. and Adams, J. (2015), On resilience and acceptance in the transition to palliative care at the end of life. *Health*, 19 (3), 263–79.

21 Wiggins, S., Whyte, P., Huggins, M., Adam, S., Theilmann, J., Bloch, M., . . . and Canadian Collaborative Study of Predictive Testing (1992), The psychological consequences of predictive testing for Huntington's disease. *New England Journal of Medicine*, 327 (20), 1401–5.

22 O'Connor, A. M. (1989), Effects of framing and level of probability on patients' preferences for cancer chemotherapy. *Journal of Clinical Epidemiology*, 42 (2), 119–26.

23 Hellman, C. M., Worley, J. A. and Munoz, R. T. (2018), Hope as a coping resource for caregiver resilience and well-being. In W. A. Bailey and A. W. Harrist, eds., *Family Caregiving: Fostering Resilience Across the Life Course*. Switzerland: Springer International Publishing, 81–98.

24 Menzel, P. T. (2011), The value of life at the end of life: a critical assessment of hope and other factors. *Journal of Law, Medicine & Ethics*, 39 (2), 215–23.

25 Palmieri, J. J. and Stern, T. A. (2009), Lies in the doctor–patient relationship. *Primary Care Companion to the Journal of Clinical Psychiatry*, 11 (4), 163.

26 Bruera, E., Neumann, C. M., Mazzocato, C., Stiefel, F. and Sala, R. (2000), Attitudes and beliefs of palliative care physicians regarding communication with terminally ill cancer patients. *Palliative Medicine*, 14 (4), 287–98.

27 Eliott, J. A. and Olver, I. N. (2007), Hope and hoping in the talk of dying cancer patients. *Social Science & Medicine*, 64 (1), 138–49.

28 Higginson, I. J., Gomes, B., Calanzani, N., Gao, W., Bausewein, C., Daveson, B. A., . . . and Ceulemans, L. (2014), Priorities for treatment, care and information if faced with serious illness: a comparative population-based survey in seven European countries. *Palliative Medicine*, 28 (2), 101–10.

29 Nicholas, L. H., Langa, K. M., Iwashyna, T. J. and Weir, D. R. (2011), Regional variation in the association between advance directives and

end-of-life Medicare expenditures. *Journal of the American Medical Association*, 306 (13), 1447–53.

30 Dolan, P., Gudex, C., Kind, P. and Williams, A. (1996), The time trade-off method: results from a general population study. *Health Economics*, 5 (2), 141–54.

31 Milgram, S. (1965), Some conditions of obedience and disobedience to authority. *Human Relations*, 18 (1), 57–76.

32 Office of National Statistics (2015), National Survey of Bereaved People in England. Retrieved from https://www.ons.gov.uk/peoplepopulation andcommunity/healthandsocialcare/healthcaresystem/bulletins/national surveyofbereavedpeoplevoices/england2015.

33 Gomes, B., Calanzani, N., Gysels, M., Hall, S. and Higginson, I. J. (2013), Heterogeneity and changes in preferences for dying at home: a systematic review. *BMC Palliative Care*, 12 (1), 7.

34 Demos (2010), Dying for Change. Retrieved from https://www.demos. co.uk/files/Dying_for_change_-_web_-_final_1_.pdf?1289561872.

35 Wong, P. T., Reker, G. T. and Gesser, G. (1994), Death attitude profile-revised: a multidimensional measure of attitudes toward death. In R. A. Neimeyer, ed., *Death Anxiety Handbook: Research, Instrumentation, and Application*. New York: Routledge, 121–48.

36 Ferrell, B., Sun, V., Hurria, A., Cristea, M., Raz, D. J., Kim, J. Y., . . . and Koczywas, M. (2015), Interdisciplinary palliative care for patients with lung cancer. *Journal of Pain and Symptom Management*, 50 (6), 758–67; Temel, J. S., El-Jawahri, A., Greer, J. A., Pirl, W. F., Jackson, V. A., Park, E. R., . . . and Jacobsen, J. (2016), Randomized trial of early integrated palliative and oncology care. *Journal of Clinical Oncology*, 34 (26), 104.

37 Halpern, J. and Arnold, R. M. (2008), Affective forecasting: an unrecognized challenge in making serious health decisions. *Journal of General Internal Medicine*, 23 (10), 1708–12.

38 Dolan, P. (1997), Modeling valuations for EuroQol health states. *Medical Care*, 35 (11), 1095–108.

39 Trope, Y. and Liberman, N. (2000), Temporal construal and time-dependent changes in preference. *Journal of Personality and Social Psychology*, 79 (6), 876.

40 Loewenstein, G., O'Donoghue, T. and Rabin, M. (2003), Projection bias in predicting future utility. *Quarterly Journal of Economics*, 118 (4), 1209–48.

41 Ganzini, L., Goy, E. R. and Dobscha, S. K. (2008), Prevalence of depression and anxiety in patients requesting physicians' aid in dying: cross sectional survey. *British Medical Journal*, 337, a1682.

42 Gopal, A. A. (2015), Physician-assisted suicide: considering the evidence, existential distress, and an emerging role for psychiatry. *Journal of the American Academy of Psychiatry and the Law Online*, 43 (2), 183–90.

43 *The Economist*, 24 and Ready to Die. Retrieved from https://www.youtube.com/watch?v=SWWkUzkfJ4M.

44 Mishara, B. L. and Weisstub, D. N. (2013), Premises and evidence in the rhetoric of assisted suicide and euthanasia. *International Journal of Law and Psychiatry*, 36 (5), 427–35.

45 Demos, The Commission on Assisted Dying. Retrieved from https://www.demos.co.uk/files/476_CoAD_FinalReport_158x240_I_web_single-NEW_.pdf?1328113363.

46 Smith, K. A., Goy, E. R., Harvath, T. A. and Ganzini, L. (2011), Quality of death and dying in patients who request physician-assisted death. *Journal of Palliative Medicine*, 14 (4), 445–50.

47 Georges, J. J., Onwuteaka-Philipsen, B. D., Muller, M. T., Van der Wal, G., Van der Heide, A. and Van der Maas, P. J. (2007), Relatives' perspective on the terminally ill patients who died after euthanasia or physician-assisted suicide: a retrospective cross-sectional interview study in the Netherlands. *Death Studies*, 31 (1), 1–15.

48 Lerner, B. H. and Caplan, A. L. (2015), Euthanasia in Belgium and the Netherlands: on a slippery slope? *Journal of the American Medical Association Internal Medicine*, 175 (10), 1640–41.

49 Williams, A. (1997), Intergenerational equity: an exploration of the 'fair innings' argument. *Health Economics*, 6 (2), 117–32.

50 Dolan, P. and Tsuchiya, A. (2012), It is the lifetime that matters: public preferences over maximising health and reducing inequalities in health. *Journal of Medical Ethics*, 38 (9), 571–3.

9. VOLITIONAL

1 US National Library of Medicine. Retrieved from https://ghr.nlm.nih.gov/primer/basics/gene.

2 Joshi, P. K., Esko, T., Mattsson, H., Eklund, N., Gandin, I., Nutile, T., . . . and Okada, Y. (2015), Directional dominance on stature and cognition in diverse human populations. *Nature*, 523 (7561), 459–62.

3 Plomin, R., DeFries, J. C., Knopik, V. S. and Neiderhiser, J. M. (2012), *Behavioural Genetics* (6th edition). New York: Worth.

4 Plomin, R. and von Stumm, S. (2018), The new genetics of intelligence. *Nature Reviews Genetics*, 19 (3), 148–59.

5 Ben-Zur, H. (2003), Happy adolescents: the link between subjective well-being, internal resources, and parental factors. *Journal of Youth and Adolescence*, 32 (2), 67–79.

6 Matteson, L. K., McGue, M. K. and Iacono, W. (2013), Is dispositional happiness contagious? *Journal of Individual Differences*, 34, 90–96.

7 Decision Science News (2015), Chances of Going to College Based on Parents' Income. Retrieved from http://www.decisionsciencenews.com/2015/05/29/chances-of-going-to-college-based-on-parents-income/.

8 Noble, K. G., Houston, S. M., Brito, N. H., Bartsch, H., Kan, E., Kuperman, J. M., . . . and Schork, N. J. (2015), Family income, parental education and brain structure in children and adolescents. *Nature Neuroscience*, 18 (5), 773; Chetty, R., Hendren, N. and Katz, L. F. (2016), The effects of exposure to better neighborhoods on children: new evidence from the moving to opportunity experiment. *American Economic Review*, 106 (4), 855–902.

9 De Bellis, M. D. and Zisk, A. (2014), The biological effects of childhood trauma. *Child and Adolescent Psychiatric Clinics of North America*, 23 (2), 185–222.

10 Dierkhising, C. B., Ko, S. J., Woods-Jaeger, B., Briggs, E. C., Lee, R. and Pynoos, R. S. (2013), Trauma histories among justice-involved youth: findings from the National Child Traumatic Stress Network. *European Journal of Psychotraumatology*, 4 (1), 20274.

11 Wegner, D. M. and Wheatley, T. (1999), Apparent mental causation: sources of the experience of will. *American Psychologist*, 54 (7), 480–92.

12 Kahneman, D. (2015), *Thinking, Fast and Slow*. New York: Farrar, Straus and Giroux.

13 Steidle, A. and Werth, L. (2013), Freedom from constraints: darkness and dim illumination promote creativity. *Journal of Environmental Psychology*, 35, 67–80; Wansink, B. and Van Ittersum, K. (2012), Fast food restaurant lighting and music can reduce calorie intake and increase satisfaction. *Psychological Reports*, 111 (1), 228–32.

14 Chiou, W. B. and Cheng, Y. Y. (2013), In broad daylight, we trust in God! Brightness, the salience of morality, and ethical behavior. *Journal of Environmental Psychology*, 36, 37–42.

15 Mani, A., Mullainathan, S., Shafir, E. and Zhao, J. (2013), Poverty impedes cognitive function. *Science*, 341 (6149), 976–980.

16 Gilbert, D. T. and Malone, P. S. (1995), The correspondence bias. *Psychological Bulletin*, 117 (1), 21.

17 Walker, D., Smith, K. A. and Vul, E. (2015), The fundamental attribution error is rational in an uncertain world. Retrieved from https://mindmodeling.org/cogsci2015/papers/0437/paper0437.pdf.

18 Crawford, C., Dearden, L. and Greaves, E. (2014), The drivers of month-of-birth differences in children's cognitive and non-cognitive skills. *Journal of the Royal Statistical Society: Series A (Statistics in Society)*, 177 (4), 829–60.

19 TED Talk. Does money make you mean? Retrieved from https://www.ted.com/talks/paul_piff_does_money_make_you_mean.

20 Vohs, K. D. and Schooler, J. W. (2008), The value of believing in free will: encouraging a belief in determinism increases cheating. *Psychological Science*, 19 (1), 49–54.

21 Leenders, M. V., Buunk, A. P. and Henkens, K. (2017), The role of the relationship with parents with respect to work orientation and work ethic. *Journal of General Psychology*, 144 (1), 16–34.

22 Moghaddam, F. M., Taylor, D. M., Lambert, W. E. and Schmidt, A. E. (1995), Attributions and discrimination: a study of attributions to the self, the group, and external factors among Whites, Blacks, and Cubans in Miami. *Journal of Cross-Cultural Psychology*, 26 (2), 209–20; Bempechat, J. (1999), Learning from poor and minority students who succeed in school. *Harvard Education Letter*, 15 (3), 1–3.

23 Catley, P. and Claydon, L. (2015), The use of neuroscientific evidence in the courtroom by those accused of criminal offenses in England and Wales. *Journal of Law and the Biosciences*, 2 (3), 510–49.

24 Farahany, N. A. (2015), Neuroscience and behavioral genetics in US criminal law: an empirical analysis. *Journal of Law and the Biosciences*, 2 (3), 485–509.

25 Cushman, F., Knobe, J. and Sinnott-Armstrong, W. (2008), Moral appraisals affect doing/allowing judgments. *Cognition*, 108 (1), 281–9.

26 Knobe, J. (2003), Intentional action and side effects in ordinary language. *Analysis*, 63 (279), 190–94.

27 Harris, S. (2012), *Free Will*. New York: Free Press.

28 Metcalfe, R., Burgess, S. and Proud, S. (2011), Using the England Football Team to Identify the Education Production Function: Student Effort, Educational Attainment and the World Cup. The Centre for Market and Public Organisation, Working Paper 11/276.

29 Dana, J., Dawes, R. and Peterson, N. (2013), Belief in the unstructured interview: the persistence of an illusion. *Judgment and Decision Making*, 8 (5), 512.

30 Ward, A. F., Duke, K., Gneezy, A. and Bos, M. W. (2017), Brain drain: the mere presence of one's own smartphone reduces available cognitive capacity. *Journal of the Association for Consumer Research*, 2 (2), 140–54.

WRAPPING UP RESPONSIBLE

1 Adler, M. D., Dolan, P. and Kavetsos, G. (2017), Would you choose to be happy? Trade-offs between happiness and the other dimensions of life in a large population survey. *Journal of Economic Behavior & Organization*, 139, 60–73.

CONCLUSION

1 Carlson, R. (2002), *Don't Sweat the Small Stuff . . . and It's All Small Stuff*. New York: Hyperion.
2 Sommers, S. R. (2006), On racial diversity and group decision making: identifying multiple effects of racial composition on jury deliberations. *Journal of Personality and Social Psychology*, 90 (4), 597; Van Knippenberg, D., De Dreu, C. K. and Homan, A. C. (2004), Work group diversity and group performance: an integrative model and research agenda. *Journal of Applied Psychology*, 89 (6), 1008.
3 Digital NHS. Survey shows one in three adults with common mental disorders report using treatment services (2016). Retrieved from https://digital.nhs.uk/article/813/Survey-shows-one-in-three-adults-with-common-mental-disorders-report-using-treatment-services.
4 Kushner, T. and Valman, N. (2000), *Remembering Cable Street*. London: Vallentine Mitchell.

Acknowledgements

I'll try and keep this bit short but also hopefully sweet.

I would like to say a very big thank you to . . .

Les; you continue to support me in all that I do. And Poppy and Stanley; you alert me to so many narrative traps.

Amanda Henwood, for your unwavering support and dedication at all stages to this project. Your enthusiasm, attention to detail, in-depth analysis and constant questioning have all helped to make the book the best version of itself. I cannot thank you enough.

Kate Laffan, for your comments throughout and for drawing my attention to so many interesting and relevant studies and articles that I would never have found without you. You make Google Scholar look ill-informed. Laura Kudrna, for your comments at all stages and analysis of the American Time Use Survey data. Your unwavering support means so much to me. Cecilia Stein, for simply being the best editor any author could hope to have. I genuinely could not have asked for a more pleasurable, purposeful and productive process. Stefan McGrath, for being so supportive of the original idea and for comments early on. And Max Brockman, for guidance on the original proposal and all things agent.

Bradley Franks, Matteo Galizzi, Dario Krpan, Grace Lordan, Robert Metcalfe, Kash Ramli, Tom Reader, Joel Suss and Stefano Testoni, Aki Tsuchiya, Alina Velias and Ivo Vlaev. It does each of you a disservice to list your names like this but I didn't want to turn this into a cheesy Oscar-style acceptance speech. Put simply, the book is better in so many ways from your various contributions.

All those who have commented on my ideas when I have mentioned this book in conversations and talks over the last year or so. I would like to single out the LSE EMSc Behavioural Science class of 2017/18 for a special mention and one student (who I won't name) who I hope has fallen in love again with David Beckham.

Thank you all so very much.